MY CIRCUMSTANTIAL ODYSSEY

Paul Nichols

MY CIRCUMSTANTIAL ODYSSEY

Permissions

A Bright Shining Lie by Neil Sheehan, copyright 1988, I Corps map permission granted from Penguin Random House

A Brave and Startling Truth poem lines by Maya Angelou, copyright 1995, permission granted from Penguin Random House

Autopsy of War: A Personal History, by John A. Parrish, copyright 2012, permission granted from Thomas Dunne Books, an imprint of St. Martin's Press

Dad's Maybe Book by Tim O'Brien, copyright 2019, permission granted from HarperCollins Publishers

The Evil Hours: A Biography of Post-Traumatic Stress Disorder by David J. Morris, copyright 2015, permission granted from HarperCollins Publishers

Dreamers poem by Siegfried Sassoon, published in 1918 — no permission necessary

The Last Ship Out (A Dream) poem, permission granted by author Gary Rafferty

Why Stories Matter quote, permission obtained from Paul Tritschler and openDemocracy

General Shoup's quotes, from Congressional Record — Senate page 3976 February 20, 1967

Concord Monitor for two items:

Saturday Monitor June 17, 1995, page A8 — image of Grateful Dead concert at Highgate, Vermont

Sunday Monitor March 16, 2003, front page — "The Conflict with Iraq" lead article with photo of Paul Nichols and others at an anti-war rally in front of the State House in Concord

Professor Sitkoff's quote from the summer 1989 UNH Alumnus magazine, permission granted from UNH

Hospital at Portsmouth Naval Shipyard photo — document stating no known copyright restrictions or restrictions on use

Viet Cong suspects photo — courtesy of US Army

My memoir is dedicated to:

My family, past, present and future, to Vietnam
veteran Brothers and Sisters and to the
Vietnamese people.

Soldiers are citizens of death's grey land,
Drawing no dividend from time's to-morrows.

First published in 1918, these poetic lines from
"Dreamers" by World War I English soldier Siegfried
Sassoon are profoundly defining.

The Last Ship Out
(A Dream)

Door gunner's bony hand,
gestures 'Hurry!'
My feet stumble me aboard,
a riddled ship
that pumps hydraulic fluid blood,
into puddles in the dirt.
Fear roots my bowels to the seat.

Stare at the aluminum deck.
Gouged by stretcher legs,
worn by boot-treads
of men now dead.
These faint clues
all that's left,
to mark their passage.

The co-pilot turns in his seat.
Skeletal hand raises the visor of his helmet.
Neatly spider-webbed by a bullet,
a third eye, between empty sockets.
He smiles a death-head's grin,
says "Welcome Aboard,
Where To?"

Poem by NH Vietnam veteran Gary Rafferty

Prologue

Ancient Greek philosopher Heraclitus said something along these lines: you can never bathe twice in the same river. Zen masters like the late Thich Nhat Hanh also ascribe to this idea of impermanence. Change is inevitable.

I began writing initial drafts of this memoir in late 1994, not knowing where it would take me or when it would end. America's ill-gotten folly in Vietnam provided grist for the mill. My original title, *One Time Too Many,* seemed appropriate since the primary focus dealt with my country's ignoble war in Southeast Asia. Long lapses of time have swirled past, and much has happened between widely sporadic writing sessions. I believe J.R.R. Tolkien is correct when he said that the job that takes the longest to finish is the one that has never been started.

Since 1994, my dad, my mom and my sister have died, as have other family members, friends and veteran brothers. I've undergone years of chronic pain remedies and psychotherapy sessions, obtained a NH medical marijuana card, earned a BS degree, and returned to Vietnam twice. The terrorist attacks of September 11, 2001 drastically changed the USA and the world. America led the way into no-win wars in Iraq and Afghanistan and prolonged the ill-advised fight supported by a comparatively minuscule allied coalition. The Islamic terrorist scourge known as ISIS has grown out of Mid-East destabilization and civil war. Worldwide climate change has hastened with calamitous results. Our country's first biracial president, Barack Obama, served two terms having been left a mess by eight years of President George W. Bush. With the 2016 presidential election the US had the four-year misfortune of a corrupt and deranged Republican Donald J. Trump, President #45, who was twice impeached. Beginning in China in late 2019 and spreading worldwide well into 2022, the deadly coronavirus pandemic COVID-19 and its numerous variants took a huge toll in lives, tanked the world's economy and disrupted normal societal functions. Following the 2020 presidential election, won decisively by Democrat Joe Biden in popular vote and electoral college numbers, right wing Republican congressmen and Trump supporters attempted to invalidate the election. On January 6, 2021 the US Capitol was attacked and besieged by rabid Trump supporters and violent right-wing militia groups causing unprecedented death and destruction. The attempted coup brought charges of "incitement of insurrection" against Trump and his domestic terrorist cult. Currently, the Eastern European country of Ukraine is being attacked and devastated, with tens of thousands killed, maimed and displaced by Russian President Vladimir Putin's troops. The US and other countries support Ukraine with weaponry and humanitarian assistance. Broad sanctions have been imposed on Russia. Fears of a possible WW III are a major concern.

Though greatly expanded from where I started out, my intention is still for my memoir to be fairly focused . . . focused somewhat chronologically on personal and societal changes within specific generations of my family's and my country's past, including our legacy with wars. It's meant only for family members' eyes and for a few close friends, not for more widespread circulation. Thinking further, who else would be interested? A few names and related details have been changed to protect the identities of those who have passed and their loved ones.

Some segments have been fast-forwarded through as they are not pertinent, insignificant, or reveal things too heavy to share. It's not my intention to delve into gruesome war story after war story. I'm not strong enough for that. Many of my specific war experiences have been addressed in poems and other writings, while some are unspeakable. If only the experiences were erasable from my memory.

Intermittently I've included little stories, which are hopefully of interest to readers. Some are foul-mouthed and may provide a dose of humor. Before my aged memory fades much further I need to finish writing this composition and get it in print. I ask for readers' forbearance if any recollections differ from mine as stated. I'm reminded of the ancient Lakota saying that memory is like riding a trail at night with a lighted torch. The torch casts its light only so far, and beyond that is darkness.

Over the years I've made corrections and deletions and have expanded details. Three supplements have been included which coincide with specific paragraphs to form an Appendix. I've amassed information obtained from family elders, extensive genealogical records, and my personal recollections. From the 1970s to present, Mary has provided invaluable clarity to some of my fractured remembrances. Old letters and photos, my military notes and documents and other sources have added accuracy to my narrative. This chronicle is entwined with my observations and opinions. It is not meant to be hurtful or disrespectful to any family member. Nor is it my intention to whine about the hand life has dealt me, for I have been very fortunate.

MY CIRCUMSTANTIAL ODYSSEY contains six chapters:
1. *What Goes Around Comes Around*
2. *The Times They Were A-Changin'*
3. *Signed, Sealed and Delivered*
4. *Homeward Bound*
5. *What A Long, Strange Journey*
6. *A Parting Glance Back and A Hopeful Look Forward*

I'm left with these thoughts from Baba Mandaza Augustine Kademwa, a spiritual leader and healer from Zimbabwe who serves as a messenger for the Ancient Ones. He makes the point that we're all future ancestors, and that things we know now will be passed on to generations who follow. He asks, as a future ancestor, is the story I have written today making me happy now?

My answer leans more towards fulfillment than happiness.

WHAT GOES AROUND COMES AROUND

Prior to the beginning of World War II my dad, Dale S. Nichols, spent a couple years in the National Guard, enlisting on October 18, 1938 in Concord, NH. While in the Guard, Dad lived in Pittsfield, NH with his mother, Grace E. (Miller) Nichols. She and Dad's father, Ned Nichols divorced in 1939. Dad was honorably discharged from the National Guard on July 25, 1940. He enlisted in the Marine Corps one day after his 24th birthday, September 14,1942, nine months after the Japanese attack on Pearl Harbor.

Many years later, I remember Dad saying he had felt that the Marines would provide the best training and have the highest quality leaders during wartime. Dad left Manchester by train for boot camp at Parris Island, SC and then on to the USMC infantry training camp at New River, NC.

Next, his outfit boarded a train to Camp Elliott near San Diego, California. He was later shipped to several island locations in the Pacific with the 3rd Marine Division, including American Samoa, Tutuila, Papua New Guinea, New Zealand and New Hebrides. Then to the Solomon Islands of Guadalcanal and Bougainville, where he experienced horrendous jungle conditions and fierce combat against Japanese forces.

More than once, I recall Dad telling about his adventure on a rubber raft offshore of some Pacific Island around the time he faced combat on Bougainville. Having a few sweltering daylight hours of inactivity and feeling extremely fatigued, Dad fell asleep on a small rubber raft in shallow water. He awoke later alarmed that the raft had drifted far out from the shoreline into a very deep, turbulent ocean. I don't remember the part of the story as to how he got back to dry land, whether he hand-paddled back or if he had to be rescued. But directly linked to that scary experience, I never saw Dad swim out into very deep water, even when swimming in our pond. It all brought back memories of nearly drowning.

Dad became seriously ill with jungle diseases (amoebic dysentery and elephantiasis) while on Bougainville. He was shipped to various military medical facilities on islands in the South Pacific, then eventually from New Caledonia to the US. After landing at Mare Island Naval Shipyard in California, Dad and other Marines received orders to escort 200 prisoners from that shipyard's Naval Prison by train to the Portsmouth Naval Prison in NH, forebodingly known as "The Castle". (I have a DVD copy of a 1973 film titled *The Last Detail*, a tale which comically relates Navy personnel bringing a military prisoner to The Castle in Portsmouth).

Dad's mother had been institutionalized in the NH State Hospital after suffering from what was termed a serious "nervous breakdown," a mental disease from which she never fully recovered. Dad had been sending his mom an allotment from his meager PFC (Private First Class) military pay throughout his deployment overseas. On military leave, he returned from the war to no home, as his younger sister Hilda had rented the house out due to financial necessity. Hilda had no way of knowing when Dad would be coming home from the war. Military service during WW II lasted for the duration of the war, rather than for a specific term.

With no home other than the Marine Corps, Dad briefly moved into the Cate farm on Loudon Ridge, the family home of his sweetheart, Virginia Mildred Cate (my mom). Soon afterwards, on April 5, 1944, Mom and Dad were married at the farm where Mom and most of her siblings were born. The wedding took place in early evening after her dad (Earle Sr.) had milked the cows. Dad's sister Hilda served as a witness to the

Dale Nichols at Parris Island boot camp

Virginia & Dale Nichols wedding photo

marriage and played the "Bridal Chorus" on the piano located in the living room as Mom's father walked her into the room, linked arm in arm. Dad was married wearing his Marine Corps uniform.

Dad spent his last year and a half in the Corps attached to the Marine Barracks at Portsmouth Naval Shipyard. While there he stood gate security duty and also guarded hard-core prisoners locked in the infamous Portsmouth Naval Prison.

Portsmouth Naval Prison ("The Castle") 1945

Mom and Dad inquired about military housing at a place in Kittery, Maine called Admiralty Village. Mom was pregnant carrying me at that time. The only available housing there were two-bedroom duplex units. Since eligibility to obtain base housing required occupancy of both bedrooms, Mom's oldest sister Viola temporarily came to live with them. Vi got a job on the Naval base. They had no car and little money so life was extremely basic. I was born in the Navy's out-patient clinic at the Portsmouth Naval Shipyard on June 15, 1945. Destiny would bring me back to this shipyard in 1967 as a wounded hospital patient.

That July, Dad was posted for transfer to a combat outfit on the West Coast readying for the impending invasion of Japan. Mom had made arrangements to move to the Cate farm with me until Dad's return. The two big US atomic bombs dropped on Japan in early August ended the war in the Pacific. They discharged dad from the Corps at the rank of PFC early that November. In being discharged, he borrowed Alvah Robinson's car. Alvah was also a war-hardened Marine from Pittsfield. Twenty years later, his son Dave quit high school, joined the Marines, and was shot thrice in Vietnam. (More about Davey later)

After Dad's death Mom gave me an old box containing a notebook with his brief hand-written recollections of years spent in the USMC, a scrapbook with photos, military records, a few mementos and several *Marine Corps Gazette* and *The Leatherneck* magazines from the World War II era. I was unaware of these captivating family keepsakes until after Dad had passed away. I also have a book from Mom titled *Pittsfield's World War II Veterans* published in 2010 which contains somewhat accurate descriptions of Dad's, Uncle Bob Nichols', Alvah Robinson's and other locals' military service during that time period.

Dad's younger brother Robert L. Nichols joined the Marines on November 11, 1942, at age seventeen. During my discussions with Uncle Bob's wife June and my mom, Grace refused to sign the enlistment papers. She later gave in after learning of Bob's intentions to live with his father, Ned A. Nichols, who would likely have signed.

Uncle Bob served in the 1st Marine Division and fought the Japanese on the heavily defended Palau Island of Peleliu. On October 4, 1944, at age 19, Bob's right arm was shot by Japanese sniper fire as he rested the flamethrower he carried. At that time, he was also wounded in the knee and nose. They crudely amputated his arm on the field of battle.

Throughout his life, the traumatic loss of the arm caused "phantom pain." He said he could feel his amputated arm and could feel the exact position his hand had grasped the flamethrower with when the bullets hit. June told me that Bob could not get a prosthesis he could wear for any length of time. The field amputation left the bone rough and near the surface, with too little tissue to cushion a wearable prosthetic arm. June claimed that Bob attempted to get Veterans Administration surgeons to trim the bone and pad his arm stub to better accommodate a prosthesis. She said the VA advised him that if they did such an alteration, his condition would no longer be considered "service connected" for compensation purposes. This is hard to rationalize, but with VA bureaucracy, such things happen.

According to June, Bob would never eat rice of any kind because it brought back horrific war memories of maggots feasting on decaying body parts.

Uncle Bob was discharged from the Marines on June 19, 1945 and became a lifetime member of the *Disabled American Veterans (DAV)* organization. He moved to Florida in the late 1940s, and I saw him only occasionally. Bob developed terminal lung cancer in 1990. Mary and I held a family farewell gathering at our place on Loudon Ridge a few months prior to his death on July 6, 1991, his last visit to New Hampshire. I remember Bob as a tall, skinny, gaunt man, with an armless shirtsleeve and distant eyes that always made him seem older than his years. Nevertheless, he had a great sense of humor and was quite a prankster. Uncle Bob became very skillful at doing work that normally required the use of two arms.

Dad's cousin, Alice M. Nichols, joined the Women Marines and also served during World War II. I have no further information regarding her military experience.

Admiralty Village apartment, Kittery, Maine 1944
L to R: Robert Nichols after losing his arm, Hilda Nichols,
my mom & my grandmother Grace Nichols

When the US entered the European Theater of Operations in 1942, it became evident that at least one of Mom's two brothers would have to leave the family farm on Loudon Ridge and join the military. James Cate, her older brother, was married to Ruth at the time. They were raising Aunt Ruth's son Richard Cutter, born when she was married to Robert Cutter. (Following Robert and Ruth's divorce, Robert married Mom's older sister Dorothy. Dorothy had been married to Clyde Nutter, who drowned when his car broke through the ice on Lake Winnisquam while he was ice fishing. Aunt Dorothy was pregnant with my cousin Jan at the time.) Younger brother Earle, Jr. was not married. One of the two boys had to remain on the Cate farm to help the elder parents. James, blind in one eye, stayed on the farm while Earle, Jr. went to war.

They sent Uncle Earle to England, where he served during the horrendous bombing of London and vicinity. His army outfit moved into France, then into Germany, where he was located in May of 1945 when the Nazis unconditionally surrendered. At that point, Earle boarded a ship expecting to eventually be part of a force invading the mainland of Japan. The two devastating A-bombs dropped on Japan ended that possibility. Soon afterwards he returned stateside, mustered out of the Army, returned to the family farm in Loudon, and married Betty. Uncle Earle died of cancer on April 3, 2011, in the home formerly owned by the late James and Ruth Cate, adjacent to where the old family homestead stood before fire destroyed it in April 1992. The Loudon Ridge Cemetery is the final resting place of many in our family lineage, dating back into the 1800s to present times, including immediate family members. Other cemeteries in Loudon contain the graves of other family members.

The majority of my generation's parents and relatives served in World War II. In one sense, everyone during the World War II years was a veteran for the cause, not just military service personnel. Nationwide, women had to do jobs formerly done by men, in addition to taking care of family. Among many instances of females working on the home front in support of the war effort were women running the sawmill at Turkey Pond in Concord and the iconic symbol of Rosie the Riveter. Common commodities were strictly rationed. Some were unavailable. Most everything of use was carefully saved. Sacrifice was universal, and everyone pulled together. Rightfully, patriotism was at an all-time high.

During part of the time that Dad was in the South Pacific, my mom went to work in Newton, Massachusetts, at Raytheon, a major weapons defense contracting company. Mom recalled the "black-out," as windows were painted black for security. Her oldest sister Viola worked there with her and they roomed together. They worked the 3pm-11pm shift. When discussing the World War II years with my mom in later years, I recall her saying, "We were all veterans during those war years." I had an interesting phone conversation with Dad's sister Hilda from her home in Georgia on April 3, 2015, regarding family connections and events from the war years. In their 90s, both Hilda and Mom contributed lots to my understanding of family genealogy and related events of those times. Their long-term memories remained quite strong.

Unlike during World War II, when women made up a huge segment of the homeland's workforce, most women of the late 1940s and 1950s were expected to be homemakers and were generally subservient to their husbands. *The Fifties*, written by David Halberstam, provides an in-depth history of that generation. I have a hardcover copy.

Between World War II and the Korean War, Hilda Nichols married Donald Jenkins, also a Marine. He was in the 1st Marine Division and served at Camp Pendleton in California and also in China. Though Uncle Don hated nearly every day in the Corps, I specifically remember the two eagle, globe, and anchor insignias centered and cemented at the corners of his outdoor fieldstone barbecue structure. Uncle Don continued his gung-ho bluster as I grew into my teens, and he continued to brandish USMC regalia throughout his entire life. Following the birth of their daughter, Judy, and years in a tumultuous marriage, Don and Aunt Hilda divorced. Don mercifully died at Concord Hospital's Hospice House in the very early hours of May 19, 2012. Over a several-month period, aggressive bone cancer had ravaged his frail body.

I have fond and humorous memories from the many years I worked for Uncle Don on weekends and during vacation time from my primary jobs. He operated a small home-based septic service and construction business. My jobs were mainly labor oriented while Don operated his heavy equipment. I remember Don saying, "Don't break your ass, it's already cracked" as I worked on his projects. Sometimes, when riding with Don in his pickup truck on the drive to his jobs, he stopped to get supplies. As soon as he got out of his truck and out of sight, I tuned the radio to a rock station and cranked the volume dial up as high as it would go before returning the key to the off position. Back in the truck, when Don went to start up the truck the ignition sent the radio blasting the music that I loved and Uncle Don hated. This sent him into a good-natured expletive-laced rant, as he quickly turned off the radio. Down the road we drove to his job.

My association with Uncle Don also included many family gatherings and restaurant dining experiences. He was a one-of-a-kind character who was very quick-witted and voiced lots of vulgar, crass, and bigoted expressions, but he often showed his compassionate side as well. Don liked being known as "The Shit King" and used to say his business slogan was, "Your shit is my bread and butter!" More than once I recall Don's humorous comment, "What's the definition of a limp dick — I've never had one!" Another of his declarations at the whiff of a smelly fart was, "That fart rolled right off the edge of a turd." Though Don and I occasionally exchanged heated banter over the years, our relationship remained affectionate right up until his death.

Upon reflection, my family's Marine Corps history had a strong influence on me during a vulnerable period in my life. One of my earliest memories from when I was very young is of Dad's Model-A truck, which someone had painted olive drab with beige camouflage-like spots. We have a photo of this truck.

Virginia, Dale and Paul, late 1940s

Years after Dad's death Mom spoke of influences the Marine Corps had on Dad. She said that he always spit shined his dress shoes as if he was about to undergo an inspection. He always kept his personal belongings very squared away and knew right where they were located. Mom mentioned other references about the Marine Corps this and the Marine Corps that which stayed with Dad throughout his life. Mom also said that Dad couldn't wait to be discharged from the Corps when his enlistment period ended at the Navy Yard. Following military service, Dad had a long career working at the Rumford Press in Concord. Our family of three at the time moved to Chichester. We lived at the lower-middle class income level.

Mary and I have done extensive genealogic investigations in recent years, records of which we have recorded in print and online at "Ancestry.com." During this process, we both had our DNA analyzed through Ancestry. No big surprises regarding our origins. We have journeyed to the Eastern Townships of Lower Canada on several occasions to research Miller family records (my paternal side). We update records as new discoveries are made. Separate from this memoir I have considerable printed family records and photos of ancestors and their gravestones.

Noted below is some of the military service information we've discovered from early wars. Several names shown are direct family blood lines, while others are through marriage.

Oscar R. Nichols was killed in France on July 20, 1918, during World War I, the *War to End All Wars*. (Oscar was Ralph Nichols' son and was killed the year Dad was born. Ralph and Ned Nichols were brothers, making Oscar a first cousin to Dad.) A further records search documents that Oscar was a US Army Corporal with Co. G, 103rd Infantry Regiment, 26th Infantry Division. He was killed on the Western Front during the "Second Battle of Marne" and is buried in Belleau, France at the Aisne-Marne American Cemetery, Plot A, Row 6, Grave 88.

Mom's maternal side of our family also includes a US Army

veteran of World War I. Harriet (called Hat), younger sister of Mom's mother Ida, married Floyd Henry Shattuck, who served in France with Co. B, 101st Ammunition Train, 26th Division. PFC Shattuck was a victim of a German poisonous gas attack and also received other wounds. He was awarded the Purple Heart medal. Mom recalls past family gatherings at the Cate farm when her uncle Floyd was present. She tells that as a youngster I used to follow Floyd around at these events and that he was fond of kids.

Prior to the 100th anniversary of the November 11, 1918 armistice, I wrote a column for the *Concord Monitor* titled "To End All Wars" honoring family members and all others who fought in the Great War. My column was published in the Sunday paper July 29, 2018. I followed that piece up with another one titled "The Positive Power of Dissent," centering on the massive 1932 demonstration by WW I veterans and their families attempting to receive their promised war bonuses. My column was published in the *Sunday Monitor* and the *NH Gazette* in time for 2018 100th anniversary Veterans Day observances. The PBS documentary titled *The March of the Bonus Army* prompted me to write my article.

In late 2018, the World War I documentary film *They Shall Not Grow Old*, directed by Peter Jackson (director of the *Lord of the Rings* trilogy), was released in the US. Though I dreaded seeing the film due to its essential graphic content, I did watch it in March 2019 at Red River Theatres in Concord. I felt that I owed it to my ancestors and the millions of others who fought in that horrendous war, which has long been so shamefully overlooked in the USA.

Through continuing Nichols family genealogical research, I have records showing that William Badger Nichols, Jr. of Bridgewater, NH served as a Union Army private in Co. B, 7th Regiment, New Hampshire Infantry during the American Civil War. William is my great, great grandfather. At this time, records are incomplete as to whether he actually served in the above outfit or merely registered for the draft. William was 37 years old when he registered, however it was common to be drafted at that age and older during the war. It seems strange that William was assigned to a specific company and regiment if he merely registered for the draft.

Interestingly, we've discovered several ancestors who fought with the Continental Army and the militia during the American Revolutionary War. Information we've found is located in our extensive ancestry files, both paper and computer.

Connected to the Nichols family name (my dad's paternal side) and in the Miller lineage (my father's maternal side) are several veterans of the Revolutionary War, some are of direct lineal ancestry and others are documented through marriage.

Research into the Cate lineage (my mom's paternal side) shows veterans of the American Revolution both through direct ancestry and through marriage.

We also found that in the Nichols lineage (through marriage), three generations of men named Jonas Prescott fought in the Revolutionary War, the French and Indian War and King William's War.

As part of a college course that I took in 1996 titled "Men and Women in Cross-cultural Perspective," I wrote 3 essays about my family's ancestry. These papers broaden the writings presented in this memoir regarding the maternal and paternal sides of my family. They are based on my recollections and discussions with close family members. Copies of the essays are kept with our slew of paper genealogical records.

Growing up, the episodes captivated me in the wildly popular Walt Disney television series about Davy Crockett, which ran during 1954 and 1955. The series was a huge commercial success, and I had all the Crockett apparel and regalia including a fake coonskin cap.

Nancy and Paul at Fort Ticonderoga, NY 1955

I even learned to play the *Ballad of Davy Crockett* by ear on my saxophone. Decades later I discovered that much of the Crockett story is based on myth.

When roughhousing with childhood friend Andy Hill and others in our rural Chichester neighborhood, we engaged in all sorts of make-believe battles. When it wasn't outlaws or Indian heathens (as Indians were portrayed on TV, except for "Tonto") that we were killing in great numbers as pretend cowboys, it was the "Japs" as pretend Marines. Ah, the feelings of pride, the illusions of glory, and always the victory we tough Marines won over those cowardly "Nips." In my room at home, I had one-on-one fights with my bed pillow, taken to exhausting levels. Usually I envisioned "Japs," one after another in hand-to-hand combat. I was always the triumphant Marine. Youthful naivety from a susceptible imagination.

At movie theaters I saw *Sands of Iwo Jima, The Naked and the Dead, From Here to Eternity,* and *Flying Leathernecks.* Particularly around Memorial Day and Veterans Day each year war movies took a dominating role on TV channels. I watched lots of them. During the late 1950s and early 60s, I read numerous books about WW II including *Battle Cry, Guadalcanal Diary, Into the Valley, Walk Into Hell* and many others.

Dad stored his sea bag in the back of his bedroom closet. Once during my youth, he showed me the contents, which included a helmet liner, his canvas leggings and some uniform components. Dad had an intricately woven wire club which he had confiscated from a "Castle" prisoner who was contemplating escape. Few inmates ever escaped from that prison with their life. Only one was never recaptured. I also recall Dad's scary-looking black woolen mask worn for warmth during guard duty at the Portsmouth Navy Yard. Winter air was brutally cutting while standing night guard on the Atlantic Coast. The mask covered the entire head with eyeholes, nose breathing space and a mouth opening. It snapped at the neck with wide flaps, which encircled the shoulders and was worn beneath the heavy green woolen USMC overcoat. (When I was in the Corps, we unofficially referred to this full-length coat as our "horse blanket".) Dad's woolen uniform hung in his closet. He said he intended to be buried in that uniform. Feeling great pride, I occasionally snuck into the closet to marvel at these things as I approached high school age.

Many, many years later Dad sold his uniform and his sea bag with all its contents for $100 to some military collector without inquiring if my sister or I cared to have his memorabilia. I regret that he sold these noteworthy things, but it was his rightful decision to make. Dad must have had his reasons. I remember him saying that moths were eating holes in his uniform.

The horrific experiences of war have produced psychological casualties as far back in time as there have been wars. Homer's epic Greek poem *The Iliad* clearly brings this into fruition, as told by clinical psychiatrist Jonathan Shay in his book *Achilles in Vietnam*. Psychiatric problems from war trauma have gone through an evolution of terms and understanding and treatment over the years. "Soldier's heart" and "irritable heart" were terms associated with traumatized soldiers surviving the US Civil War. In World War I the terms were "shell shock" and "war neurosis." "Combat fatigue" became the common term for psychiatric casualties during World War II and the Korean War. In 1980, prompted by extensive research on widespread chronic trauma from Vietnam War experiences, "post-traumatic stress disorder (PTSD)" became a new classification in the *Diagnostic and Statistical Manual of Mental Disorders* (DSM). The DSM has evolved and gone through several changes over the years.

Just as physical injuries can be painful throughout life, so can psychological wounds. The late Donald M. Murray was an army paratrooper who experienced fierce combat in Europe during World War II. He became a distinguished journalist, an admired UNH English professor, and author of several books on writing. Murray was a member of the *Veterans for Peace* organization. For two decades he authored a popular column in the *Boston Globe* newspaper. I have a folder full of his writings. In one of his "Over 60" columns from February 1996 he wondered how he could make youngsters understand his perspective from the war as being more immediate at times than where he lived in the countryside of New Hampshire. Even after more than a half century, an edge of his steppingstone revealed by melting snow caused him to stop until he was sure that the stone was not a land mine.

As I struggled with war-related PTSD from the Vietnam War, I became certain that Dad suffered deeply from the stress of the World War II years. Several instances in the past make this personally recognizable. Dad seldom mentioned his war experiences to me as I was growing up, though toward the last few years of his life he did share some of what he went through. He refused to watch a war movie except for once when, at my youthful nagging, he took me to see *The Naked and the Dead*. I remember Dad's strong criticism of some unrealistic aspects of the film, which my unknowing senses couldn't understand.

Over the years Dad often made references to certain war-related anniversaries, such as at Thanksgiving and Christmas, bringing him back to difficult times he couldn't forget. Occasional sleepless nights reliving long ago jungle experiences took a toll on Dad. I specifically recall stopping by his house when he was in his 80s and finding him painting trim while standing on a short ladder. I mentioned his apparent unsteadiness on the rungs and asked if I could help. His reply was that he was weary because he had spent the night on Bougainville in the Solomon Island chain.

Dad was hypervigilant. Anger sometimes flashed, seemingly out of nowhere. He had strong tendencies toward isolation. Dad wanted nothing to do with tents, camp food, or wet, bug-infested conditions. The jungles of the South Pacific Islands had cursed the otherwise fun adventures of camping. One spring, a neighbor convinced Dad to take me on an overnight fishing trip with him and his sons. We set up the tents, it rained continually, the black flies ate us alive, we caught no fish, and headed home earlier than planned. I camped out often with friends growing up, but never again with Dad.

Driven by staunch cold war fears of communism, a nasty slew

of paranoid hate-mongers gained prominence in the late forties and on through the fifties, fueling America's nationalistic, defensive fire. Republican Wisconsin Senator Joseph McCarthy actively spread red menace hatred, wrongly accusing many US citizens, journalists, art celebrities and politicians he suspected of having communist ties. Republican US Senator Styles Bridges of NH held that position for 24 years. He was a member of the party's conservative wing and was an unwavering defender of Joseph McCarthy's "red scare" investigations. Richard Nixon, a key member of the House Un-American Activities Committee, fanned the flames. Other unsavory zealots of this period include US Secretary of State John Foster Dulles, CIA Director Allen W. Dulles and the infamous FBI Director, J. Edgar Hoover. High-level positions of these low caliber men blazed the trail that America trod.

The Korean War (1950-1953) took its deadly toll with me hardly realizing it, though I was quite young, and we didn't have a television back then. Shamefully, very little history of this war had been taught in schools, and its veterans have received sparse recognition. Regrettably, the Korean War has been termed "The Forgotten War." It was settled by an armistice, not a victory. The historic downplaying of the Korean War likely has to do with the scope and victorious outcome of World War II. In 2022 Korea remains a hostilely divided country, North and South. To this day, the US maintains several thousand troops from all branches of the military for defensive purposes on South Korean bases. Thankfully, decent bookstores now carry some excellent books about the Korean War. A powerful national monument has finally been erected on the Washington, DC mall in honor of those who fought and suffered in Korea. And many states have now erected monuments to honor Korean War sacrifices.

The Cold War grew icier as the fifties decade wore on. Tension, paranoia, hatred and weapons buildup between East and West burgeoned. Annihilation of life on the planet weighed heavily. "Mutually assured destruction" became a doctrine of military strategy thought to prevent deadly buttons from being pushed by opposing sides. News commentary fanned the flames of fear, distrust and the inevitability of a disastrous confrontation. "Better dead than Red" was a common slogan. Dad was unabashedly verbal of his intense abhorrence of communism and its perceived threat to humanity. His Republican ideology was somewhat comparable to that of the John Birch Society. The late gossip commentator, Walter Winchell, provided flagrant, often inaccurate news through his radio and television broadcasts, which were rife with anti-communism rants. I remember seeing Winchell on our small black-and-white TV screen when Dad tuned in to the broadcast. Winchell was a powerful supporter of Senator Joseph McCarthy's infamous communist witch-hunt activities.

All through elementary school we feared an atomic bomb attack. Regular survival drills announced by shrill siren blasts sent us kids diving under our tiny desks, crouched with hands folded over our heads until all-clear was signaled. These exercises were referred to as "duck and cover." Those of us from that time period clearly recall these drills and the fears they generated.

Overall, the fifties and early sixties was a very drab, puritanical stretch of time. At Chichester Central School, my first-grade teacher Mrs. Merryfield taped our mouths shut if we were caught whispering to one another. Many of us mischievous elementary school boys got the red-ass treatment at the hands of Miss Walker's big wooden paddle down the hall in the teachers' room. Unheard of in generations that followed! Corporal punishment was also quite common within some family homes.

Underground fallout shelters were widely promoted. The US Department of Defense published family fallout shelter design plans containing technical data, construction models and bills of materials. Everything from the very basic to the ridiculously elaborate. Quantities of non-perishable food, water, batteries, radios, air filtration systems, first aid kits and such essentials were stocked. One year, my junior high school class science project was a scale-sized Styrofoam model of a family bomb shelter featuring earthen blast protection and intricately equipped long-term survival provisions.

My whacked-out neighborhood friend, Darrel Kennison, spent weeks digging a huge deep hole out in the woods, planning to shield it from radioactivity with a thick lead lid to escape the civilization-ending bomb that he felt was surely coming. Bizarre extremes and conspiracy theories were not uncommon during those fearful times.

Community Civil Defense shelters were ramped up and emergency survival exercises were carried out. Everyone had to be ready for that communist attack, most likely from the Soviet Union, but perhaps from China. Worse yet, it was surmised, maybe from both in tandem. In reality, this dual threat was extremely unlikely, as those two superpowers had competing interests.

In light of real and imagined foreign threats, a morbid climate of war inevitability haunted the fifties. Patriotism ran full strength for the America we believed in. Fear and anxiety, however, did not dominate our lives.

Great optimism prevailed with promise of a bright, prosperous future for Americans. White Americans! By the mid-fifties, the civil rights movement had steadily strengthened in the South as racially significant events took place, most scarred by hatred, prejudice and severe acts of violence. Courageous Black leaders and followers gained prominence in the long struggle toward racial equality. Many were beaten, lynched and otherwise murdered in the process. Thousands of white citizens also supported the Black leaders' causes and took bold actions in solidarity. Many paid a dreadful price for doing so.

It would be inaccurate to say that the Cold War influences I've described overwhelmed the many joyous events of my childhood in rural New Hampshire. Sometimes on summer nights Dad and I went hornpout fishing at Lily Pond in Pittsfield and Sanborn's Pond in Loudon. We took the traditional family Sunday drives except for when Dad had to work, usually with a stop for ice cream. On rare occasions, due to significant financial limitations, Mom and Dad brought Nan and me to a restaurant for a nice meal. During our younger years, Mom used to buy us kid's shoes that were seconds in order to save money. I often received second-hand presents for Christmas and birthdays. For example, I never had a new bicycle, but instead got one bought from the parents of a kid who had died following surgery. Also in the used category were my set of lifting weights, a punching bag and downhill skis. That said, Christmases were very special in our family. Excitement built each year as the 25th of December approached. On a monetary scale I would place us as having been always significantly lower middle-class. My parents worked diligently and provided for our family as best they could. Like so many, they had been brought up in hard times and wanted more prosperous lives for following generations.

Growing up in a small-town neighborhood of close friends, I often went hiking, camping and exploring in the surrounding wooded landscape. The Hill family's home was across the street from our house. My best friend Andy Hill and I had a great time fishing the local brooks and tearing down the steep hills of Webster Mills Road from top at Nudds Hill to bottom just past the Suncook River on our homemade motorless buggies. We pushed our buggies to the top of the incline, then set off rolling down the hills. This involved a long downhill run with subtle curves, and our buggies rolled very fast until the road's steep incline brought us to a stop just past the river. There were far fewer cars and trucks on the road back then. Fewer cops too!

Unfortunately, such a fun experience would be out of the question nowadays.

Down the road from my family's house across the Suncook River were railroad tracks that ran through Epsom, Chichester and on to Pittsfield. Occasionally, a train still traveled on these tracks. Close by the tracks was an abandoned mica mine, which we youngsters explored and referred to as a silver mine. Steep granite embankments rose far above the railroad tracks in the area of the mine. Andy and I had youth-type bows and arrows. A few times when playing on the high rocky cliffs we lurked in wait for a train to pass through. When the train came close enough, we pretended to ambush it by zinging arrows at the passing cars. Unfazed, the train kept going along its way toward its destination.

To pass the winter months, Andy and I often snowshoed into the woods, built a campfire, cooked hot dogs and toasted marshmallows. We also skied and tobogganed on the nearby hilly fields. On big sheets of cardboard, we screamed down steep snow-crusted slopes. We skated on icy ponds and meadows, and we played hockey with neighborhood kids having no rules and using empty boots as goalposts. Shots wide of the goalposts buried the puck into the snowbanks.

Rural life was good, and the times were relatively simple. Boredom was seldom an issue. Andy was a couple years older than me. When he got his driver's license, we sometimes went skiing at Gunstock and other in-state recreation areas. We became increasingly interested in girls. In fact, Andy had a good-looking sister Karen who was my age.

During summers, our family occasionally spent overnights at Uncle Bob and Aunt Dot Cutter's camp on Pleasant Lake in Deerfield. I loved the smell of the knotty pine interior and the rustic nature of the cabin. Hanging out there was great fun for my sister Nan and me. We swam, fished and played games with our two female Cutter cousins. We even learned to waterski.

My first summer employment began at age 13 at a Chichester chicken farm on Pleasant Street, where I could commute from home by bicycle. My job was renovating chicken houses, painting creosote on wooden floors and whitewash on the walls. I got a captivating eyeful in the owner's egg packing room, where the walls were covered with posters of quite nude pin-up girls. In later years, before and after I had a driver's license, I worked summers, school vacations and weekend days at Uncle Bob Cutter's diverse farm in Epsom.

Hunting was by far Dad's favorite sport, especially deer hunting. He occasionally took me on bird hunting jaunts when I was quite young. He carried his old single shot 20-gauge Iver Johnson shotgun. I carried no gun, so for me this was a hunting walk, a learning experience to observe and feel the excitement. In later years, it was I who carried the shotgun. Dad bought me a used Winchester single shot .22 rifle when I was about 12 years old, and he taught me how to shoot. I have that rifle to this day. I also have the Iver Johnson.

Deer hunting was an intensely serious annual event for Dad and the three Bartlett brothers who he most always hunted with. There was a split season for deer, first in northern NH followed by a more southern in-state season. As I reached my early teens, I was invited to join Dad and his companions on the hunt. Leaving home well before daylight, Dad drove much faster than usual to a location in the town of Errol north of the White Mountains, where we met up with the Bartletts. Dad's rifle was a .45-70 Winchester lever action that was long ago given to him by his father. I used the 20-gauge shotgun mentioned above. Cocking the hammer on this single shot gun was difficult, especially with half-frozen hands, because at some point in time the spring mechanism had been replaced with parts that didn't fit properly.

When the southern season opened, I was sometimes allowed to skip a school day, particularly if a good tracking snow had fallen. The hunting plan was for a couple in our crew to locate quietly apart on "stands" at spots where deer often crossed. This wasn't a tree stand, but just a knoll or place allowing fairly good visibility. The other hunters in the group followed fresh deer tracks in hopes of driving deer in the direction of those of us on stands. This strategy worked well. Dad and the Bartletts shot a deer most every season. I never shot one.

Invariably, the hunt began at the first hint of daybreak and continued until heavy dusk. The night before, Mom packed Dad and me a sandwich and a few fig newton cookies each, which we stored in the game pouch of our hunting jackets. This course of action wasn't altered by frigid or stormy weather.

During my high school years, I worked one day of each weekend at my uncle's farm. The other day was spent hunting with Dad until the season ended. Even if Dad had shot a deer, he continued hunting more in the role of a scout. As time went on, my interest focused on girls, mostly my girlfriend Carol. I no longer burned for the hunt. I stood silent on my frigid outpost not thinking about deer, not caring if a damned deer came running by or not. Instead, I wrote dreamy notes of affection in my mind to Carol, just wanting to get out of the fucking woods to spend time with her.

My girl-oriented dread of the hunt built as each weekend approached. This situation presented a vexing dilemma in that I didn't want to disappoint Dad by declining the chance to spend time hunting with him. I don't recall exactly when this quandary got settled, but I think it faded gradually rather than coming to an abrupt halt. Once I broke loose, however, I never again went deer hunting. And several years later Dad lost interest in hunting and didn't renew his license. Following my experiences in Viet Nam, I've never bought a license and have never gone hunting for sport or for food.

High Schools had strict rules — no dungarees (called "jeans" nowadays), no T-shirts, no untucked shirttails or upturned collars, no sandals or flip-flops, no shorts and no longish hair for boys. I once got sent home from Pittsfield High School for having my hair too long, Elvis-style. I soon had it slightly trimmed but wasn't allowed back without a note from home saying I had indeed been to the local barber. I recall a girl in my class being sent home for wearing culottes. Culottes looked like a short skirt but had a sewn-together crotch, exposing nothing but legs!

The pop music scene turned livelier during the second half of the fifties, as rock and roll soared. It was wonderfully refreshing to our youthful ears listening to Elvis Presley, Jerry Lee Lewis, Chuck Berry, Fats Domino, Buddy Holly, Bill Haley and the Comets, and others on the radio. During my high school years in Pittsfield, I bought lots of new and used 45 rpm vinyl records. I could buy them used for 25 cents from the jukebox at Hemeon's store, a high school student hangout. Television access had gradually become widespread, so I could watch occasional rock and roll performances at home. The majority of our generation's parents were not pleased with the new direction that music was taking.

My sister, Nancy Dale Nichols, was born on November 28, 1947, at the Giles private birthing house in Pittsfield, NH. Our brother, Larry Keith Nichols, was born on December 3, 1956, at Concord Hospital. There was great excitement in our family, though Nan was really hoping for a sister. Mom and Dad were thrilled to have a third child, though the pregnancy was unplanned. We were all blessed with this beautiful baby boy.

The paragraphs I'll now attempt to write are the most tragic and emotionally devastating of any in this memoir. The siege is so dreadfully heartbreaking that I will spare some of the most wrenching details.

Larry became sick in the early spring of 1960 and was transferred from Concord Hospital to Boston Floating Hospital for Children on June 4th of that year. He was diagnosed as having a nasty, highly malignant stomach cancer (neuroblastoma). Over time, Larry underwent two major surgeries, many radiation treatments, experimental drug dosages and excruciatingly severe pain. While in the Boston hospital, Larry became afraid to go to sleep for fear of what doctors and nurses might do to him next. He once asked Mom if he was going to die because he had overheard discussions to that affect between doctors. This from a child under four years old.

After Larry left the hospital for home the final time, Mom had to administer needles of pain medication into his frail little body. Before long, the shots became necessary in shorter duration due to increased pain. Larry's condition got to the point where there was little flesh to inject. In discussions decades later, Mom recalled that I left the room whenever she injected Larry with pain meds. The continued injections were more than I could bear watching, adding credence to Mom's strength during such dire circumstances. His crib was located beside Mom and Dad's bed, so he could be readily tended to. At times during the night, Larry asked Mom to press on his tummy. Mom reached from her bed through the crib rails and applied light pressure, which somehow comforted Larry a bit until the next shot took hold.

Larry's death occurred at about 1:00 PM on Sunday, January 29, 1961, in our Chichester home. I had been outside and happened to come into the house as he lay dying. Nan was away visiting our cousin Judy Jenkins. Mom, Dad and I were lovingly with Larry as he passed. In my file of family papers is a folder titled "Larry's folder." Among other things, it contains some photos and my hand-written chronological account of Larry's sickness, his operations and treatments, his suffering and his death. Larry is buried at the Nichols lot in the Loudon Ridge cemetery just up the road from where Mary and I have long resided.

This tragic ordeal aged Mom and Dad by at least a decade in my estimation, sapping their hope, their energy and robbing their smiles. Of course, it was profoundly life altering. They lived with cruel survivor's guilt, wondering why the horrific disease had struck little Larry rather than them. They lived and relived the horror, the helplessness and the hopelessness. And those hateful, useless "what ifs" persisted. Though heartbroken in grief, Mom's strength weathered the devastation better than Dad's. Poor Dad had no time or energy for anyone or anything except his deep despondency. Yet he had to steadily work to provide enough money for us to carry on. At that sorrowful time, we all needed each other.

In the decades since Larry's death, and since Dad's 2005 death, Mom has spoken to Mary and me many times, reliving some of the traumatic experiences our family endured during Larry's sickness. I don't recall Dad ever speaking of the family tragedy after Larry passed. I think he was unable to confront it in conversation. Mom told us that one day during Larry's cancer hospitalization, her dad and her youngest brother Earle came to their home offering to mortgage their Loudon farm in order to pay for Boston hospital costs. They were concerned that the costs would overwhelm our family's ability to pay for continued treatments. Mom said she and Dad much appreciated but refused the offer, deciding that they would make payments as they could for as long as necessary to pay all bills incurred.

Larry's death was very difficult on Nan and me too, exposing us to tragedy, desperation, and loss we could not have imagined. Though there were many years between us, Larry and I were particularly closely bonded.

I became deeply despondent due to the senseless inevitability of his plight. I felt sad, angry, useless, guilty and spiritually lost. Uncle Don Jenkins was of great help to me by offering a measure of solace where Dad remained void. Mom reminded Mary and me of my rage during the home gathering following Larry's funeral service, when out in the garage I repeatedly beat my speed bag with furry and helpless frustration. Uncle Don came out to where I stood and calmed my anger.

Larry, Paul and Pal the dog June 1960

Down back at the foot of our hill near the brook laid a big fallen red maple tree. It was down but not flat down, as its mangled limbs allowed the main trunk to sort of levitate. I spent hours with my hatchet meticulously carving the name "Larry Keith Nichols" along the huge stem. I felt that I was with him there and the place became my refuge. There was a connection between a fallen tree and a fallen brother. To some extent this lengthy physical activity temporarily helped relieve my anger and grief.

Mom convinced Dad that our family needed to get away from our house for a while. She and Dad scraped enough money together for us to drive to Florida to visit Dad's brother Bob and his father Ned. Overnight during the drive south, Mom, Dad and Nan slept in our 1957 Chevy station wagon. Having no room for me, I slept outside of the car on the ground.

I vividly remember seeing the squalid living conditions of the Black population along the roadside. This was before big interstate highways bypassed such poverty and was before the many civil rights activities in the immediate years following. Before the 1964 Civil Rights Act aimed towards ending segregation and race discrimination. The drive through the southern states was a real eye-opener for us, coming from white populated New Hampshire.

Years later, Mom reminded me of a conversation I had with her soon after Larry's death concerning my fear and anxiety about future prospects of having any kids of my own. In her sensitive way, Mom tried to assure me that the chances of having a child developing cancer at an early age were very remote. "We've all got to try and move on," she said. Yet in late 1967 when Cheryl was quite pregnant with Shawn, our firstborn, I again expressed my trepidation about childhood cancer to Mom. Again, she was reassuring. And her reassurance proved to be correct.

Our next-door neighbors, Andy and Karen Hill, and I attended the Concord school system after grade 8 at Chichester Central. Andy drove Karen and me to school in their dad's car. I was attending Concord's Rundlett Junior High School (grade 9) when Larry got sick and, ironically, I was completing an oral science report about cancer. Mercifully, I was excused of an oral presentation and passed in a written version.

During my year at Rundlett I often saw a tall, thin man constantly wearing sunglasses walking around the streets of Concord, always alone with a briefcase in hand. From his mannerisms, it was obvious that he wasn't a lawyer or a businessman. Known in town as "Nervous Ned," he was teased ruthlessly by many of the kids during after-school encounters. Though I often saw him, I didn't join in the torment of the quaint-acting man. I was aware that he had survived the Bataan Death March during World War II and that the trauma of the experience imprisoned his life. I had read about Bataan, and though war nevertheless seemed glorious in my naivety, I felt empathy for "Nervous Ned." Treatment of prisoners of war by the Japanese is vividly depicted by the books *Unbroken, Too Dead to Die, Ghost Soldiers* and *The Railway Man.*

Continuing at Concord High School became impossible for me when my ride disappeared due to Karen's unexpected pregnancy. Karen was quite alluring and very bright, attaining the highest grades in school. Small town societal pressures in those days shunned unwed mothers, and the Hill family abruptly moved out-of-state early in Karen's pregnancy to escape negative public scrutiny. I transferred to the less distant Pittsfield High School that fall as a sophomore and most days caught a ride that year with the Ryan boys who lived a short distance up the road. Though five years apart, my mom and dad had both graduated from Pittsfield High School.

Pittsfield and its surrounding towns largely consisted of conservative, patriotic, low to middle class blue-collar workers. Local factories and mills employed much of the population. Late each summer during sweet corn season the B&M canning factory in Pittsfield employed folks from several nearby towns. This short-term source of employment generated supplemental income for the purchase of back-to-school clothes and other household expenses. Some strange characters found much needed work doing various jobs that the factory provided. Local farmers, including my grandfather Earle Cate, benefitted from this unique market for their acreages of sweet corn.

Mom said that working at this canning factory is where she and Dad first met back in the early 1940s. Previously, she knew Dad's sister Hilda and brother Bob, but hadn't yet met my dad, since he was older. In fact, Bob worked at the canning factory after losing an arm during World War II. According to Mom, he operated a chute which delivered corn ears in bulk directly to the line of husking machines. As we kids were growing up, Mom and Dad worked at the factory as many hours as possible for extra income. I worked there also, as did many fellow high school students. The pay was minimal, but long hours provided us with seasonal spending money. Sometimes, when a hard frost was forecasted during peak corn production, high school officials let us students out of class early in order to help get the corn processed. Eventually, the processing machinery became old and frequent breakdowns occurred. In its final few years of operation, the workforce sat idle for extended periods while still in pay status on the time clock until the machinery was repaired. The factory finally shut down, marking an end of an era for the community.

Our graduating class was small, consisting of only 26 students, the one just prior to the "baby boom" (those born between 1946-1964). I developed tight friendships, both male and female, within our class and at levels above and below. Our cars, many of them rust heaps with big engines, were customized with suicide knobs, fender skirts, full moon hubcaps, whip antennas and Glasspack or Hollywood mufflers. My first car was a much-used black 1951 Ford with a flathead V8 engine, almost identical to the one my good friend Mike Wade had at the time. This was great, because Pittsfield cops and irate citizens had trouble placing blame as to which of us was raising hell around town. Usually, both of us were! The floorboards of my Ford were so rusted out that I could see pavement in places from the driver's seat.

With few exceptions, we teenaged boys were quite undisciplined and macho, with anti-establishment attitudes. During my high school years, I became increasingly interested in girls, beatnik culture, fast motorcycles and customized cars. Back then, driving impaired from alcohol was not nearly as serious an issue with the local cops as such offenses later became. There were far fewer cars on the roads, for one thing. Finding a friend who was 21 years of age to buy booze for us underaged rascals was quite easy. Like most high school kids, indulging in cheap beer, rot gut wine and hard stuff when available was commonplace. It was fun to buy a case of beer and cruise the back roads with pals while listening to the radio with the beer box sitting open on the car seat and uncapped bottles in our hands. Life was more carefree in those days.

Most students at Pittsfield High School were residents of Pittsfield and Barnstead, but a few came from Chichester, Gilmanton, Loudon, and Northwood. Considering how conservative the towns' people were, we teenagers were a wild bunch, tearing around in loud ramshackle cars and lots of partying. The few from more wealthy families had fancier cars, and some even had motorcycles.

Nearly all cars had a full bench-type front seat with the shifting lever located on the steering column instead of bucket seats and stick shifts typical of sports cars. Also, cars had no seatbelts. This allowed girlfriends to sit nearly on top of their boyfriends who were usually the drivers. Seeing couples motoring down the road nearly as one was ordinary to the culture of the times. Such a scene is nearly unthinkable nowadays since most cars have front bucket seats with a console between them plus usually the shifting lever. Besides, driving with a girlfriend sitting close as was common in the past would now be considered a serious driving hazard. Actually, it was! Going "parking" with a girlfriend at an off-road spot is another bygone happening. Today, public and police suspicions have grown to such rampant levels that an out-of-place vehicle is a serious cause for concern. A concern to be investigated!

I skipped school occasionally, got many detentions, and began listening to Bob Dylan, whose raw folk songs were just beginning to appear on vinyl records. Several of his early songs were forcefully antiwar and spoke clearly of social injustice and racial inequality in the US. I especially loved Dylan's second album titled *The Freewheelin' Bob Dylan* released in May 1963. All songs on the album were great but three were particularly telling (they still are all these decades later), "Blowin' in the Wind," "Masters of War," and "Oxford Town." Paradoxically, I continued to hold the Marine Corps in high esteem. I was still naively clinging to the pride that had been instilled from my younger years, and of course I had no inkling as to the direction our country was barreling toward.

Dad worked the night shift at the Rumford Press, often six nights of the week, so I saw relatively little of him. He needed to sleep well into the morning, and generally I would be gone by the time he got up. Mom was absolutely the greatest. She was kind, loving, and understanding. Unlike Dad, she was not of strict authoritarian disposition. Mom's more lenient outlook couldn't subdue my wild ways. I had trivial behavioral problems in school and minor scrapes with the law, most always in conjunction with my equally wild friends.

By working weekends and school vacations at Uncle Bob Cutter's farm, I had enough money to keep my old cars on the road most of the time. During my years working on the farm, I learned how to operate a chain saw and a brush saw. I did chores at the big chicken houses and in the dairy barn. I shoveled shit. I drove tractors and old dilapidated farm trucks. I helped with logging, cordwood harvesting, haying, picking rocks in crop fields, packing eggs and garden work. Uncle Bob had a diverse farm, at one point called Cutter Enterprises.

During late winter and early spring many times I rode in the cab of big box tractor-trailer trucks, usually driven by a farmhand named Glen, hauling loads of sawdust or shavings to farms in surrounding towns. The journeys were cold, as the old truck cab sputtered and provided little heat for us or the windshield defroster. Most were chicken farms, as I recall. This operation took place when the houses were empty awaiting new flocks of chicks. The body of the truck had been blown full of the sawdust or shavings and overnight the stuff had often partially frozen.

Glen backed up to the open bays of huge chicken houses at lower levels and upstairs. We pieced together sections of the 8 - 10-inch diameter steel conduit from the rear end of the truck body and connected it to the blower engine. Clamped together with extended sections, we aimed the free end into each pen. Breaking apart frozen chunks of bedding material with heavy pitchforks and shovels and forcing them into the conduit was hard, dusty, loud work, more tiring as we reached the farther end of the truck body. Using this method, we got the right amount of bedding blown into each bay. Glen had a foul mouth, which made me laugh. I remember him exclaiming, "This fuckin' shit is frozen *tighter than Tom Cunt's dog."* He used the 5-word description on different occasions, and I never asked him who Tom Cunt was or if he even had a dog! (Mary and I have used the phrase over the years in various situations.) After filling the pens, Glen and I headed off to the next farm needing delivery to repeat the process until the truck body was empty.

Without question, the most dreaded job I got involved in was at Uncle Bob's slaughterhouse. When it came time to populate the chicken houses with new birds, the old hens were jammed into wooden crates, trucked to the farm's slaughterhouse and slaughtered by the hundreds. Broilers came to the same fate as did turkeys around Thanksgiving time.

This was a truly messy and brutal operation, requiring several workers taking on various jobs. It began by yanking the thrashing birds from wooden crates, hanging several at a time by the legs just above their feet on a line of ropes, and cutting their throats with a knife as they flailed wildly in the bloody throes of death (with turkeys, the metal killing funnels were used). Occasionally, a bird escaped the crate and tried unsuccessfully to escape the carnage. Squawking escapees were caught and harshly hung by their legs with others on the slaughter ropes. The sometimes not quite dead birds were then tossed into the scalding tub, then grabbed by the legs and run individually through the defeathering machine. By the end of the slaughtering operation, blood, chicken shit, and feathers were everywhere.

The chickens' innards were removed by hand and their feet were chopped off atop a long bench. The foul smell of chicken guts over a prolonged period of time was quite nauseating. The birds were then packed in the big freezer for later delivery to markets and restaurants. High pressure hoses were used to wash down our boots, rainwear, sections of walls, equipment and the floor. As much as I hated doing henhouse chores, this brutal killing job increased my dislike of anything to do with chickens. I still dread thinking about it today.

The good times rolled perpetually through high school graduation in June of 1963. I barely made it to my commencement ceremony since it took place during "motorcycle weekend." I had spent the previous wild night at the Weirs in Laconia with older friends and had to hitchhike home, since my friends had the cars and were staying at the race scene. Mom and Dad were having a fit, afraid that I was going to miss the graduation ceremony that they had long looked forward to.

During the summer of 1963, I bought a used 3-point hydroplane (called a pumpkin seed) and a trailer to haul it on. Dad heard of a used Mercury Mark 25 outboard engine for sale from a guy who worked with him in Concord. I bought the motor and worked long hours fixing the boat up and painting it a combination of bright red and white. It looked great!

Jean Stimmell, one of my wildest and closest classmates, lived at his parents' home with property leading to the shoreline of Jenness Pond in Northwood. I brought the hydroplane to Jean's, where I stored it conveniently at the pond. The Mercury was really too heavy and powerful for my little boat, but that's what I had. When first cranking the motor, the front of the hydroplane rose out of the water, drastically lowering the back end until flattening out and streaking across the surface of the pond. Jean and I often raised hell taking turns screaming across Jenness Pond that summer. From the shore, all that could be seen of the boat once it planed was a rooster tail of water spraying from the revved engine.

Over the winter of 1963-4, Dad fashioned stabilizers onto my boat to allow it to plane sooner when the engine was cranked. We fastened one stabilizer rig to the bottom of the hull, equidistant on each side of the motor. That spring, I found that the addition of the stabilizers had minimal effect on the boat's operation, as the motor was simply oversized for the tiny hydroplane.

One summer day in 1964, after drinking far too many beers, Jean and I decided that maybe we could both take a fast trip across the pond in my pumpkin seed. Even though it was a one-person boat! After climbing aboard and accelerating to the max, the boat labored for several feet, then upended and sunk into the shallows of the pond. Jean and I were thrown into the water roaring with laughter, not at all concerned about the submerged boat and motor. The gas tank floated close to where the boat went down, still attached to the fuel line. This made the event even funnier to us.

That was the final adventure with my hydroplane. We got it hauled out of the pond and onto my trailer. I took the motor to Green's Marine in Hooksett where it was dried out and tuned up. I sold the whole outfit well before college called Jean and me off in different directions.

During these transitional years, I often heard angry remarks from Dad about how I needed Marine Corps boot camp discipline to straighten me out. I got brief lectures on how "today's youth" had no respect, no direction, and how a few weeks at Parris Island was what we all needed. Such reprimand was indeed brief because it abruptly ended in a pissed off confrontation.

At some point during this clamorous period I decided to take off. I secretly packed up a few belongings that I could carry on foot (including my 16-gauge Mossburg shotgun wrapped in a blanket) and began hitchhiking. California was my intended destination. I managed to catch rides as I thumbed along with the choked barrel of the shotgun protruding from my armful of blanket. Having little cash, I pawned the gun in Boston and continued onward. In Hartford, Connecticut I realized how worried my parents would be, so I phoned them only to let them know that I was okay. Mom tearfully begged me to return, which ended my great adventure west. Mom and Dad drove to Hartford late that night and brought me back home. I now wonder where my life would have taken me had I not called.

I gave serious thought to joining the Marines immediately after high school graduation, mostly as a catalyst to get far away. At school's annual recruiter day events I had always liked the Marine's uniform and glorified line of shit the best. A couple years later, when my draft notice arrived, I felt that maybe I could honor Mom and Dad through military service. Maybe I could compensate for some of their emptiness from losing Larry by making them proud of me, now their only son.

40

THE TIMES THEY WERE A-CHANGIN'

The bland, conservative culture of the 1950s sowed the seeds that gradually sprouted the 1960s. Major changes usually arrived late in the "Live Free or Die" state. Prior to Governor Meldrim Thomson's quirky ultraconservative tenure during the seventies, our state's number plates more palatably read "Scenic" New Hampshire. Instead, Thomson ordered the state's Live Free or Die motto be emblazoned on our number plates. This caused quite a stir among many residents, but unfortunately there was not enough dissension to restore the former "Scenic" wording. I knew some folks who put Duct Tape over the motto on their plates, which provided fodder for cops to pull them over.

Even in NH a big shift was happening within our generation. We couldn't have identified or described what was happening if we had tried, but a generational clash was definitely underway. Ours was a generation that questioned authority. In many ways we loathed authority. A small wave was becoming a tsunami. The standard white picket fence, the *little boxes on the hillside made of ticky-tacky and they all looked just the same*, the cookie-cutter societal mindset of the Fifties - early Sixties was coming unraveled. The radios blasted, and vinyl records spun steadily, playing a rapidly expanding array of folk and rock and roll music. Generally, town cops were loose and State vehicle inspection laws were quite lax. As an alternative to driving cars, hitchhiking near and far was commonplace by both genders, so mobility was not a problem. The novels *On the Road* by Jack Kerouac, Aldous Huxley's *Brave New World* and others spurred excitement. Restlessness was rapidly growing. Trying to accurately describe the wild, rebellious atmosphere to those not of the Sixties generation is impossible. One had to have been there, had to have lived during those extraordinary times.

The young vibrant President John F. Kennedy was in charge of our country as of January 20, 1961, with new and far-reaching dreams for the future. However, Cold War fears continued to dominate foreign policy. The Army's Green Berets had been born, and most Americans were feeling patriotic and positive. Nationally, racial unrest spread rampantly, and the associated violence increased. Societal boundaries were increasingly tested . . . and breached. In thinking back, I define the Sixties as running from 1963 through 1974. I mean in spirit rather than in terms of the standard ten-year decade. After all, the 60s were not standard by any measure.

Bob Dylan's folk song, "The Times They Are A-Changin'" from his third album released in January 1964 was astoundingly prophetic. The song's entire lyrics are profound and warn mothers and fathers of societal changes coming in their kids' thoughts and actions.

Electric activity drenched the air — revolutionary energy. Four books I have: *The Sixties: Years of Hope, Days of Rage*, by Todd Gitlin, *Witness to the Revolution* by Clara Bingham, *The 60s: The Story of A Decade* by authors of *The New Yorker*, and *You Say You Want A Revolution?*, an illustrated history edited by Victoria Broackes and Geoffrey Marsh provide excellent accounts. For the most part, I'm glad I had the chance to live through that tumultuous period from age 18 through 29 as it raged by. It was a time like no other. I have included an extensive listing of political and societal events of the Sixties generation, both positive and negative, in the Appendix of this memoir.

Uneasy and uncertain, I decided to try college instead of joining the Marines after high school. Jean Stimmell headed for Columbia University. Another, Mike Wade, enlisted in the Army.

Like most graduating high school classes, we dispersed.

I entered the two-year forestry program at the Thompson School of Agriculture at UNH in September of 1963. The little money I had scraped up, plus a small "dollars for scholars" loan, barely paid tuition and book costs. Living on campus was financially out of reach. A Pittsfield friend, Rip Perrino, enrolled at the Thompson School that semester and was in the same monetary bind as me. He and I commuted together from our parents' home (Pittsfield and Chichester respectively) to Durham, alternating cars between his old Ford and my 1961 VW beetle. We gained many friends on campus and often flopped overnight in Durham and vicinity. The partying was nearly steady, which was the main contributing factor to my nearly flunking out that first semester. I was attending a dendrology lab deep in the UNH woods on November 22, 1963, when, from a fellow student's transistor radio, came breaking news of President Kennedy's assassination. The lab was terminated, the campus was still, and our country was in shock. Vice President Lyndon B. Johnson was immediately sworn in as President.

The University of New Hampshire was a far cry from liberal universities like Cambridge, Columbia, Madison, Ann Arbor and UC Berkeley during my two years there. For the most part, the only "long hairs" were a few art students. Political activism and demonstrations were rare. The campus was short on racial diversity. NH, like most of northern New England, was very "white."

The music of The Kingston Trio, Bob Dylan, Joan Baez, Peter, Paul and Mary, Phil Ochs, Dave Van Ronk, The Kingsmen and many others was extremely influential to the times. However, smashing sound and mind barriers was music by British rock groups, especially The Beatles and The Rolling Stones, which was new to the US in early 1964. On this side of the Atlantic we had never experienced anything like these tremendous bands.

I had an older friend from Pittsfield who was in the Air Force stationed in England or Germany. When home on Christmas leave in 1963, he spoke of an English band from Liverpool called The Beatles who were rocking many small clubs in Europe. He mentioned that we would soon be hearing them in the US. My friends and I guffawed at a band named Beatles thinking that our Air Force friend was full of shit! However, before long "Beatlemania" was the musical rage across America. In early 1964, The Beatles and The Rolling Stones appeared separately on television's popular *Ed Sullivan Show*. Their prolific songs filled the air. Music was embarking on another radical shift, a fantastically innovative transition so welcome to our generation.

As second semester began in January 1964, I owned a 1955 Crown Victoria Ford, which would have been a snazzy car if it hadn't been so badly rusted. Soon after the first Beatles hit album *Meet the Beatles* became available, I raced from the Durham campus toward Concord to buy a copy of the album before it was sold out. Along Rt. 4 in Epsom, I got a speeding ticket, but I managed to get the vinyl LP record at French's music store on State Street, Concord. Beatles music filled the airwaves.

During my commutes to UNH, I noticed a very attractive high school girl waiting for the bus along Route 4 in Northwood. I began regularly hitting the horn and flirtatiously waving as I passed by. Back then such antics were commonplace. Before long she was waving back. One late afternoon I stopped at Johnson's Dairy Bar, a short distance east of where she stood on school days. To my surprise, I saw her waitressing behind the counter. Her name was Cheryl Ann Noyes, and she was a junior at Coe-Brown Academy. Soon, I met her family, and we began dating. I got along very well with Cheryl's mother (Mary) her father (Charlie) and her three brothers (Buzz, Leslie and Andy). Later, I had a good relationship with Carroll Bailey, Mary's husband following her divorce from Charlie. The romantic relationship between Cheryl and me grew hot and heavy. We were together as much of the time as was possible.

In the spring of 1964, prior to the end of my second semester (in which I scholastically made the Dean's list), I took out a high-interest loan and bought a 1961 Harley-Davidson XLH Sportster. The previous owner had modified the 900cc engine, making it faster than factory grade. The bike had a kick-start and a "suicide" throttle. This was the first motorcycle I had ever driven, and a wild summer ensued. I made many a trip on that bike to visit Cheryl, waking her parents with the Harley's loud pipes as I rolled down the driveway late at night.

In accordance with requirements of my college program, it was necessary that I find summer employment somewhat related to my course of study. To fulfill this obligation, I worked that summer for the NH State Parks Department. I also worked on Uncle Bob's farm one day each weekend. I was unable to make payments on my Harley while continuing at UNH, and by late summer a period of uncertainty weighed heavily. I returned to college two weeks late after making the agonizing decision to sell my bike.

During 1963's first semester commutes to Durham the old VW Bug radio told of US military advisors being killed in some far-away place called Viet Nam. A US covert war was underway there, run mostly by spooks of the CIA and Army Green Berets and Ranger outfits in conjunction with South Vietnamese forces. They reported the casualties in increasing numbers as the semesters rolled around. Where the fuck is Viet Nam, I thought, and what's this all about? No one in my circle of friends had reason to be personally concerned, and we partied on. When war doesn't directly affect a person, he or she tends to remain oblivious to the violence, pain and destruction that ravages all sides. On March 8, 1965, Marine units from the Third Division landed in Danang, becoming the first overt US ground combat forces. Shortly thereafter, US combat forces in addition to advisors were dying steadily in Viet Nam.

From March through April 1965, I worked weekends doing timber stand improvement on Jack Heath's Epsom woodlot. As with other fairly secluded places, Cheryl and I went "parking" as far into the forested access road as I could drive my car.

In early April, following a night of rowdy partying at UNH, I drove my Crown Victoria barely off campus toward home and got stopped by the Durham police. Being under 21 years of age, I was charged with illegal possession of alcoholic beverages. I was found guilty by the Durham District Court and fined. Soon afterwards, I got placed on disciplinary probation by the UNH Men's Judiciary Board, a common occurrence for students back then charged with such offences. The restrictions at UNH were of little bother since I was about to graduate that May. Fortunately, I wasn't charged with driving drunk. Cops were much more laid back about such things than in the society of today.

Immediately after earning my Associate Degree from the Thompson School, I took a summer job as a surveying aid in Sullivan County NH with the Soil Conservation Service (SCS), an agency of the US Department of Agriculture (USDA). In Claremont, I moved into an upstairs apartment in a Polish family's home. One day while working in the field with the SCS geologist, I climbed a tall white pine tree and snagged two fluttering young crows from their nest. It seemed like every adult crow for miles around was pissed off at me and were loudly letting me know. We shut the excited young crows in the official government sedan and finished our work at the site. Having been free to flit throughout the car's interior, we found bird shit galore when time to quit for the day arrived. Shit from the rear window to the dashboard! The geologist kept one crow and I brought the other one to Mom and Dad's house, where over time it became a quite tame pet. Outside, Mom cawed a few times and the crow swooped in near the house for the snacks she offered. One day it was discovered dead beside the road, hit by a car not far from the house.

I contemplated returning to UNH for a four-year degree that fall, but in early October I transferred to a better position as an engineering aid with SCS out of the Plymouth, NH office. Preliminary studies were being conducted for a proposed federal watershed dam project. My job involved remote field monitoring and retrieval of rock core samples from private sector bedrock drill teams, often under frigid conditions in high forested terrain as winter approached.

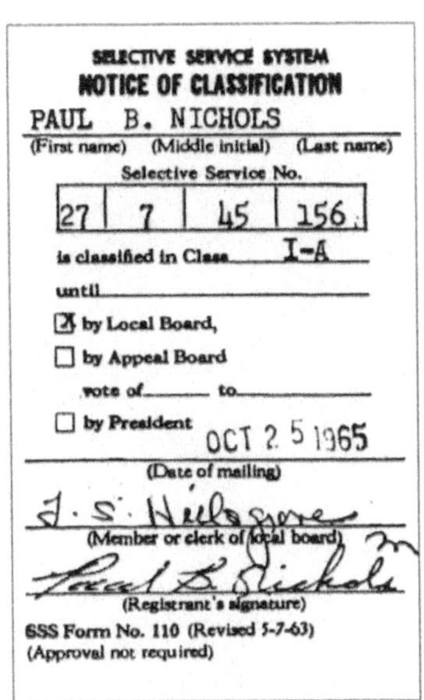

Paul's 1965 military draft cards

The US war in Viet Nam was heating up at a steady pace. So was my romance with Cheryl. President Johnson doubled the draft quota during the summer of 1965. On October 25, 1965 my 2-S (student deferment) draft classification became 1-A (available immediately).

Our military needed a renewable supply of young bullet stoppers. Things moved fast in the conscription arena back then. Concord's draft board #7 sent me orders dated October 27 to report for an Armed Forces induction physical in Manchester on November 5th.

I passed the physical and was about to be drafted into the military.

My draft reclassification came as a disturbing shock to Cheryl and me. We hadn't expected it; hadn't given the possibility any consideration. At that point in my life, I had no intention or desire to join the military. Confusion and uncertainty occupied our thoughts. Plans we had for our future were suddenly turned upside down. This situation was very stressful to us.

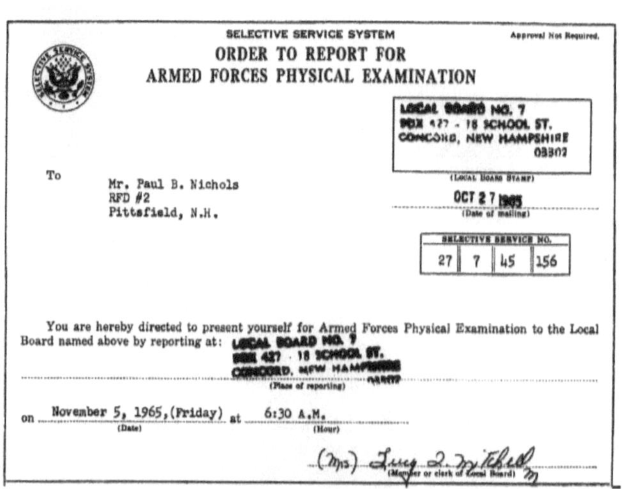

Selective Service Order to Report

STATEMENT OF ACCEPTABILITY

LAST NAME · FIRST NAME · MIDDLE NAME	PRESENT HOME ADDRESS
NICHOLS, PAUL BRUCE	RFD #2, Pittsfield, NH

SELECTIVE SERVICE NUMBER				LOCAL BOARD ADDRESS
27	7	45	156	LB #7, 18 School St., Concord, NH

THE QUALIFICATIONS OF THE ABOVE-NAMED REGISTRANT HAVE BEEN CONSIDERED IN ACCORDANCE WITH THE CURRENT REGULATIONS GOVERNING ACCEPTANCE OF SELECTIVE SERVICE REGISTRANTS AND HE WAS THIS DATE:

☒ 1. FOUND FULLY ACCEPTABLE FOR INDUCTION INTO THE ARMED FORCES.
☐ 2. FOUND NOT ACCEPTABLE FOR INDUCTION UNDER CURRENT STANDARDS.

DATE	PLACE	TYPED OR STAMPED NAME AND GRADE OF JOINT EXAMINING AND INDUCTION STATION COMMANDER	SIGNATURE
5 Nov 65	AFEES, Manchester, N. H.	JACK E. SHULER 2d Lt., AGC	

DD FORM 62 1 MAR 59

PREVIOUS EDITIONS OF THIS FORM ARE OBSOLETE.

REGISTRANT COPY 2

Any inquiry relative to personal status should be referred to your Local Board

Statement of Acceptability

In 1965 I felt that answering my country's call was noble. Though I didn't want to go, I gave little thought to any alternative. Resisting the draft didn't cross my mind. My youthful years mirrored those of most youth of our times. We had an accepting and trusting form of patriotism. Sort of an innocent blind patriotism, unaware or unappreciative of the historic underpinnings that opposition and protest had in our country's founding. After all, the years leading to the Revolutionary War and the war itself, which several of my ancestors fought in, were based on opposition and protest! We didn't give the historic value of open protest the thought it deserved. All that drastically changed as the Sixties decade moved onward.

Undoubtedly, our families' honorable military history influenced our acceptance of the situation we were in. For so many young men of the Sixties generation, our fathers and uncles had fought in World War II, the "good war." We were steeped in pride for the great victory they had achieved against the evil forces of Germany and Japan.

At about the time my draft classification changed, I received word that I had been accepted in a New England training program with the USDA's Agricultural Stabilization and Conservation Service (ASCS), a sister agency of SCS. A position with ASCS assured greater advancement in the absence of a four-year college degree. The Durham hiring office offered to attempt an unlikely draft deferment, but I declined. At this point I still had faith in our country's values and leadership.

If pursued, I may have been able to avoid the draft because I was the sole surviving son to carry on the family name. By getting sucked into the military in the early war years, I was spared the agonizing, soul-searching decisions of those who came later, as the Sixties gradually melted into the Seventies. I've often wondered what course I would have taken if my draft notice had arrived in 1968 or later years, when the lunacy of the USA's role in the war was plainly evident. There were no easy options for America's youth.

During the 1960s, avoiding the draft involved difficult decisions or good fortune. Thousands fled to Canada or European countries. Many went to jail as a life-altering option. Others remained exempt in stateside colleges or faked illness, homosexuality, or purposefully injured themselves. Those convincing authorities of conscientious objector beliefs escaped the draft on moral or religious grounds (many in this category did alternative service, such as serving in the Peace Corps). Young men who were politically connected or had wealthy or influential parents or knew the right doctors to get a 4-F classification (unfit due to medical or psychological conditions) had the means of beating the dreaded conscription. Other schemes were tried, sometimes successful and sometimes not. There was also the possibility of joining a military reserve unit, the "weekend warriors." National Guard, Army Reserve and other armed forces reserve outfits were flooded with frenzied enlistees seeking sanctuary from the war. Enlistment quotas were jammed full to the point where only the privileged or extremely lucky slithered into such outfits. Those who did had sort of a best-of-both-worlds option; they had a good chance of staying clear of the war in Viet Nam, while gaining the honor and record of serving in a military branch. My Pittsfield friend Rip Perrino managed to slip into a reserve outfit and thus remained free of the war. A proportional few National Guard troops served and died in Viet Nam.

Public condemnation of US involvement in the Viet Nam "conflict" was relatively scant in 1965, especially in rural areas. Openly opposing this growing US aggression was a lonely endeavor north of Boston, however many sizable protests were taking place in big cities across our country. Among Americans who did come out against US intervention were followers of Quaker beliefs, folk musicians, enlightened students, poets and those considered activists of the radical left fringe. Some World War II and Korean War vets, journalists, religious leaders and politicians also opposed US involvement in Viet Nam's affairs, though only a scattering. The general populace stood by our country's leaders when it came to matters of foreign policy. Bad tastes were swallowed, trusting that the cause must be honorable. The "domino theory" was erroneously believed to be a valid concern — soon the commies would be at our door, so we had to extinguish the little "brush fire" in Viet Nam before Marxism engulfed the world. Who else was up to the task but the kick-ass USA? The prevailing Cold War mindset was that "might makes right." (It's interesting to note that in an 1860 speech at Cooper Union, NY, Abraham Lincoln stated that "right makes might.") "Better dead than Red" was a common refrain during the Fifties and early Sixties. Years later, conservative columnist Max Boot referred to the Vietnam War as "a sideshow in the Cold War against communism." Some sideshow!

Adding to the patriotic zest was Barry Sadler's song, "The Ballad of the Green Berets" which was released in January 1966. The song soon became a number 1 hit single, and for a while Sadler turned into a celebrity for magazine articles, radio and TV coverage. Sadler had served as a Green Beret medic during his tour of duty in Viet Nam in 1964-1965. Incidentally, when I was in the Marine Corps we changed part of the song's lyrics about one hundred men testing today, but only three qualifying to wear the Green Beret to "One hundred Marines will shit today and wipe their ass with the Green Beret." I like to tease my former Green Beret medic friend John Jones with the revised lyrics!

I hold no animosity toward draft resisters and evaders who genuinely stood by their convictions that the war in Vietnam was hideously wrong. Many Americans, including thousands of veterans, hold deep hatred of actress/activist Jane Fonda for her antiwar activities, particularly her visit to North Viet Nam during the summer of 1972. Among other derogatory images of Jane Fonda, I recall seeing a bumper sticker on a car which read "Viet Nam vets aren't fonda Jane." There were urinal bowl decals and other such demeaning visual statements directed toward her. I feel that she showed extremely poor judgement by allowing herself to be photographed sitting at a North Vietnamese antiaircraft gun on the outskirts of Hanoi. But, other than that big mistake, I believe her intentions were valid in opposing the war. Over the years she has attempted to atone for the unfortunate incident. I have her 2005 memoir explaining her wartime visit.

Most despicable, in my mind, are those of the Dick Cheney ilk, who reaped multiple draft deferments while enthusiastically cheering on the war suffered by multitudes less fortunate. Our country has been led into far too many wars by such "chickenhawk" leaders. Far too many in this despicable category sit unfazed, safely chirping for war from lofty seats of power.

Much has been documented about how class and race determined who was drafted and who fought in America's war in Viet Nam. One of the best references regarding this was featured in the March/April 2017 issue of *The VVA Veteran* magazine, which I have in my files. This excellent synopsis lays out the class selection process based mostly on racial, monetary standing and educational scrutiny. Minorities, poor and working-class whites, and those less educated bore the brunt of the draft and were sent into Viet Nam's meat grinder.

Three-year or four-year enlistments often provided an opportunity for schooling in some field of benefit to the military; training which could possibly be of use in life following discharge. This chance was greatly diminished for draftees, who served only two years. The military knew better than to spend time and energy on those of us who would become civilians as soon as possible.

In 1969 the Selective Service began drafting men under a new system based on the birthdate of potential inductees. Called the draft lottery, specific dates were drawn using a procedure designed to make the outcome random. Men whose birthdate matched the number drawn in 1969 were selected for conscription into the military during 1970. And so on through 1972.

As US combat involvement in Viet Nam was winding down, the Nixon administration ended the draft completely on January 27, 1973. Both the draft lottery system and the total elimination of the draft were slimy political acts designed to fulfill Tricky Dick's presidential election and re-election promises. He strategized that ending conscription would ease tensions and curb the intense nationwide opposition to the highly unpopular war.

SIGNED, SEALED and DELIVERED

Before continuing chronologically with the events covered in this memoir, I feel that it is necessary to include the following few paragraphs which will clarify to future readers some of the narrative that follows.

The country of Viet Nam written as two words is standard in that country, with appropriate accent marks. In the beginning years of the war, the country was expressed in the US as Viet Nam. Over time, the Americanized version commonly became expressed as one word, Vietnam. Both expressions will be used in this memoir based on different timelines.

Myriad books have been written and continue to be written about the Vietnam War. In Vietnam it's known as the "American War" and is referred to as such by many US veterans who served. These include historic nonfiction accounts, magazines, novels, textbooks, self-help books, journals, memoirs, books of poetry and books of art. Several authors are Vietnamese. Some authors are Vietnam veteran brothers and sisters who I know well. I own a considerable library of such books, many of which I have read and some I'll never read. Numerous movies and documentary films have also been produced about the war. I have a collection of those on DVD that I consider most factual. Paintings, drawings, photographs, sculptures, music and other art forms also tell the story.

My library is important because the contents convey what happened during a long, nasty, immoral, unpopular, and unwinnable US war . . . a criminal war begun and perpetuated by lies. They provide a history with profound personal connections. The books hold ghosts and reflections of the strong bonds of brotherhood and sisterhood that developed during war. The war was intimate and life-altering though no two experiences were the same.

In a strange way that's difficult to clearly describe, this library is a part of me and my path through life. It was through these books and associations with other Nam vets that I was led to understand that I wasn't alone with my intense emotions and conflicted feelings. In the decades since the war, I've felt that I would hate to be the last living Vietnam War veteran. Considering everything, that dread is unlikely to be the case. Nam vets covet the profound connections with fellow Nam vets (brothers and sisters), the only ones who can possibly understand.

My library of books, films and related artwork is definitely a part of US history, and I feel strongly that they should be preserved. The books have also served as an excellent reference source for my own writings and for my work with high schools, universities and at various public forums over the years.

The US became entangled in Viet Nam's civil war due to fears promoted by the domino theory (referred to in the second chapter of this memoir) and thus supported the Army of the Republic of Vietnam (ARVN), the South Vietnamese Army. Many ARVN units fought valiantly and admirably, but others proved cowardly, with inept or corrupt leadership, little commitment and weak convictions about the war's objectives. Often times during heavy fighting, ARVN soldiers dropped their weapons and ran for cover. Desertion was commonplace. Similar to the American Civil War, some Vietnamese families became divided with members fighting for the north and others within the family supporting the south. Most families felt trapped, simply wanting to live their lives free of foreign interference. Le Ly Hayslip's haunting memoir *When Heaven and Earth Changed Places* provides a personal record of this.

South Vietnamese presidents were fraudulently elected and

were contemptibly corrupt, generating a problematic fighting force. The situation wasn't helped in that a succession of South Viet Nam's presidents had direct ties to the USA, making them widely considered as unsavory puppets of the US. Being a Catholic president in an overwhelmingly Buddhist population furthered the mayhem, as was the case with nefarious, corrupt Presidents Ngo Dinh Diem and later, Nguyen Van Thieu.

North Viet Nam's war with America was led by President Ho Chi Minh, affectionately known to his followers as "Uncle Ho." His untiring lifelong dream was for Viet Nam's unification and independence. Ho Chi Minh sought US support in this endeavor but was blatantly disregarded. Historic records make this very clear. He then formed the National Liberation Front consisting of communist Viet Cong (VC) peasant guerrilla fighters and regular army cadres. Also under Ho Chi Minh's control was the North Vietnamese Army (NVA), a formidable force well trained and well equipped with Russian (formerly USSR) and Chinese weaponry. Such weaponry included highly efficient AK-47 rifles, long-range artillery, rockets, mortars, tanks, grenades, mines and other explosives, and a limited number of MiG aircraft. The enemy we fought was often brilliantly led, strongly nationalistic and infinitely determined to defend their country from the onslaught of their newest foreign invader, the United States of America.

French colonialists were defeated in 1954 northwest of Hanoi at Dien Bien Phu. It is important to note that the USA had been somewhat covertly supporting the French from the end of World War II through subsequent years, leading to the French defeat by the Viet Minh. The victorious top commander throughout the French and US wars was NVA General Vo Nguyen Giap.

The infamous "Gulf of Tonkin incident" of August 1964 opened the floodgates for overt US war in Viet Nam. Covert pursuits had been continued since the French defeat. The 1964 presidential election had strong implications. Vice President Lyndon B. Johnson had become President immediately following JFK's assassination. The 1964 presidential election featured Johnson against hawkish archconservative Arizona Republican Senator Barry Goldwater. The "incident" came about due to an attack by North Vietnamese torpedo boats on US Navy Destroyer *Maddox* on August 2, 1964, followed by alleged attacks on the *Maddox* and *Turner Joy* on August 4. In fact, no second attack took place. Furthermore, the North Vietnamese had been provoked into retaliatory strikes in reaction to earlier clandestine raids by US Navy ships on the North Vietnamese coast. Challenger Goldwater had been loudly claiming that Johnson was weak against communist aggression in Vietnam and advocated to employ low-grade nuclear weapons. With all this disruptive political misinformation, the upcoming presidential election triggered pressure for escalation of US war against Vietnam.

The vast majority of the American public had little understanding of what was happening, as our country was led into the quagmire... sucked increasingly deeper as if in quicksand. On August 7, 1964, Congress overwhelmingly passed the Gulf of Tonkin Resolution. The vote was 416 to 0 in the House and 88 to 2 in the Senate. The only no votes came from Senators Wayne Morse of Oregon and Ernest Gruening from Alaska, both Democrats. The Resolution gave Johnson a "blank check" to wage war against North Vietnam, though records show that he was deeply conflicted about escalating. He had no desire to be a war president, but political forces led us deep into the mire. Johnson won the presidential election in a landslide.

Our political and military leaders misjudged their war of attrition approach, using enemy "body count" as a measure of success. Widespread "search and destroy" missions of suspected VC hamlets and the designation of "free fire zones" intensified the killing. Dead Vietnamese of any age or gender were tallied as enemies. Thus, the sum of dead Vietnamese determined the measure of body count. All the while, intentionally erroneously low US casualty figures disclosed to Americans back home were common through deviously filtered media reports. For example, battle accounts of enemy dead might declare 243 killed, while US casualties were vaguely reported as being "light."

Correspondents and photographers pretty much had free rein to travel throughout the war zone; access unlike during any US war activity before or since. Graphic prime time television news coverage was broadcast on a daily basis. Newspapers and popular magazines carried shocking reports and visuals. Eventually, all this strengthened antiwar sentiment nationwide and pressured our warmonger politicians.

The heinous "Phoenix Program" run by the CIA in conjunction with the Republic of Vietnam used extreme terror and psychological operations to achieve murderous results. Hallmarks of this evil program included widespread disinformation tactics, torturous interrogations, assassinations and "kill quotas."

Under the code name, "Operation Ranch Hand" (formerly known as "Operation Hades"), the US military sprayed approximately 20 million gallons of "Agent Orange" and several other extremely toxic defoliants known as the "Rainbow Agents" over much of Viet Nam's countryside, as well as parts of Cambodia and Laos. Extensive aerial spraying, mainly from Air Force C-123 aircraft, took place from 1962–1971 poisoning forests, jungle, cropland, and waterways. They also sprayed these herbicides from helicopters, riverboats, trucks, and individual backpacks. It covered people and entered the food chain. The defoliants (produced primarily by Dow Chemical and Monsanto Corporation) contained dioxin, one of the deadliest known cancer-causing compounds. Chemical company boardroom discussions, secret pentagon reports and political warmongers were aware of the calamitous peril caused by the Rainbow Agents. The criminal legacy of these monstrous chemicals continues to this day, horribly affecting a multitude of US veterans and their kids, and Southeast Asian people and their offspring. Diseases from Agent Orange poisoning have been proven to sometimes skip a generation, striking grandchildren of war survivors. Medical studies have long recognized that thousands of Vietnam War veterans have died from Agent Orange exposure. Local vets I knew well who suffered and died of cancer brought on from Agent Orange exposure were Bear Jenisch, Dwight Graves, Rick Ducey, Russ Dunn, and Bobby Corliss. It's as though these vets were killed in Viet Nam and didn't know it! This defoliation program was a form of chemical warfare.

Our military's widespread use of the incendiary napalm and incessant high explosive carpet-bombing by B-52 bombers, known as arc light operations, caused untold devastation to the people, their countryside and their heritage. Viet Nam is a country only slightly bigger in area than the state of New Mexico. More US bombs were dropped on this little country over the course of the war than were dropped during both theaters of World War II combined. Former US Air Force Chief of Staff Curtis LeMay is on record stating, "We're going to bomb them back into the Stone Age." Regarding fighting the Vietnamese, Army General Glenn Walker advised, that "You don't fight this fellow rifle to rifle. You locate him and back away. Blow the hell out of him and then police up." Famed AP news correspondent Peter Arnett reportedly wrote, "It became necessary to destroy the town to save it." These headlines were published in newspapers in February 1968 reporting on the battle of Ben Tre.

The war resulted in thousands of Amerasian children (those born to Vietnamese mothers who were fathered by Americans) belonging to no one. Those rejected kids were known by the Vietnamese as "children of the dust" and were helpless, hopeless street children.

The "Strategic Hamlet Program" launched in rural areas early in the war proved disastrous, causing increased alienation toward ARVN and US goals. Vietnamese village families and their belongings were rounded up and forcibly moved into protective hamlets. The objective was that by uprooting and corralling peasant villagers in controlled hamlets, Viet Cong influence and support could be eliminated. This cruel displacement program proved unworkable and was eventually terminated. The "winning hearts and minds" strategy to gain support of the Vietnamese people was morally and effectively bankrupt.

Secret illegal bombings and troop incursions into the adjoining countries of Cambodia and Laos expanded the war's carnage to no avail. As the war raged on, US political and military leaders declared that we must "stay the course." They lied about there being "light at the end of the tunnel" which would bring "peace with honor." All were catch phrases of doom.

The late, highly acclaimed historian and Pulitzer Prize winning author, Barbara W. Tuchman, in her book *The March of Folly* puts forth a concise, condensed account of misguided US involvement in the affairs of Vietnam from 1945 to 1973. She does so brilliantly in her Part 5 chapter aptly titled *America Betrays Herself in Vietnam*.

Below are May 1966 quotes from USMC General David M. Shoup, Congressional Medal of Honor recipient for WW II heroism on Tarawa, Commandant of the US Marine Corps (1960-1963).

These quotes were printed in the Congressional Record February 20, 1967:

"I want to tell you, I don't think the whole of South East Asia, as related to the present and future safety and freedom of the people of this country, is worth the life or limb of a single American."

Furthermore, General Shoup said:

"I believe that if we had and would keep our dirty, bloody, dollar-soaked fingers out of the business of these nations so full of depressed, exploited people, they will arrive at a solution of their own. That they design and want. That they fight and work for. And if unfortunately their revolution must be of the violent type because the 'haves' refuse to share with the 'have-nots' by any peaceful method, at least what they get will be their own, and not the American style, which they don't want and above all don't want crammed down their throats by Americans."

General Shoup remained in strong, outspoken opposition to America's war in Vietnam. The second quote was originally part of a speech he delivered on February 12, 1966 at a World Affairs Day event at Pierce College in California.

The Marine Corps offered a two-year enlistment having a 120-day delayed entry option. Rather than be drafted for two years in the Army, I hurriedly swore the oath becoming USMC property in November of 1965. Cheryl and I had become engaged, and we decided to be married within the 120 days prior to my leaving for boot camp. In addition to my day job in Plymouth, which lasted well into December, I took a night job at Pittsfield's leather tannery. At the tannery, I spread and piled suede leather hides across wooden horses on a piecework basis after they had been dyed in huge wooden rotary mills. By that time, I had replaced my Crown Victoria with a fast (Thunderbird engine), but decrepit, 1957 Ford convertible. Putting the top down on the car required tricky ingenuity because one of the roof support structures was broken. Plus, the manufacturer's electronic system was inoperative. To engage the power apparatus to lift the roof back I laid a knife blade across the dashboard terminals. Then the top's framework had to be helped down into place by hand on the side that was broken.

Cheryl and I were married in a little church in Northwood on New Year's Day 1966. We were very young, quite common for marriages during this time period. She was 18 years old and I was 20. We believed that we were a perfect match. We had a conventional wedding ceremony for the times with family and friends present. Reverend Parker from Chichester's Congregational Church performed the marrying ceremony, and my cousin Judy Jenkins sang a love song. Following the wedding, Cheryl and I spent that night at the Wayfarer Inn in Bedford, then drove on to Boston for our brief honeymoon. We had rented a mobile home for the month in Boscawen for privacy's sake during our brief time together.

Feeling sad and apprehensive, I boarded a train in Manchester, NH on January 26, 1966, en route to Beaufort, South Carolina. I knew no one on the train and took a seat beside a scared-looking kid named Robert Daigneau. He said that he lived on a farm in Gilmanton and was also headed for Parris Island.

We were picked up by seething Marine DIs (Drill Instructors) and were hastily loaded into "cattle trucks" and driven to the USMC Recruit Depot receiving barracks. This took place in the wee hours of the morning, and it infuriated the DIs to greet us clad in our civilian clothes and with civilian hairstyles.

We were all made to stand at attention on Parris Island's traditional yellow footprints painted on the pavement while being verbally trashed. Bob Daigneau and I were both assigned to the 3rd Recruit Training Battalion, S Company, Platoon 332. Bob was granted hardship leave during training due to his father's serious illness. His dad later recovered, and Bob returned to Parris Island, graduating with a different platoon. Ours had moved on. I didn't see Bob again until many years later when he visited me in Laconia. More about Bob later.

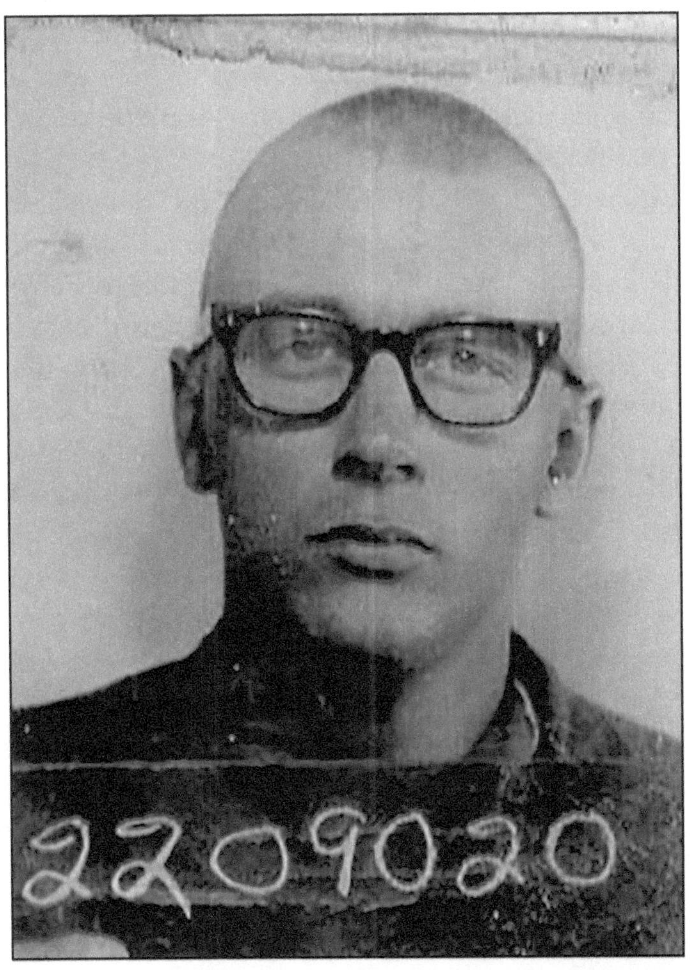

Paul's Parris Island ID photo

USMC boot camp lived up to its reputation. It was a harrowing, unforgettable experience about which any number of words could not adequately describe. Personal identity was stripped away from recruits and was replaced by group identity. The training ordeal was pure indoctrination into the Marine Corps way. Deviations prohibited! This was true from arrival at the receiving barracks and issuance of "782 gear" all the way through to graduation day. Vile torment from our DIs did somewhat diminish as graduation day approached when we "turds" came closer to being Marines.

Having grown up in rural "white" New Hampshire, I was ignorant of races and cultures different from mine. Big city life was foreign to me. Other than rare attendances at Fenway Park to watch the Boston Red Sox play, I had never seen a Black, Hispanic, or Asian person. This lack of diversity brought a momentous awakening right from the start, as I was in the company of recruits from all walks of life. Platoons included youth from the deep south through northeastern states. Recruits from the countryside and from big cities. And from the Caribbean Island of Puerto Rico, a US territory since 1898. Interactions with Blacks and Hispanics were common during basic training. I'm not aware of any Native Americans and Asians in Platoon 332, though many trained in other platoons. Recruits from western states went through basic training at the Marine Corps Recruit Depot in San Diego, California.

Since the USMC is a part of the Department of the Navy, the use of nautical terms was standard, and we soon learned the meanings of each. "Port" for left and "starboard" for right are examples. A bed was a "rack." A bathroom was a "head," so when in our squad bay (barracks) a DI would yell to recruits, "Port side, get your swinging dicks to the head." Or "Get outta that rack," no questions were asked!

Writing a detailed account of the boot camp adventure could serve as a mini memoir and would hardly portray the intensity of the experience. The DIs zeal was especially harsh with a burgeoning war underway. The following paragraphs offer a partial account of what happened within our platoon during those early months of 1966.

The standard twelve-week ordeal was compressed into eight, and platoon size was increased due to the war's hungry demand. I was number 75 in a platoon of about 100. We slept on narrow steel framed bunk-type racks (one above the other with very thin mattresses) that ran the length of our squad bay on both sides, with a fairly wide aisle down the center. The DI's office was at one end. Our day began prior to daybreak. The platoon was often awakened as overhead lights suddenly came on with the crashing sound of a big metal trash can rolling down the squad bay between the rows of racks. The can had been hurled by the DI as a startling wake-up call. When inspections were ordered, our clothing and equipment had to be displayed in a very neat and specifically aligned arrangement on our meager mattresses. All USMC-issued clothing had to be stamped with our name in black ink placed at specified locations on each piece. (Following boot camp, our unofficial slang terms for such inspections were "junk on the bunk" and "things on the springs.")

In addition to severe discipline, hardline regimentation, brutal harassment, and grueling physical and mental exertion that define Marine Corps boot camp, DIs primed us for war in Viet Nam. This was obvious, and we were told that most of us would be going "across the pond." The pond being the Pacific Ocean.

It was demanded that we use a very minimum (like two sheets) of toilet paper when taking a shit. This would get us used to the tiny roll of toilet paper contained in each individual cardboard box of C rations. They taught us that Marines are "highly trained, paid-by-the-government killers," a quote I clearly recall. In bayonet drill we slashed, jabbed, smashed and butt stroked dummies designed in the likeness of Vietnamese people. The Vietnamese were referred to in derogatory versions of "gook," most often, "Luke the Gook." We learned little about Vietnamese culture and values. Instead, our enemies were dehumanized as though they were evil subhumans.

Running was integral to boot camp training. When running, our DIs often chanted "One, two, three, four — I love the Marine Corps," at which recruits shouted the refrain as the platoon ran to its destination. Very silently under my breath, I chanted "One, two, three, four — fuck the Marine Corps." I suspect others did likewise! Running chants at times contained variations of killing VC (Viet Cong).

When we weren't outside running, we marched. Marching cadence varied depending on which DI was in charge. One cadence version was: "If I die in a combat zone, box me up and send me home. Place my arms across my chest. Tell the world I've done my best."

We were marched past the infamous Ribbon Creek, the tidal wash into which a DI marched his platoon of recruits in 1956, drowning 6 of them. On a couple occasions when our platoon was learning to march during the early weeks, we couldn't perform to the satisfaction of our DIs. We were made to pull our wrinkled utility hats ("covers") way down onto our heads and walk along as a disorganized mass. They forced us to call out mooing sounds, as if we were a herd of cows. The DIs angrily shouted that we animals were headed for the barn (our barracks). Our platoon was viewed in this manner while other platoons in various stages of training marched in strict formations. This was especially degrading when we came alongside marching platoons in immaculate utility uniforms nearing graduation and looking very "AJ squared away." DIs fostered competitiveness between their platoon and others.

I had little trouble with the physical exertion of boot camp, but the strict regimentation and harsh discipline were oppressive. All of our DIs were strict hard-asses, but Sgt. P. W.

Gigler was downright sadistic. He never once giggled! Recruits who drill instructors deemed fat, out of shape or unmotivated were sent to STB (Special Training Branch). Threatening descriptions of what took place during time spent at STB brought about tight conformity. No one wanted to be transferred to STB!

During February, I got called before Sgt. Gigler who informed me that the dispensary had found that I had some sort of venereal disease (VD). I knew this was impossible, but Gigler would hear of nothing I attempted to say. Trying to explain that I was married less than a month before arriving at Parris Island meant nothing to him, and words were few. Gigler led me to his car, which was a Volkswagen Beetle. Immediately when the bug started up the Lovin' Spoonful song *Daydream* began playing on the car radio as we headed for the dispensary. The radio was quickly turned off, but the lyrics of the jovial, whimsical song danced through my head, recalled from days prior to Parris Island. Under the circumstances, the song about a boy lost in a daydream while envisioning his sweetheart reminded me longingly of how much I missed being home with Cheryl.

At the dispensary it became clear that a records mix-up had occurred, and it wasn't me who had VD. There were no apologies for the error!

Most always, when one or more platoon members screwed up, even in a minor way, the entire platoon caught the wrath of our drill instructors. There was no room for individualism. They considered the platoon as being one transformed body. Punitive pushups, many of them, in our squad bay were a common result of the slightest transgression. Once, our platoon was made to stand in front of our racks and hold our bath towels by the corners with outstretched arms for a long period of time. With aching fingers and shoulders, we had to keep that position while the DI ridiculed us for being weak "cheese dicks."

When our platoon was going through the chow line at the

mess hall, our trays were held perpendicular to our bodies, with our eyes staring straight ahead while we silently continued sidestepping down the length of the line. Food items were flopped onto our trays by the attending mess duty recruits on the other side of the line. The stainless-steel trays were segmented, but the food served didn't always land in an empty segment. We ate with our platoon members at cafeteria-style tables aligned in the spacious mess hall. Mealtime was short, and they forbid us from saying a word to one another. Other platoons sat at adjacent tables as directed by their DIs.

On one occasion, several of us had gone through the chow line and were seated with our food, while some recruits from our platoon were still going through the line. Evidently, someone at our table must have said something or done something that alerted the ever-watchful Sgt. Gigler. He strode quietly to our table. Without word or warning, he reached down and quickly tipped our table over. Silverware and trays of food landed on us and on the floor. At that point, Gigler shouted orders for our entire platoon of "maggots" to get our "swinging dicks" out of the mess hall. This included those who had still been standing in line without a bite to eat. Chow time had ended abruptly. Once outside, they hurriedly marched us to our barracks. Harassment and many pushups followed.

One day, a solemn drill instructor faced us with news that tragedy had struck a recruit in our platoon. Bobby Lee was briefly called from our squad bay and notified that his brother had been killed in Viet Nam.

On Sundays came the chance to attend a religious service. Religious or not, this offered a short break period from the harassing DIs. Recruits were ordered to fall out into groups depending on their religious denomination. Catholics were referred to as "mackerel snappers."

On Platoon 332's graduation day in late March, tens of thousands demonstrated in the second "Days of International

Protest" against the Viet Nam War in big cities across the US, Canada, Europe and Japan. The drill instructors didn't tell us this news, of course!

Following Parris Island came several weeks of advanced infantry training at Camp Geiger, a satellite of the larger Camp Lejeune in North Carolina. The barracks at Geiger were shabby, and I recall seeing cockroaches on the mess hall floor. Platoon 332 from Parris Island was no longer a unit, and I didn't see anyone from my weeks in boot camp.

At Camp Geiger I trained in K Company. The "K" designation stood for "Killer," not kindness! This period was known as ITR (Infantry Training Regiment), and it was even more strongly geared toward combat in Viet Nam. The intense focus of this training was fighting and surviving the war.

At the time of my arrival the training fields were overcrowded, so new units could not immediately be formed. They ordered newcomers to serve on mess duty (KP) or other shit details in the interim. I got assigned to be in charge of an overnight armory crew. Our job was to clean a huge assortment of weaponry used by outfits already in training. The work was arduous.

A white Marine from a southern state (Virginia, I think) refused to pull his share of the workload. He may have resented my northern roots. Tempers flared as I tried to convince him to get busy. We got into a scuffle and tipped over a barrel of solvent as we flailed across the concrete floor. I got the better of the fight by putting him in an unyielding headlock and breaking his nose with my fist. There was a saying common among Marines at the time relative to one not looking so good, that saying being, "You look like you've been in an entrenching tool fight without an entrenching tool." The Marine I thrashed looked like he had been missing his entrenching tool!

Continuing on from Parris Island, ITR training took on the near constant dehumanization of the Vietnamese, the Vietcong

(VC) and North Vietnamese Army (NVA) in particular. My copious hand-scribbled notes reflect some of what we were taught. They read like this: *The VC guerrilla stands about five feet tall and wears black pajamas — very vicious, cruel people armed with anything, even spears and crossbows — creative minds make menacing traps — terrific endurance — masters at ambush and camouflage — 96% of all Vietnamese women have VD* (blatantly untrue) *of which 50-60% are incurable types, like the deadly "black syph."* Servicemen contracting black syph, we were told, never make it home. Instead, they were sent to some island off the coast of Viet Nam to die. Since the disease was deadly with no chance of a cure, families of such victims were informed that their sons were missing or had been killed in action. This we were told, but I've never seen it recorded as fact. We were warned that if captured: *Luke the Gook will cut you four ways — long, wide, deep and continuously.* And maybe even worse than that!

Viet Nam's varied geographic features and uncomfortable climate conditions were described in graphic detail. We learned about the country's bugs, leeches, snakes, rats, water buffalos, rock apes, elephants, and tigers. They schooled us in mapping, camouflage, carrying out vertical assaults, amphibious landings, search and destroy operations and dealing with the extensive VC tunnel systems and booby traps. Of search and destroy operations, my scrawled notes say: *search an area and kill everything in sight.*

We practiced using many types of fully operable weapons and explosives. Again, I will refer to one of my handwritten notes from explosives training. While discussing detonation cord and its destructive uses, the instructor stated: *Det. cord detonates at 21,000 feet/second and makes a good clothesline for your pregnant girlfriend.* Later, during ITR training, we were required to go through the dreaded "gas chamber" filled with tear gas.

Absent was information about Vietnamese language, history, culture, and spiritual values. We had no idea about the importance of family reverence or the significance of Tet festivities. Vietnamese Tet began the lunar new year and signified the advent of spring. The holiday had powerful spiritual meanings. The Vietnamese zodiac sign for the year 1966 was Horse, which had specific values in their culture. We knew nothing of the rich and ancient history of the people we were being sent to kill. Tet of 1968 (year of the Monkey) is recorded as "The Tet Offensive" in US history books and relates to fierce countrywide battles, omitting the cultural meanings of the annual holiday.

As training was ending, they advised those of us who were married to execute a power of attorney and prepare a will. Being mostly in our late teens, we owned nothing to will!

Decades later, I've found myself reading letters from family and friends written during my training at Parris Island and Camp Geiger. The many back-and-forth letters between Cheryl and me are heartbreaking. It was torturous being so deeply in love and recently married, then being torn apart by distance and uncertainty about what our future would hold. Especially at a time when a faraway war was rapidly escalating. Such separation was a tough way to begin a marriage, and our letters poignantly relate intense longing for one another. Letters to my parents brought Dad back to his experiences at Parris Island from 1942. It is obvious from his letters in reply that my accounts of boot camp rigors nudged Dad's own memories to the surface. In a few places, he offered brief notes of humor.

After completing ITR, standard procedure allowed me several days of military leave from late April into May. I knew that Cheryl was at her mother's house, and I hitchhiked there from Manchester. It was great to be temporarily free of the Corps and with loved ones on home turf. Orders for my first regular duty station sent me to Camp Lejeune with the 2nd Marine Division.

Based on testing, my two-year college degree, and the luck of the draw, I was assigned the 1413 construction surveyor MOS (military occupational specialty). Cheryl and I had bought a brand new green 1965 Volkswagen beetle. She quit her job and we drove south in our VW crammed with all our belongings we could fit. At Camp Lejeune we moved into Knox Trailer Park, base housing for low-ranked Marines. Our very basic but livable trailer was #417 in a sea of other dull gray-silver abodes. We had little money over and above survival. For low-cost recreation, we drove to nearby Topsail Beach in Surf City outside of Lejeune whenever possible. At one point, we got so broke we pawned my alto saxophone and tape recorder in the off-base town of Jacksonville (referred to as "J-ville") to get by for the month. Pawnshops and sleazy bars were common fixtures in towns located close to military bases. Needless to say, we never retrieved these things from the pawnbroker.

A few Marines in the outfit I was assigned to had returned from combat in Viet Nam. They were worn and appeared far older than their years. Stories of their experiences were gruesome, and we were warned to stay clear of Viet Nam if possible.

By mid-June I received orders to report at Camp Pendleton in southern California, where I was to join an FMF (Fleet Marine Force) "West Pac" ground forces replacement draft for Viet Nam. I was going "across the pond" as the Parris Island DIs predicted.

On June 17th Cheryl and I drove our VW straight through from Camp Lejeune to Northwood, arriving the next day. We attended the big motorcycle race at Bryar Motorsport Park in Loudon on June 19th.

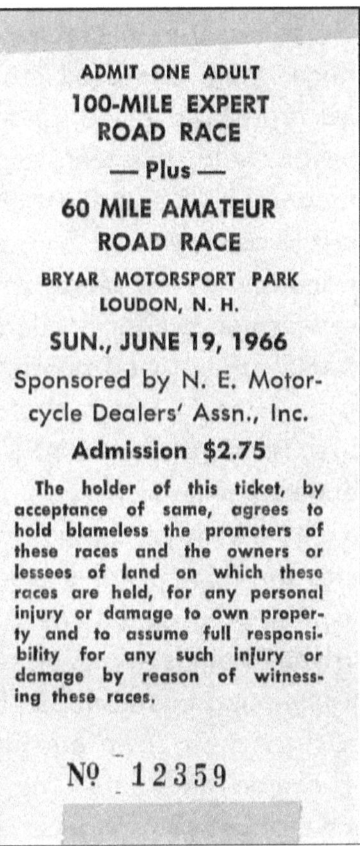

1966 race ticket at Bryar Motorsport Park

US casualties from the war were accelerating, and my time at home was dwindling. The imminent reality of my 13-month tour in Viet Nam generated feelings of pensive anxiety in Cheryl and me, as my departure date grew closer. Significant changes had come into our lives during the past six months, and our future was further clouded by the uncertainties of war. We vowed that our deep love for one another would sustain us through the difficult period ahead.

Nationwide, a commercial airlines strike was in progress when it came time for me to leave for Camp Pendleton in July. I had to catch a series of standby military flights beginning at Hanscom AFB (Air Force Base) in Massachusetts. The goodbyes were tearful as Cheryl, Mom and Dad stood waving while I boarded the C-130 transport plane and taxied down the runway, trying my best to hold back tears as the three faded out of sight. From Hanscom AFB I shuttled on C-130s to several military bases across the country.

The first stop landed me in New Jersey at McGuire AFB. That night a few of us servicemen caught a ride into Trenton where we visited several bars. I recall that Trenton was a shithole of a city. The next flight took me to Wright-Patterson AFB in Ohio, followed by another to Richards-Gebaur AFB in Missouri. The C-130s had no conventional seats for troops. Along both walls of the fuselage olive drab nylon strapping was attached, upon which we sat close to the floor jammed side-by-side with little elbow room. Not comfortable conditions for long continuous flights. I finally arrived exhausted at Travis AFB near San Francisco. I took a Greyhound bus from San Francisco down the California coast to Oceanside, a town outside Camp Pendleton, arriving on base a couple days late. The journey had been chaotic with little sleep between flights, as servicemen and women tried to reach their destinations on time. Checking in a few days late was excused because of the huge airline strike.

At Camp Pendleton I was assigned to a staging battalion in an area of Quonset huts called Las Pulgas — a training area designed exclusively for Marines destined for Viet Nam. Those responsible for our training were relentless combat-hardened survivors of the Viet Nam and Korean Wars, and they treated us like shit. For about four exhausting weeks, Las Pulgas proved to be the most grueling conditioning yet, especially brutal during mid-summer in the brown Southern California mountains. We took long forced marches into the hills with little water, few C-rations, and full packs. The dust under our boots billowed up like talcum powder with each step, and the hills were abundant with rattlesnakes, scorpions, and tarantulas. I recall that one time when we caught a scorpion and a tarantula we sprayed them with lighter fluid and set them afire.

A mock Viet Cong village had been set up, complete with tunnels, spider holes, punji pits and booby traps. We underwent POW training, exercises in escape and evasion, assaulting fortified positions, camouflage, gas warfare, and extensive experience with explosives and infantry weapons. We dug foxholes with our entrenching tools. We crawled under live machine gun fire. Nearby explosions erupted, adding to the training's real life feel. They showed us graphic films revealing the types of VD common in Viet Nam. Our hatred of "Luke the gook" intensified as the VC and NVA were dehumanized as godless heathens.

Three especially harsh incidents during my time at Las Pulgas come to mind:

During a live field demonstration of the C-4 plasticized explosive, one of the instructors noticed a fatigued young Marine in the bleachers dozing off. The pliable nature of C-4 had just been covered, and a sizable charge was about to be set off a safe distance away from the benches where we sat. The instructor walked up into the stands and molded a block of C-4 around the awakened Marine's head, shaped roughly similar to a set of headphones. Within seconds, a tremendous explosion was detonated at the pre-determined site. The ground heaved and debris flew. The young Marine sat stunned. He and the rest of us in the bleachers stayed very alert throughout the remainder of the explosives class.

On another hot day of training midway into a poisonous snake class, an inattentive Marine was singled out and made to hold a rambunctious rattlesnake. Those sitting next to him edged aside a bit. With one hand on each end of the squirming rattler, arms held a distance from his body, the Marine maintained his grasp until the session ended. Heat and fatigue were no excuse in the minds our hard-assed instructors.

At Camp Geiger's ITR training I had my first encounter with the "gas chamber," as previously mentioned. The second time at Las Pulgas was a much more punishing experience. We had been briefed on how to "clear" the gas masks that we were temporarily issued. Soon afterwards we were directed into a Quonset hut, where we were lined up around the inner walls. Next came instructions that a live gas mask exercise would be taking place in the gas chamber where we were assembled. Suddenly smoldering pellets of tear gas landed amidst us. They made us to walk around the interior of the hut in single file while singing a few bars of the Marine Corps Hymn. At a point when the instructors observed that we were sufficiently coughing and burning, we were ordered to remove the gas masks from our belt pouches and fit them over our faces, then to clear them of the tear gas and put them back on so we could supposedly breathe. For most of us, this procedure didn't work out well since gas remained in or leaked into our masks. We were allowed to run out through one opened end of the chamber into fresh air. We ran with outstretched arms coughing and wheezing. Our eyes, underarms and crotch were most irritated until the effects of the gas wore off. There were no long-lasting effects of this uncomfortable episode.

Our white USMC issued underwear was dyed green making it less visible to enemy eyes, and typical Marine skinhead haircuts were compulsory. When weekend leave was available, we sharply contrasted with the California surfer-boy crowd. We felt envious of their freedom. Anti-war sentiment was surging across the country. I wasn't aware of the extent of the discord, being so insulated from national news and so inescapably immersed in all that was going on at Las Pulgas. One weekend while doing my laundry in an Oceanside laundromat, I glanced at a news magazine with Bob Dylan on the cover. He had barely survived a serious motorcycle accident in Woodstock, NY and was recovering from his injuries. It was heartening to have this remote connection with the poet/musician who I greatly admired.

Our lot hung together for obvious reasons, and we managed to have a few wild drunken times on our last weekends in the USA. During mandatory weekend morning musters for shit detail assignments, we would show up to be accounted for, then a few of us would quickly fade away out of formation and out of sight of those in charge. Those who remained in formation got stuck with shit details. Under the circumstances, our attitudes were such . . . we didn't really give a fuck!

One particularly crazy episode was a hitchhiking journey to Tijuana, Mexico, a destination prohibited for Marines in our deployment status. Three or four of us who eluded a Las Pulgas shit detail that day thumbed our way to Tijuana. TJ wasn't that far from Camp Pendleton, and I remember being picked up by a crazy guy in a Plymouth Fury (a huge boat of a car with monstrous tail fins). He blasted us to the Mexican border at a chilling rate of speed, and we managed to get through the SPs (Navy Shore Patrol) guarding the gate. We had a wild time for several hours drinking rotgut tequila in seedy bars lined with raunchy whores. Since I was married, I stayed clear of the whores. Two bars we spent time in were The Blue Fox and The Chicago Club. While sitting in the bars, club women sat on our laps. They also fondled those who were standing. Somehow, we managed to stay clear of the clink. Crowds of poor Mexicans on the streets hawked all kinds of stuff, including kids trying to sell their sisters for sex. I bought a cheap switchblade. I don't recall the trip back to Pendleton.

Los Angeles was off limits too, and a few of us went there by bus one weekend. Being a country boy, I recall feeling overwhelmed by the huge city and all the activity happening everywhere. We went to lots of cheap bars, as money was scarce, and got back to the base with pounding heads.

The military's concern about weekend leave destinations was that of "missing movement," the serious punitive Article 87 under the Uniform Code of Military Justice (UCMJ). In other words, bad behavior in town might land us in civilian detention, causing us to miss our trip to Viet Nam. Our favorite mutinous saying was "What are they going to do, send us to Viet Nam?"

In August 1966 we departed from Camp Pendleton on military buses to San Diego. Among the few onlookers gathered to see loved ones off was some Marine's mother, who was crying frantically and threatening to kill herself if her son boarded the war-bound ship. We were to board the *USNS General Weigel*, a dilapidated troop transport ship that was first launched in 1944. My early August letters to Cheryl describe the delay in getting on the "old tub" due to steering mechanism, generator, and electrical malfunctions in sailing merely from San Francisco to San Diego! The letters further state that there were about 3300 of us who finally got on board. Of those, 1184 were Marines, the rest being army soldiers plus the sizable Navy crew that piloted the ship. Unlike traditional celebratory war send-offs, no deployment ceremonies were held as we left for Viet Nam.

I managed to secure a top rack in the cramped quarters above other racks. My reasoning was that if seasickness became a problem at least no one would be puking down on me. The downside of this choice was that my rack was next to a big heat duct, causing further discomfort from heat and noise. Also, right over my head was a loudspeaker, which blared seemingly nonstop. The plus sides of this sea journey were beautiful sunrises and sunsets, boundless starry skies, silvery schools of flying fish, occasional huge ocean sunfish basking near the surface, and not being killed or maimed in combat. There was plenty of time for writing letters. Whenever possible, a bunch of us spent night hours relaxing in the balmy Pacific air on the ship's fantail gazing at the stars and thinking of home. It is amazing to be on the sea day after day and not get sight of land in any direction. Just seemingly endless ocean.

Sea duty was another drastic lifestyle change as my old letters attest: extremely cramped quarters, rampant seasickness, cold saltwater showers, racks five-high and close in all directions, never-ending chow lines and hours of standing fire nozzle guard. The big solid brass fire nozzles attached to coiled hoses at various stations along the length of the ship were being stolen, creating a serious safety hazard. Marines blamed Navy personnel thinking that they probably hoarded and sold them at huge black-market profits when reaching port. As usual, Marines got stuck pulling guard duty at various posts.

The thin mattresses aboard the ship were encased in what were referred to as "fart sacks." Several of us lower-ranked Marines, me included, got assigned to "KP duty," commonly called "mess duty," for a few days. We spent hours laboring in the galley area where the ship's food was stored and prepared. Knowing that we were destined for Viet Nam where chow would be scarce and horrible, we naively came up with the idea of hoarding a nonperishable stockpile of the ship's stores. We amassed a hefty load of food items, loaded them into a fart sack that one of us had ripped off, and hid the stash away for safekeeping. Exactly how we figured we would ever get the bulky sack off the ship into the war zone is now immaterial, and of course it remained on the ship. In reality, maybe it was just the boredom and the thought of stealing from the Navy was fun enough for us.

Our immediate destination was Viet Nam, but somewhere en route orders mysteriously changed. Rumors passed that the ship might dock briefly in Hawaii. No such luck! After two weeks at sea with no land in sight we docked at Naha Harbor, Okinawa.

Okinawa is a beautiful island in the East China Sea under Japanese governance, with widely scattered US bases. From Naha we were trucked north to Camp Schwab, a Marine base named after USMC Medal of Honor recipient PFC Albert E. Schwab, who was killed during the Battle of Okinawa in the spring of 1945.

We stood with our gear spread out at our feet on an asphalt expanse in blazing sun for hours before being trucked to Camp Hansen, a USMC base named after Marine Private Dale M. Hansen. Hansen was also a Medal of Honor recipient killed during the Battle of Okinawa.

I was attached to A Company, 5th Engineer Battalion, a combat engineer outfit (MOS 1371). For a short period of time, I was assigned as a driver of a Mighty Mite jeep. In this capacity, I traveled to several US military bases, including Kadena Air Base, driving bigwigs around. The one good thing about this job was that I saw some of the island's gorgeous rural countryside. Many fortunate military personnel (mainly Air Force) had regular duty stations on Okinawa. Some of the married ones had their wives living there with them. On rare occasions, I saw attractive "round-eyes," our benevolent slang term for American women or any non-Asian female. It was obvious why service in the Air Force was considered being in the Cadillac of military branches, whether stationed stateside or abroad.

Animosity between branches of the US military goes back at least to World War II times, probably earlier. Usually taunts were good-natured, but not always. Navy personnel were unflatteringly known as "Squids" or "Anchor Clankers." Air Force members were "Flyboys" or "Wingnuts." Army soldiers were known as "Ground Pounders." Rancor toward Marines from other branches included derogatory terms like "Jarheads" and "Seagoing Bell Hops." As Marines, our curt response to being called a bell hop was, "The only bell I ever hopped was your mother!"

Strange how certain sayings come and go in casual communications across generations. During the Vietnam War era it was common to say, "You're fuckin' A" or "Fuckin' A right" when expressing total agreement with something said or written. Another term considered cool during the 60s era had a "go-go" suffix. This originated with scantily dressed female "go-go dancers" wearing "go-go boots" performing in "go-go bars." From those terms "a-go-go" commonly got added to nouns as a suffix. For example, on my sea bag I had written "Viet Nam a-go-go." Late during my enlistment, I also had written "Eat the apple," short for "Eat the apple, fuck the Corps" on my sea bag, one of our several favorite references to the USMC!

Before long, higher-ups curtly informed me that surveyors were not needed in Viet Nam, and I received intensive guerrilla warfare training in conjunction with the 1371s. Our company consisted of green troops fresh from the US plus the shattered remnants of a combat-scarred outfit on "float" after months at war in-country. These bedraggled Marines were regrouping to finish their 13-month tours in the Nam. They were our age in calendar years but were prematurely old in body and spirit from horrors they had endured. Their worn frames, changing temperaments, far-away unfocused stares, and nervous uneasiness gave us a close-up view of reality — features impossible to reveal through previous training. Their ghastly, fragmented stories reinforced our anger toward the "gooks" and our determination to kill as many of them as possible. Gaining close bonds with the combat-hardened Marines was difficult. We newcomers became FNGs (fuckin' new guys) in the outfit even before setting foot on Viet Nam's soil.

During that month at Camp Hansen, most of us were allowed time to raise hell on weekends. We piled into tiny "skoshi" cabs driven by Okinawans, who taxied us to town at incredibly fast speeds on narrow, steep winding island roads. Above, I've described some of the sayings of the times we were living in and how they came about. Another such expression we picked up from the skoshi cabs was the term shortened as "skosh." So, when getting across something little, we might say, "The sergeant was a skosh pissed off." Or, "Hold on a skosh, I'll be right with you." At especially sharp corners, big convex mirrors were positioned to show oncoming traffic, which included small busses jammed full of people. Traveling to locations off base in cabs, I sometimes saw cars and even busses crashed off the side of the winding roads.

The local eateries served scrumptious, inexpensive native oriental cuisine beyond anything I could have previously imagined. Open sewers called "benjo" trenches ran along the ville streets. Okinawa was definitely a new cultural experience. Sometime during September, a beer bash was held for A Company at Ishikawa Beach. My Marine friends and I had a great time that day. The turquoise ocean water was clear and warm, the beach was expansive, and the beer was cold and plentiful.

Since our company was part of a BLT (Battalion Landing Team), we were always on standby status. Only "Cinderella liberty" was authorized, which meant we were to be back on base by midnight. Occasionally one of us knew the desk duty NCO, enabling us to sneak back in the early hours from a wild night of carousing in nearby Koza or Kin Town. Small restaurants, shops, tattoo parlors, bars and whorehouses lined the streets. At one of the shops, I bought Cheryl a couple items of clothes and mailed them to her. Under the influence of beer, I came close to getting a tattoo on my arm of the Marine Corps' eagle, globe, and anchor emblem. Many drunken servicemen got tattoos and the clap (VD) that they later wished they hadn't!

Most bars doubled as brothels. Those having a sign prominently lighted with a large "A" above the entrance meant that these establishments were monitored and determined to offer sex free of venereal diseases. Such designation could not be guaranteed, however. In Koza (now renamed Okinawa City), BC Street was one of the most famous streets for carousing. A favorite bar among many along the street was called "Club MG."

In this bar, typical of most, attractive young prostitutes socialized with horny Marines, coaxing us to buy them drink after drink. Being in cahoots with the bar proprietor, they stayed relatively sober by either getting watered-down drinks or by not finishing them. But we did finish ours. We got drunker and our thin wallets got thinner! In most cases, next came the short jaunt down the hall to a tiny bedroom that wasn't for sleeping.

Late one night I dragged one of my buddies out of a Koza whorehouse in order for us to make it back to base before the midnight curfew. Months later he was killed in Viet Nam. Though I got drunk many times and, despite tempting opportunities, I remained completely faithful to Cheryl. For this I caught lots of shit from my compatriots, some who were married, as they raved about banging so many gorgeous bar whores for little (or "skosh") money.

Clubs on base at Camp Hansen were rowdy, with one-armed bandit slot machines, jukeboxes and charming oriental waitresses serving unlimited beers. Club Oriental, the enlisted man's bar, was known unofficially as "the animal club." Drunken brawls between transient troops were frequent.

After many rumors and a couple false starts, they rushed our outfit to the White Beach Naval Facility to board the amphibious assault ship *USS Thomaston*, LSD-28. Some of us (me included) received orders of our immediate departure verbally by bullhorn, as MPs (military police) in vehicles wove through the narrow streets of nearby villages rounding us up.

An LSD (Landing Ship Dock) had the capability to lower its stern into the sea, thus allowing landing craft to disembark independently to make amphibious landings. The ship had a small helicopter deck, which made sporadic mail service possible. Our command ship, the *USS Iwo Jima* (LPH-2) with its many helicopters, could be seen in the wavy distance, as could the *USS Vancouver* (LDP-2). These three ships served as part of the US Navy's Seventh Fleet.

Marines' living conditions were even more miserable on the LSD than on the General Weigel. The amphibious assault ship was much smaller, and we were combat loaded. Navy personnel had far more comfortable living conditions. We slept on narrow canvas tarps laced over piped frameworks connected with 90-degree elbows. These racks were situated closely together above, below, and laterally. The top racks and all available space nearby were packed with helmets and other combat gear ready for quick departure.

LSD-28 sleeping quarters, Edgar, Paul and Ted Buckner

Our individual seabags were packed on military vehicles in another area of the ship. Following extended time spent in Okinawa, where there was an abundance of whorehouses, cases of crabs (pubic lice) were discovered on the ship. We were subjected to crotch inspections, as crab infestations spread quickly in such cramped quarters. One by one, we had to drop our drawers while a corpsman searched our crotch for crabs using a flashlight and wooden tongue depressor. Gung-ho Marine Captain J.J. Carroll had us out on the fantail doing daily calisthenics, and we peons caught the usual USMC shit details. Captain Carroll was killed shortly thereafter by a "friendly fire" short round on a hill southwest of Cam Lo, later named Camp Carroll in his honor. Most of my closest friends from the month on Okinawa were aboard the LSD. These friends included Buckner Crump and Charlie Burns, both later killed in the war.

For nearly a month we sailed in the South China Sea close enough to Viet Nam's shores to see and hear the vivid light shows of war's destruction. Like silver streaking darts appearing from nowhere and diving earthward, US air strikes were hammering the countryside. Hell was raining on whoever was caught in the distant fireballs. Eerie feelings about our impending fate clashed with our urges from boredom to get off the ship. The one positive aspect of being stuck aboard the ship for so long was that our tour of duty in Viet Nam would be one month shorter. We were in enemy waters. We had no idea when or where we would make a landing, or under what conditions.

On a couple occasions, close to the mainland in near-darkness, I saw Navy SEAL UDTs (Underwater Demolition Teams) dressed in black drift from the ship toward shore in small black rafts. They carried M16 assault rifles, the first I had seen (Marines were issued M14s until March of 1967 when the seriously defective M16s became standard issue). Since then, I've wondered what became of those brave young SEAL teams. I doubt that they returned to the ship.

At one point our LSD got caught in a typhoon and was tossed wildly on high seas. The below deck turbulence where we stayed made walking very difficult. I recall trying to eat in the mess area during the violent commotion. Dishware and food flew around as we a clung to the bolted down seats and tables.

No one went topside during the fierce storm.

Our rapid departure from ship occurred in late dusk aboard several LCUs (Landing Craft Utility) similar to those I'd seen in World War II movies years back. We traveled from the South China Sea into the Cua Viet Estuary and westerly up the Cua Viet River toward the Dong Ha combat base in I Corps. One landing boat in our group got stuck on a sandbar and was immediately hauled into deeper water. After stepping on land, we slogged in darkness along a narrow trail for a considerable distance, heavy with gear through chilly rain and mud. Our first miserable night was spent inside the perimeter wire at Dong Ha.

The DMZ (demilitarized zone) was a demarcation line roughly following the seventeenth parallel, along the Ben Hai River and west to the Laos border. The DMZ separated North and South Viet Nam, and Marines often referred to it as the "Dead Marine Zone." The US military designated four tactical areas in South Vietnam: I Corps, the northernmost of these regions, bordered the DMZ and consisted of five contiguous provinces. From north to south they were Quang Tri, Thua Thien, Quang Nam, Quang Tin and Quang Ngai.

Running southerly from I Corps were II Corps, III Corps and IV Corps. IV Corps took in the Mekong Delta at Viet Nam's southernmost tip.

Dong Ha is located along Viet Nam's main north-south road, Highway 1 (also known as "the Street Without Joy"), and at the junction where Route 9 heads west to Laos. The Dong Ha combat base formed the southeast corner post of a perilous area known as "Leatherneck Square." Cam Lo on the southwest, Con Thien to the northwest and Gio Linh to the northeast formed the "square." Our military's matted metal airstrip at Dong Ha, when not under repair from rocket, mortar, and artillery attacks, allowed crude access for mostly twin-engine C-123s, four-engine C-130s and helicopters. I first saw lumpy body bags containing dead Marines near this strip, stacked on pallets like cordwood ready for graves registration and a final flight home.

There was an area completely barricaded off with tall, ominous concertina wire coils. Hanging on the wire was a sign with the word "min" in big red print above a skull-and-crossbones image also prominently outlined in red. This served as a warning for mines left over from when the French colonized Viet Nam back in the 1950s. Looking through the wire I saw numerous sets of prongs sticking up out of the ground made evident where the soil had receded over time. These could have been harmless duds, or they could have exploded at the slightest nudge. We stayed away from this area, which I think must have been eventually blown in place by our troops.

Very shortly after arriving at Dong Ha, young Marine enlisted men who I had trained with and partied with on Okinawa and accompanied on the LSD were scattered to various assigned outfits, some in distant locations. The abrupt fragmentation and placement with unknown troops was difficult at first. In previous US wars, and later US wars in Iraq and Afghanistan, military units trained together at various stateside bases and elsewhere. They traveled to the battlefield and fought as a cohesive group. Unless members became casualties, they came home as a unit. Such tight cohesion was lacking in America's war in Viet Nam. Nothing was conventional about this damned war.

For branches of the service other than the Marines, the standard tour of duty in Viet Nam was twelve months. For Marines it was thirteen. Since we received orders for deployment on an individual basis, servicemen sporadically joined their assigned units, then rotated out as dictated by the number of days they had served in country. Hence, there was a continuous straggling flow of FNGs (fuckin' new guys) and short-timers (those nearing the end of their tour of duty) mixed with those falling somewhere in between.

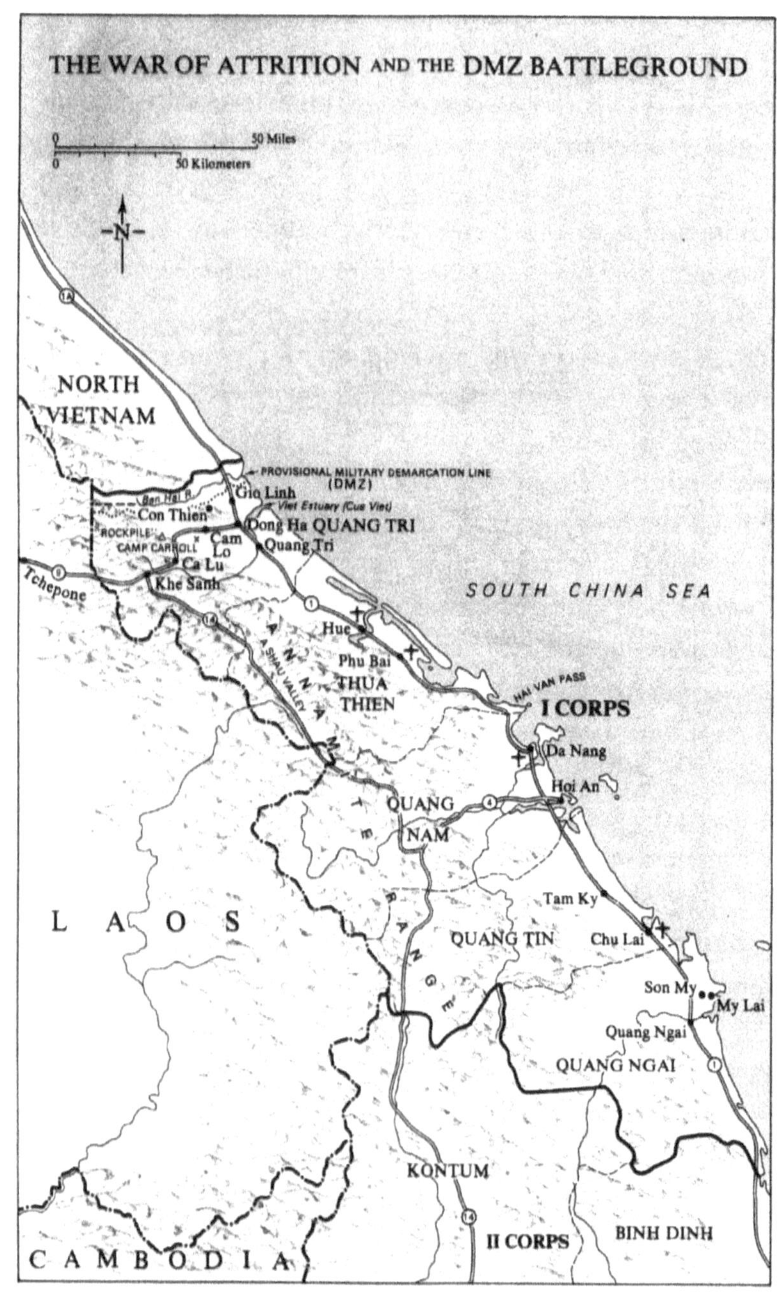

I Corps map and DMZ

We all kept close track of the days until DEROS (date eligible for return from overseas), the date when we could head home. This strange rotation system did little for unit solidarity. Transfers between outfits within the war zone were quite common and created further disjointedness.

In the fall of 1966, the North Vietnamese sent large fighting units south across the DMZ. The NVA had acquired powerful long-range artillery, and their big guns, rockets, and mortars regularly hammered our combat base. The base consisted of a maze of green canvas tents with nearby sandbagged bunkers in a sea of monsoon season mud. When possible, scrounged pallets served as crude tent flooring. During my earliest days there, fellow FNGs and I filled hundreds of sandbags. Visible by day, when the fog wasn't too thick over huge coils of concertina wire which ringed the base, was an expanse of rice paddies. On far edges of the paddies were ominous tree lines. The squalid town of Dong Ha languished a short distance outside our perimeter wire. Hungry little Vietnamese kids in ragged clothes begged for food through the wire and in town. Speaking few words of English, they repeated over and over in pathetic monotone voices, "You give me chop-chop, you give me chop-chop." Chop-chop was their word for food. Tagged villagers with conical hats picked the battalion dump under close watch by Marine guards. Extreme poverty was plainly evident.

The monsoon season occurred during mid-fall, lasting into the first months of winter throughout northern Quang Tri Province. Weather conditions were miserable, with nearly constant gray skies, frequent wind driven rains, slimy stinking mud, and surprisingly cold temperatures. The chill felt colder than actual thermometer readings, especially since we were always somewhere between damp and soaked, muddy and living in wet canvas tents or holes dug in the ground. A warm shower or a dry change of clothes was nonexistent.

*Our Dong Ha tent and bunker during the monsoon season 1966.
Piss tubes in background.*

We often got stuck with overnight perimeter guard duty. Sandbagged bunkers were located at specific intervals along perimeter lines. Danger lurked on the other side of concertina wired barriers. Directional antipersonnel Claymore mines were set to help prevent being overrun by enemy infiltrators. Long nighttime hours manning one of these bunkers was a miserable experience in raw, wet, and windswept conditions. Old sheets of metal roofing rigged above the bunker helped keep some rain out and allowed better visibility. Rats and biting bugs added to the wretchedness. Two men were assigned to each guard post and were equipped with a PRC-6 walkie-talkie, pop flares, rifles, a .45 pistol, an M60 machine gun, plenty of ammunition and hand grenades.

Paul during nighttime perimeter guard in Dong Ha January 1966

A suspicious sound or movement in the distance prompted the use of a pop flare, which when ignited became suspended in the air by a small parachute. The flare swung slowly and illuminated the area for a while until it burned out. This scene looked quite freakish through tired, straining eyes, as shadows seemed to move with the flare's sway.

"Shitters" were crude little wooden shacks—dank and smelly. Excrement was caught in two halves of rusty 55-gallon drums. Catching "shit detail" meant dragging the barrel halves out, dousing their contents with diesel fuel, lighting them afire, then tossing the halves back in the shitter until next time. Truly a chore that none of us wanted!

"Pissers" were sparingly installed at various locations throughout our encampment. They consisted of a 3.5-inch rocket launcher barrel dug into the ground and angled to accommodate average crotch height. Our nearest "piss tube" had a metal screen fashioned across the open end to prevent rocks and junk from being tossed into the tube. At some point, a disgruntled Marine threaded a USMC eagle, globe, and anchor emblem—the big one meant for a barracks cover (service uniform cap)—onto the screen facing outward. Those of us who used this tube pissed on the insignia with a measure of gratification. The emblem was eventually removed by someone more affectionate to the Corps than we were, probably a lifer.

Particularly during the first weeks at Dong Ha, chow was pathetic. We traipsed through the mud for a canteen cup full of thin lukewarm pea soup broth made from treated swamp water. This, plus one or rarely two C-rations each day comprised our diet. Of the 12 individually boxed meals in a case of C-rations there were few good choices. Eventually, occasional "care packages" containing canned beans, fruit cocktail and other non-perishables sent from family members back home were gratefully received. These packages brightened our day, and we shared our treats with others in our outfit, some who never got any.

There had been no exaggeration during training about Viet Nam's curse of leeches, rats, snakes, mosquitoes, centipedes, lice, and ticks—insects of all descriptions. Huge buffalo leaches latched onto us from paddies and streams. Small land leaches dropped on us from jungle vegetation. Rats were commonplace, and they tended to be big rats. Ravenous mosquitoes thrived. In some areas, tigers roamed. There's record of a Marine PFC killed in Quang Tri by a tiger. Though rare, most likely there were other such casualties from tiger attacks. And though not proven, hostile "rock apes" inhabited the remote jungles of Viet Nam. There were several accounts of rock ape encounters, but I never saw one. Elephants existed mostly in central Viet Nam.

Malaria, dysentery, ringworm, immersion foot and jungle rot were quite widespread. Our feet stayed wet and muddy for such long periods of time that the soles became parboiled, conditions similar to what are called "dishpan hands" with kitchen help. As a result, the wet wrinkled skin peeled off and feet became sore. Even when otherwise healthy, the drizzling shits were common due to the poor living conditions. A Marine named Skinner from our unit came close to dying after contracting Rocky Mountain Spotted Fever, a serious disease acquired from tick bites. We had suspected malaria, which was common. Delirious from high fever, nausea, and diarrhea, he was flown to a Danang hospital where he was packed in ice and treated back to health. Five Marines in our area got bitten by a rabid puppy and had to undergo the required series of stomach shots at the muddy medical tent. As with all poverty-stricken countries, the Vietnamese people suffered malnutrition and many diseases. There were active leper colonies in some areas of the country.

I remained with a combat engineer outfit in the 3rd Engineer Battalion, 3rd Regiment of the 3rd Marine Division. The FNGs among us were fortunate to be in the company of and learn from battle-tested Marines who had survived months of war and had suffered many casualties. Combat engineers were not "grunts" (infantrymen) but were often assigned to infantry outfits for unspecified periods of time specializing in demolitions.

On infantry operations our jobs were varied and dangerous. We cleared jungle LZs (landing zones) necessary for medevac, troop reinforcement and re-supply "choppers" (helicopters). We cleared fields of fire, built bunkers, stood six-hour security guard shifts, installed perimeter wire and set trip flares, deployed anti-personnel mines for defensive positions, swept roads and trails with mine detectors. We also conducted visual sweeps for mines and booby traps. We blew lots of things up with high explosives. Suspect VC hamlets populated by just elders, a few women and youngsters cast ominous vibes as we approached. Their thatched hooches (dwellings), animal shelters, tunnels, bunkers, munitions and food and water supplies were destroyed. Sometimes live people were in places we wiped out, as were their domesticated animals (pigs, chickens, ducks, cows, dogs, and water buffalos) — hence the term "search and destroy" operations. The monsoon rains and enemy activity required frequent repair of roads and bridges. Most were remote and precarious. With the unconventional nature of this war, combat engineers took on nearly anything else thrown our way, including patrols.

When captured VC suspects were loaded onto helicopters destined for interrogation it was said unofficially, with a hint of dark wit, that captives were counted after the chopper landed, not before. The insinuation was that the head count could be less upon arrival. A push out the door far above the ground likely caused suspects inside to talk plenty! I have no personal experience of this occurring, but recorded testimony from first-hand accounts is credible. Most often, VC suspects were turned over to South Vietnamese or Korean interrogators, who were merciless and used brutal, torturous methods of information gathering. Execution often followed.

Peasants suspected of being Viet Cong 1966 US Army photo

Our enemies were very ingenious at devising booby traps and land mines. They were extremely resourceful at assembling innovative traps from the most commonly available materials, in addition to those manufactured by the Chinese and Soviets. Punji stakes made from sharpened bamboo were hardened over fire, sometimes dipped in excrement to cause infection, and placed in concealed holes along foot tails. Once stepped on, the bamboo pierced a combat boot into the foot or snapped laterally into the leg. Sometimes a grenade was attached below the bamboo in such a manner that when the victim's foot instinctively pulled up, the grenade detonated. Other bamboo and spiked antipersonnel booby traps included Malayan whips and mace traps suspended from the jungle canopy. Explosive devices such as cartridge traps, rigged C-ration cans and the "daisy chain" (a string of grenades lashed to foliage along a trail) were common. When activated, the grenades exploded in rapid succession causing multiple casualties. Clever traps were also made from artillery and mortar rounds. Mines and booby traps were activated by rigged trip wires, or from pressure release, or from command-detonation electrically. Another danger to passersby on a trail were "spider holes". These were holes having camouflaged lids dug next to a trail. They were typically just big enough for one Viet Cong fighter to hide in. A VC waited patiently hidden until an unsuspecting American walked past, then he popped up from his hole with rifle for the surprise kill.

The Vietnamese people were also very ingenious in their daily living situations, being mostly poor farmers throughout the countryside, and living for so long with the turmoil of colonization and wars. These people were mechanically astute, having the ability to improvise and fix nearly anything not working properly. They could get by with little from the outside world and devised living improvements from things they salvaged. One example of this was making sandals from discarded tire treads, which served as soles. Strips of inner tubes were inserted through the tire pieces and fashioned as straps to fit around feet and ankles. Jokingly, we Marines termed these sandals "Ho Chi Minh" flip flops. I bought two pairs of the sandals from villagers and mailed them home. They serve as one of the very few physical artifacts I was able to send home from the war zone.

Vietnamese sandals made from tire treads and tubes 1966

Throughout the war, US injuries and fatalities from booby traps (antipersonnel mines) and land mines were of staggering proportions. Their cruel erratic nature magnified fear and anxiety among our troops. Casualties from explosions of mines and booby traps were severe due to the concussion of the blast and widespread mangling, as hot jagged shrapnel tore through whatever was in its path. Severe wounds slowed the advance of a squad or platoon.

Paul with mine detector November 1966

Mine detectors were often scarce, and operating one was highly stressful. The person operating the detector became a valuable target. A careless mistake could mean instant death to the operator and others nearby. Random harmless scrap metal fragments such as pieces of shrapnel or barbed wire were fairly common along trails and roadways. Such rubble set off intensified tones into the headphones of the operator.

The exact location indicated by the detector was marked. Following a distance behind, the next Marine knelt and delicately probed the marked spot in an angular direction with his bayonet to determine the metallic source. After several false alarms, the elevated level of caution sometimes diminished with disastrous results. In our outfit, we took turns using the mine detectors, not wanting to press our luck by using the rig for too long a period of time. Discovered booby traps and mines were usually blown in place but, if necessary, they were disarmed and removed by the better trained and more experienced among us.

Combat engineers were generally better off than our infantry brothers. After completing an operation or a field assignment we usually returned to a relatively safer area with lousy, but improved, living conditions. Extended periods spent in the boonies were wretched. From Dong Ha we operated westerly in the vicinity of Cam Lo, toward the Rockpile, Ca Lu and northerly toward a Gio Linh outpost at the DMZ's door.

Vietnamese woman with child - Cam Lo vicinity November 1966

Our principal enemy was the NVA, though VC cadres and sympathizers were prevalent, active, and treacherous. Operation Prairie (stages I and II) was ongoing during this period, mainly fighting the NVA 324B Division, which attempted to move south across the DMZ into Quang Tri Provence. Third Marine Division combat engineer outfits participated in these operations. My commanding officer was 1st Lieutenant Armstrong, who had received two Purple Hearts by the time I arrived. After the second one he could have gone home, and he should have. Number three cost him both legs.

My first experience under fire came in early November from a sniper attack near the Cam Lo River. We were attempting to free a deuce-and-a-half truck bottomed out in mud when the bullets began coming our way. Fortunately, none of us were hit. Thick vegetation prevented us from laying eyes on the sniper(s), but we cut loose with several rounds into the assumed direction. Reality struck—never before had I felt that bone-chilling fear, knowing that somebody out there would love to blow me away. Boot camp bravado had vanished.

We continued creating drain trenches in the flooded roadway using picks, shovels and detonating cord packed with mud, but we kept a more cautious eye toward the thick foliage and increased guard security.

In typical USMC fashion, the Corps' birthday was heartily celebrated on November 10th with a huge drunk, even in monsoonal Dong Ha. Ingrained slogans like "Semper Fi," "Uncommon valor was a common virtue," and "The few, the proud, the Marines" were brought to light by the most gung-ho lifers. Early on in our enlistment, most of us from the rank of private to at least corporal detested being in the Marine Corps, which we termed "The Crotch." A common refrain among us was "Eat the apple – fuck the Corps."

The beer tent was usually stocked with cans of Korean Crown beer and an occasional USA brand. Higher-ups did not consider the consumption of alcohol while in fairly secure areas taboo during this war. Sometimes we could buy rotgut whiskey and marijuana across the concertina wire or in the ville from the Vietnamese. The whisky bottles read "Canadian Club" or "Seagram's VO," but the contents were not. The whisky was nearly blinding, about like drinking barbed wire! Inside a "Winston" or "Marlboro" cigarette box were stuffed fat, poorly rolled joints. Usually, the pot was coarse and harsh, but smokable. Once, when dealing through the perimeter wire, we got tear-gassed from the Vietnamese side of the coils, which really pissed us off and quickly sent us out of the area with burning eyes and shortened breath.

Servicemen having a specialty MOS went through Vietnamese language school and could communicate quite well with the locals. But such servicemen were few and far between in our area. I still have the USMC issued "Leatherneck Fire Team Phrase Book," which covered English/Vietnamese translation of several basic words and phrases. Certain words, slang terms and pronunciations came to be understood between Americans and Vietnamese. Even among the engaging young kids. I'll list a few that I remember below, some with a phrase to exemplify:

> *Di di,* (pronounced dee dee) meant beat it, move, get out of here. Dee dee mau meant make haste, move fast.
>
> *Beaucoup,* (pronounced boocoo or bu cu) meant many, lots, plenty.
>
> *Dien cai dau,* (pronounced dinky dow) meant crazy in the head. You bu cu dinky dow!
>
> *Boom-boom,* (pronounced boom-boom) meant to have intercourse, to fuck.

The Vietnamese used a sliding scale between one and ten to describe or signify something as being bad or good. Number one was the best. Number ten was the worst.

So, someone might say, "She number one bu cu boomboom."

Letters from family, lovers, and friends back in "the world" (our term for the US) were of utmost importance to troops stuck in Viet Nam. I was fortunate to get many loving handwritten letters from Cheryl and others back home. They came sporadically, sometimes weeks after being postmarked. Often, they arrived in batches having been mailed on wide-ranging dates.

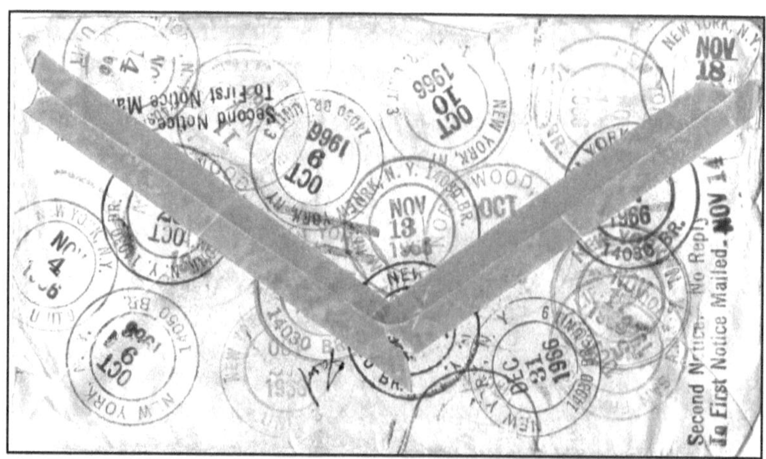

Envelope from letter sent by Cheryl in 1966

I wrote to Cheryl and others whenever I had a chance. Several good friends from high school had gone into the military before I was drafted and were stationed in Europe and South Korea. Without exception, letters from these friends bitched in vivid detail how much they hated the military and couldn't wait to get free of its grasp. Letters sent from the war zone required no postage, instead "Free" was written where stamps would normally be placed. Phone calls to or from home were impossible and unheard of. There were no phones in the remote areas where I served. Cell phones and emails didn't exist.

I spent a miserable Thanksgiving Day, Christmas, and New Year's Day (Cheryl's and my first wedding anniversary) in the chilly rain, feeling scared, angry, and despondent. Years later I wrote this poem in expression of my lament:

Quang Tri New Year

Incoming,
that familiar scream.
In scramble's blur
we hug the sandbagged wall.
Mud clings to mud
Fear clings to refuge
Which blast will
shred life's tour
in monsoon darkness?
Fresh vents in canvas,
spared of flesh designs.
A new year begins.
The first of seven wedding anniversaries
survives.

These holidays arrived under threats of being hammered by artillery, mortars and rockets or being infiltrated by sappers.

At Christmastime, in a sandbagged bunker near the one I frequently dove into, a young Marine shot himself to death. Word passed around that he had recently received a "Dear John" letter.

Christmas day 1966 at our bunker

Just before Christmas, some ARVN soldiers broke into the mail tent. At least that's who we blamed, though we never found out for certain who the culprits were. They stole our undelivered holiday goodie packages and scattered our precious unseen letters and cards to the soaking winds. ARVN forces were who we were supporting in their fight against communism. Experiences more deadly in nature involving the ARVN intensified our hatred. Our standard terms for all Vietnamese were gooks, dinks, slants, slopes, rice rats, and angle eyed shower shoe propelled rice rats. Luke the gook was reserved for VC and NVA soldiers. Increasingly, it became evident that this war was a worthless cause. Our anger grew as our morale plummeted. While in Dong Ha I wrote two very dark poems, which reflected my state of mind. One was titled, "Hell Has No Boundaries." The other was titled, "Plague Nowadays." I mailed hand-scribbled copies home to Cheryl, but to my knowledge, no copies of these poems exist now. Just as well!

Renowned author and Vietnam War combat vet Tim O'Brien said it this way in his 2019 book titled *Dad's Maybe Book*:

I had been in-country only a couple of months, but Vietnam was already a stone in my stomach. I hated the place. I hated myself for being there. Beyond that, as a purely practical problem, we were caught up in a confusing and deadly civil struggle. No front, no rear, no clear battle lines, no clear military purpose, no way to distinguish friend from foe. The enemy was everywhere and nowhere, vanishing into tunnels and popping up behind us and then sliding away again. We didn't know the language. We didn't know the culture. We didn't know where we were at any given time or why we were there.

Buddhism is the predominant religion of the Vietnamese population. I recall seeing bald Buddhist monks clad in bright yellow/orange robes standing in silence amidst the bombed-out ruins and tattered gardens of a small monastery in the vicinity of Cam Lo. I was shamefully ignorant of the ways of Buddhism and therefore lacked appreciation of its values. I felt contempt toward the plight of the monks, who I considered weird, and of their ravaged pagoda. Enlightenment was a concept beyond me.

Our battalion area was in the expansion process. Many Vietnamese graves located in this area had been indiscriminately bulldozed away, causing diplomatic concerns somewhere up the line between South Vietnamese and US governments. To help appease such concerns, grave removal was ordered when possible.

I was sent to the outskirts, barely within the coiled concertina wire perimeter to guard Vietnamese peasants while they dug up remnants of buried family members.

Vietnamese ancestor removal January 1967

As I stood near them with my rifle in hand carefully watching their every move, I had no empathy for what they were forced to do. I had no knowledge of ancestor reverence which, linked to ancient Confucian beliefs, was of monumental importance to Vietnamese culture. Even had I been aware of these values, my disdain would have been fueled by ingrained ethnocentrism, anger, and hatred.

My job was to assure that these peasants weren't Viet Cong digging holes and burying mortars or other weapons for use in planned attacks under the darkness of night. It was nearly impossible to tell who was VC among the general population. The Vietnamese dug into the red soil at various gravesites extracting fragments of ancestral bone and body parts for relocation elsewhere. They caringly placed bone in small wooden boxes similar to the stone core sample boxes I used with my 1965 job with SCS. The Vietnamese jabbered and mouthed a handful of rice during the digging. I watched, void of compassion. We had often been rocketed at night. Compassion was just a word from dictionaries.

Years after I left the war, this experience remains very troubling to me. Occupying large areas of Vietnamese land, disfiguring it and the intrinsic values it held, and inhumanly assaulting sacred ground to establish "our" combat base instills no pride in me.

I had brought a cheap plastic camera with me from home when I left for Camp Pendleton. The camera accommodated no adjustments and took a roll-type film. I used this camera while in California, at Okinawa and in Viet Nam, sending exposed films back to Cheryl for developing. Most were taken with black and white film and visually support minimal parts of this memoir's narrative. My opportunity to take pictures in Viet Nam was quite limited, but I managed to get several until late February 1967. I have no idea what happened to my camera after the day of the mine explosion or if there were potential photos on a film roll inside the camera. I never again took a photo in wartime Viet Nam.

In the war zone we commonly dreamed up special nicknames

for our fellow troops — often a weird variation of a last name, a home state, or some crazy trait or connection we conjured up. Written record of our compatriots' full names and stateside addresses were scant. Those we had easily became lost. Whatever happened to *Mongoose, Camshaft, Kentucky Burnett (wounded three times), Lightning, Dizzy Dean, Doublehung, Water Bull, Rail Job, Pvt. Medicine Bear* the Native American, or the Southern Baptist Cpl. we called *Hereafter?* As mentioned previously, the sporadic rotation system in place during these times meant that close buddies were constantly leaving the war when that magic DEROS rolled around. Or when they became casualties. Such departures left gaping holes behind. On the other end, when an individual's going home day arrived, he lifted out of the Nam leaving brothers behind to unknown fates. Glad to escape the war, a hole nevertheless nagged… a strange loneliness, a feeling of survivor guilt. Keeping in touch usually didn't happen.

In time, my original surveyor MOS caught up with me. Despite an attempt to remain with my combat engineer outfit, they transferred me to a more conventional engineering team. Leaving my former unit hurt deeply, as I had formed tight and trusting connections with those guys. I lost track of most of them after being reassigned. Midstream transfers were common to this damned war and created profound disjointedness. My new outfit operated out of Dong Ha, and the transition ran its course.

My high school friend Jean Stimmell had dropped out of Columbia University and joined the Navy prior to my military induction. He sailed on the *USS Westchester County*, an LST (Landing Ship Tank) to rivers and ports in Viet Nam, Japan, the Philippines, and other Pacific Islands over an eighteen-month period, which overlapped with my months in Viet Nam. Jean's outfit traveled dangerous rivers and delivered Marines and supplies into various battle zones. He also spent time on coastal bases and in Saigon. On November 1, 1968, while the LST was anchored in the My Tho area in Viet Nam's Mekong Delta, two powerful mines set by Viet Cong divers exploded, killing 26 sailors. This assault was the US Navy's deadliest single incident of the Vietnam War. Fortunately, Jean had been discharged from the Navy sometime prior to the explosion.

R&R was a term used to denote "Rest and relaxation," sometimes called "Rest and recuperation" or "Rest and recreation." Generally, US troops in Viet Nam were permitted one R&R break during a standard tour of duty. Several cities served as destinations for a 5 to 7-day out-of-country getaway from the war, including in Hawaii, Sydney, Bangkok, Hong Kong, Manila, Taipei, and Tokyo. A quota system was used to determine who got to go where and when. Quotas for the most popular locations got filled, so wait periods were set up. Or one could choose a second or third destination and hope for the best. R&R was famous (or infamous to certain segments of the host cities) for rowdy servicemen in need of warm showers, good food, well-stocked bars, and whorehouses, which were abundant and busy. Not that much rest, but lots of recreation!

Envelope from Jean Stimmell's letter 1966

Rarely, Jean and I communicated by mail but at one point in 1966 we conjured up a dreamlike plan to try for a coinciding R&R quota at the same city. We hoped for a get-together in Okinawa's port city of Naha where his LST would be landing. We fantasized raising big hell while drinking the war from our heads. However, by the time I received his letter I had left Okinawa and had landed in Vietnam's I Corps area.

No such rendezvous took place.

Reality was that I hoped to meet Cheryl in Hawaii for a week (more on that later). She had been working hard, trying to pay off the last of my UNH expenses and a high-interest loan that was outstanding. She saved my pay sent from war service intended for our dream reunion in Hawaii. One Marine I knew who was from California had an R&R quota for Hawaii. He planned to go there and disappear, never again returning to Viet Nam. I don't know how his idea worked out, but for his sake I hope it did.

By far, my most enjoyable couple of days in Viet Nam came about unexpectedly when I was ordered to Danang. Because this experience was so abnormally different from the rest of my time in the country, I'll elaborate. These happenings are much easier to write about than deathly stories from Quang Tri Province. I flew from Dong Ha's shaky metal matting airstrip south to the massive US Danang Air Base in Quang Nam Province. My temporary assignment was to guard a huge supply of beer and liquor, which was stockpiled for a journey north by way of a barge.

The base at Danang was gigantic, not at all resembling Dong Ha. Instead of muddy, rat and mosquito-infested canvas living quarters stood plywood buildings with sheet metal roofs called strongbacks. The monsoon season had left south of the Hai Van Pass where Danang is located. Serving on this base provided a higher comfort level but was much more formal and regimented than I had been used to up north. Military apparel was more squared away, for example, and saluting officers was mandatory. I swear I remember shower stalls and flush toilets there. It was mind-boggling to me that I was in the same war less than 100 miles south of where I had just come from. There was an in-country R&R Center at Danang's beautiful China Beach. This said, the war raged mercilessly in all directions off the confines of the base. Attacks from nearby Marble Mountains and from within the base were also common.

When on land in Viet Nam or offshore within established distances considered as the war zone, service personnel received "hostile fire pay" also called "combat pay." Such pay consisted of a standardized sum which was added onto one's regular pay based on rank. Troops serving in dangerous areas with horrid living conditions griped that servicemen who spent their tour of duty in relatively safe and cushy locations received an equal amount of combat pay. Either way, the extra pay fell far short of the danger we were all subjected to.

The beer was stockpiled on wooden pallets and encased in sheets of cardboard banded tightly with metal strapping. It needed to be guarded from the Vietnamese, who would sneak in with knives, cut through the cardboard and steal quantities of beer to sell on the black market. US service personnel likewise stole the beer, but not to sell! Located nearby was the extensive Danang PX (Post Exchange). This PX resembled a large retail store back in the US and was like nothing I had seen in Viet Nam. It had a cafeteria with milk dispensers, hamburgers, ice cream, etc. Even US civilian clothes and merchandise were sold there. I bought a Western Bowie knife at the PX. The leather sheath was sort of a calfshit brown color. At the PX I bought some black dye. I spread the dye covering the face of the sheath making it more difficult to see when hanging from a belt. I identified the back side of the sheath with my name, service number, and outfit. Later, a friend wove a laced rawhide leg tie at the tip of the sheath.

Outside the PX young Vietnamese kids gleefully slid down an embankment slippery with red mud on scraps of cardboard. Years later, I wrote a poem about this scene titled "USA Cardboard." Older girls stood nearby eating lice they had picked out of each other's hair. The poverty was profound here, as it was everywhere I had been in this war-ravaged country. Many people were savagely displaced from destroyed villages elsewhere in the province. They had little to bring with them. They struggled to survive.

Close to the PX sat a conex box, a small rectangular corrugated steel shipping container having a big, hinged door used for shipping military cargo and for storing supplies in country. This closed container served as a whorehouse for a young Vietnamese woman who we Marines called "Suzy the Skivvy Girl." During daylight hours while guarding beer, I saw Marines enter and exit the windowless box in quick succession. I remained outside of the box. Suzy was making money inside. And probably sharing a dose of gonorrhea! I had my camera with me and took a photo of Suzy exiting her conex box enterprise.

A USO (United Service Organizations) show featuring the skimpily dressed Nancy Sinatra was taking place at a distant end of the base. I had some free time and decided to check it out. I thought of one of her hit songs, "These Boots Are Made for Walkin" as I began hitchhiking. I got picked up by a Marine officer who gave me holy hell at the edge of a squalid village called Dogpatch. Horny American GIs often vanished when venturing into Dogpatch. Rumors told of whores infected with the dreaded "black syph" and with razor blade inserts fastened in their vaginas. Occasional snipers also took their toll. Like other villes near US bases, peasants survived by hustling anything they could. I didn't make it to the USO show thanks to the officer's interference.

One last note about Dogpatch: I saw shanties that were totally sheathed with beer cans which had been cut down one side, flattened, and tacked to the outside walls. The Vietnamese could make something out of nothing, from booby traps to shower shoes, to irrigation systems. Vietnamese were clever, patient, nationalistic and determined; important traits obviously overlooked by arrogant US leaders who got us involved and kept us embroiled in Viet Nam's affairs for so many years.

When off-duty, my quarters were a strongback cramped with transient Marines. Most of us passed around marijuana joints and hash laced with sticky opium. We laughed, told hometown stories, and listened to rock and roll music. One night while there I talked with a gaunt, glazed-eyed lance corporal who was rotating back to the US the next day. He showed me a plastic bag full of severed Vietnamese ears sloshing in a formaldehyde-like liquid, which he had packed for the trip home. The war brought on such morbid things.

I stood long stretches guarding a sea of beer pallets and a lowboy trailer stacked high with cases of top-labeled hard liquor destined for Marine officers and high-ranking NCO lifers. We who pulled guard duty made a respectable dent in a pallet of beer, hitting it especially hard during night shifts. Often, we shared a beer or two with fellow Marines wandering by.

Late one night, a canine Marine (dog handler) patrolled near where I stood guard. He had a monstrous German shepherd on a leash. These dogs had important missions during the war. They were highly trained and were unconditionally loyal to their handler. They were also extremely intimidating and vicious toward Vietnamese on the receiving end. I asked the K-9 Marine, who was a short distance away, if he wanted a beer. He did. These beer cans had no pop-tops, requiring an old-fashioned pointed opener. Not thinking of the consequences, I tossed an opener toward the handler. The beast of a dog saw the motion and immediately lunged at me, thinking I might be tossing a grenade in their direction. Fortunately, the dog was muzzled and under complete control of his master. Another scary experience of a different kind!

Intentions were that after the pallets of beer and boxes of liquor were loaded on a barge, me and the other guards would accompany it north to Dong Ha. We had plans to confiscate as much of it as possible. Alas, I got ordered to fly back to Dong Ha before the barge ever left shore. Too bad, because I looked forward to the barge trip and especially wanted to smuggle some of the officers' liquor. Whether or not the barge ever got underway is unknown to me.

The C-130 roared out of Danang's big airport, and before long it came down hard on Dong Ha's rough perforated metal alloy matting strip. From first impact until the plane came to a stop it sounded as though we had no landing gear, and there was damn little strip left ahead of us. The mangled remains of an Air Force F-4 fighter lay strewn in the countryside a short distance past where the matting ended. The strip wasn't built for landing fighter planes. I had no idea that I would return to Danang under drastically different circumstances.

A couple guys from our tent inside the wire at Dong Ha had been to one of the R&R getaways. They returned with wild tales, women's bikini underwear from whorehouses they had visited and a few music recordings. I recall hearing songs from Bob Dylan's *Blonde on Blonde* album and from *Out of Our Heads* by the Rolling Stones. This music, plus pot and beer when available, offered a brief make-believe escape from the war zone.

I passed up an R&R quota for Bangkok, Thailand and instead waited for the chance to get a Hawaii destination. Hawaii R&R was scarce and difficult to acquire, but eventually I got placed on the quota listing. Cheryl and I planned to spend some long-awaited time together, and we had most of the details lined up as to where we would meet, etc. The reunion never happened.

An exploding land mine changed our lives forever during the Vietnamese zodiac year of the Goat.

On February 20, 1967, I accompanied an advance party from our outfit traveling in a personnel carrier (PC, a 3/4-ton military truck) by "Rough Rider" convoy south from Dong Ha on Highway 1. Though small by military standards, PCs were quite heavy and very ruggedly built. I rode in the back with a few other Marines and lots of gear. We crossed the wide Quang Tri River on a floating pontoon bridge, past ravaged Quang Tri City and through the old imperial city of Hue in Thua Thien Province. We continued south to the Marine combat base at Phu Bai, where we spent the night getting our gear in order and reviewing the details of our mission.

At daylight, a squad of us moved to a remote location northwest of Phu Bai called Gia Le (Gia Le Thuong). We spent the next few nights in relative safety inside a concertina wired Seabee encampment, where they operated a big rock crusher. I believe this was Naval Mobile Construction Battalion Three (NMCB 3). During night hours we shared perimeter guard armed with pop-flares, PRC-6 walkie-talkies (which we termed "prick-6s") and lots of firepower, keeping vigil for VC sappers and rocket and mortar attacks. The Seabees treated us well, sharing hot but humble breakfasts. They warned us about the abundance of lethal land mines and booby traps so commonplace in the vicinity. Marines had been blown away from the infestation of enemy mines in the area where we were headed, and we were crazy to venture outside the wire, the Seabees said. Our assignment took place far outside of the wire.

Early mornings, our survey team loaded up the PC and drove along the very narrow meandering hard-packed dirt road into the boonies. The road was about the width of our driveway on Loudon Ridge. It was obvious that this road into the hinterlands was rarely used by motor vehicles. Peasant foot traffic, bicycles and oxcarts were fairly common. During the few days I spent in the area our small truck was the only motor-driven rig I saw.

The terrain and vegetation in Gia Le were different from northern Quang Tri Province, with more rolling hills having bushy ground cover. Most trees were scrubby in comparison. The monsoon rains had dissipated, and the days were sunny and hot. The creeks were full of leeches, and the snakes were poisonous.

War was very evident here. Graveyards with battered shrines and monuments were numerous, as were scatterings of mounded earthen graves.

There were many US bomb craters.

We often saw Vietnamese peasants at work on the land, frequently with water buffalos. These huge, ox-like animals had a menacing dislike for Americans. It was as if the sight of us or our smell pissed them off. Wary of this, US troops kept a watchful eye for water buffalos. We liked neither the Vietnamese, except for the kids, nor their buffalos! These beasts were indispensable to Vietnamese agrarian culture. There were no tractors or other mechanized equipment. Water buffalos were very docile toward their masters, including children who rode and tended them. During the early war years, Americans killed many water buffalos indiscriminately, sometimes as if for sport. Later, as a diplomatic gesture, official US policy tightened, allowing the destruction of buffalos only in life-threatening situations or in collateral damage situations. That was official policy! Word passed that our government paid cash reimbursements in certain cases for buffalos slaughtered by US forces.

Our mission was to map the topography of a large remote acreage slated to become the new 3rd Engineer Battalion area when it moved south from Dong Ha. In later months, this area grew into the Gia Le Combat Base. Elements of B Company had joined us on the convoy from Dong Ha to support Operation Chinook II, which was ongoing in the Phu Bai/Gia Le area.

Highly acclaimed war correspondent and author Bernard Fall was killed after stepping on a Bouncing Betty booby trap on February 21, 1967. The explosion also killed a Marine combat photographer. They had been covering the operation.

Paul sitting on Vietnamese grave near Gia Le,
Thua Thien Province February 23, 1967

We felt uneasy, being few in number and so isolated without the accompaniment of infantry and extra firepower. Especially after being told by the Seabees that we were crazy to be going where we were going. In typical Marine Corps fashion, mine detectors were in short supply. We didn't have one, so we visually swept the dry, hardened road each day checking for surface disturbances, wires or anything that looked suspicious. From our visual checks, things seemed ok.

At most, three of us could fit in the truck's cab, in addition to a PRC–25 portable field radio, which we called a "prick-25." Personnel carriers had a hinged bench running along the length of the bed on both sides. One or two of us always stood "shotgun" (security) as we rode along, locked and loaded and keenly alert for anything dangerous. Others sat on the benches with our gear piled on the floor between. Travel to portions of our mapping site were impassable due to a bombed-out bridge. At that point, we drove randomly into the countryside as far as possible, then hiked. The savagery of war was all too evident here and most everywhere.

Tello, my young Puerto Rican comrade, and I humped the hills with the stadia rod, essential to the survey process. He and I switched off between carrying the rod and providing security. The rod carrier wore a .45 caliber automatic pistol, and his sidekick carried an M14 rifle with plenty of full magazines. The magazine inserted in the rifle had a second loaded one inverted and taped to the operable one enabling quick replacement. Another loaded magazine in its canvas pouch was looped through the rifle sling.

We communicated with those at the distant surveying locations through use of "prick-6" walkie-talkies.

One day while I led the way, cautiously walking along a narrow brushy footpath, Tello and I came within inches of tripping a booby-trapped 105 mm artillery round.

We were constantly tense and vigilant as we slowly headed up a scrubby hillside trail. Miraculously, as I looked at the ground before each step, I noticed a thin trip wire ahead of my boot leading across the trail to a hidden, lethally rigged charge. A harbinger of things to come. We flagged the location, and the howitzer round was later blown in place.

*Paul wearing life-saving flak jacket at outskirts of
Gia Le February 23, 1967*

The morning of February 27, 1967, began like any other of the few days we had spent at this new location. Our few personal belongings and extra military gear were left in our tents at the Seabee base camp. With loaded truck, we headed out to resume mapping where we left off the previous day. As always, we visually checked the hard-as-concrete road ahead for disturbances in the roadbed where land mines could have been placed. Randomly along the way, Vietnamese men and women worked busily in the countryside. For reasons I can't recall, a decision was made to move to a different site by late morning.

After receiving the PRC-6 signal to return to the truck, which was a considerable distance from Tello and me, we were threatened by a hostile water buffalo. The buffalo's Vietnamese master did nothing to restrain the encircling beast, and we readied to shoot if it attacked as we cautiously edged toward the truck. This episode slowed our departure, and I've since wondered if it was a primitive diversionary tactic allowing time for mining the road nearby. Tello and I joined the others at the truck, thinking that this was just another bizarre Viet Nam experience. After all, the water buffalos held a strong dislike of Americans.

It was a hot day and the stiff abrasive weight of my flak jacket had been irritating my sunburned shoulders. I tossed my flak jacket on the personnel carrier floor and stood on it amongst our gear. As we started down the road, I stood riding shotgun in the back of the truck directly behind the driver, holding onto the cab with one hand and my M14 in the other. Squad members not in the cab sat on both sides of the truck's benches. We traveled down the same section of road we had driven over early that morning.

A horrendous explosion erupted beneath our truck just behind the cab below where I stood, leaving a deep crater in the packed gravel. The PC was blown sideways across the elevated roadway, and I landed halfway off the sprung tailgate.

A wheel with a section of axel and frame were blown off along with other truck parts. All this was cast quite a distance from the roadside into the brush. The body of the truck was bent and riddled with shrapnel holes. The truck's benches where others in our squad were sitting were mangled. My recollections immediately after the blast come from an in-and-out haze. However, some are all too clear.

The deafening blast ripped through the truck. My clothes were tattered. Dirt was embedded in my skin. My head rang relentlessly. I bled from shrapnel wounds, one on the inside of my left arm near my elbow (the arm that held my rifle). I got quite a shrapnel gouge on my right shinbone, and I had no idea what my left foot looked like. Half-conscious and in agony, I flopped onto the ground, afraid to feel for my legs; then, finding them attached, wondered if I still had my balls. A jagged shard tore through the steel magazine in my rifle, jamming the cartridges. The good fate of having my flak jacket under me when the mine exploded undoubtedly saved my legs, and probably my life. Like other stuff in the truck, my flak jacket was thrown out and laid shredded on the ground.

We who had been in the rear of the truck lay sprawled on the ground, dazed, wounded, and groaning. Those in the cab were less seriously injured. Fortunately, the PRC-25 in the cab was operable and someone radioed Phu Bai for a medevac chopper.

Rounds from unseen snipers spun the ground around us as we crawled for cover in the brush and under the truck's rubble. Leaking fuel was a concern, but zinging bullets were the greater threat. Those who could, fired into the hills where the sniper rounds seemed to be coming from. Dazed in a state of shock, my final recollections from this scene were the hovering Huey chopper followed by the scrambling "dust-off" crew rolling us onto litters and quickly loading us in the chopper. I'm sure the corpsman injected me with the first of many hits of morphine, and I have no memory of the flight to Phu Bai. Any attempt to describe the corpsmen or conversations any of us may have had draws a total blank. Records show that five of us were medevacked. One was an African American, one was Hispanic, and the other three of us were Caucasian.

I regained consciousness on a canvas cot in a sizable floorless hospital tent at the Phu Bai combat base. The tent was divided. The part I was in was packed with Marines in and out of morphine sedation groaning from wounds of varied severity. On the other side of a partial divider flap were the triage cases, where desperate life-and-death decisions were being made to help the poor souls with a chance of survival, while letting go of those beyond hope.

Dedicated Navy doctors and nurses worked tirelessly under dreadful conditions. Many Marines were hurt far worse than me, so the most I could expect were shots of morphine as often as possible and bandages for my shrapnel wounds. This was a tent full of blood, agony, and death. Outside were the familiar sounds of helicopters. A horrific, indescribable night passed. I desperately had to take a shit. With no one available to help me, I struggled onto a "silver saddle" (stainless steel bedpan), which I attempted to balance on an upright 105mm artillery casing. Under normal conditions, such a balancing act would be tricky. Hampered by a smashed lower extremity, I fell to the ground a few times before involuntarily shitting my ragged pants and the immediate surroundings.

Years later graphic nightmares of the casualty tent still haunt. Below is a journal entry I wrote following one near-sleepless night:

Intrusive visions, sounds, feelings, smells, and even tastes grabbed me like it was yesterday: the dead, the dying, frantic doctors, crude medical conditions, dangerous makeshift casualty tent—flap dividing the triage cases from those of us with a chance. Sounds of moaning, groaning, crying, screaming, praying, desperate calls for Mother and morphine, comforting and cursing half-sentences from over-tired corpsmen, clinks and clanks inside the tent—wap-wap-wap of choppers outside. Wondering, how badly am I really hurt, how many of us lying here are dead now and how many will be within the hour, will we take a direct hit in the dark from a mortar or rocket— sometimes not caring if we do, what happened to the others when the mine exploded—I don't think they're in this field unit with me, why don't they give me another needle—the last one has worn off, when will morning come, do Mom, Dad, and Cheryl know I've been hit—they couldn't know yet, what's this whole fuckin' thing about, anyway? The smells and tastes hit at the same time—what I can smell here also tastes. It goes beyond inhaling. Blood, burned flesh, guts, rot, sweat, shit, piss, puke, medications, cigarette smoke, mud, wet canvas—on and on.

To further describe the dreadful impact of casualties on corpsmen and doctors, the following excerpt is from a book review (*VVA Veteran* magazine, July/August 2012) titled "Autopsy of War: A Personal History," a memoir by John Parrish, M.D. Parrish arrived in Vietnam in the fall of 1967 as a barely (and inadequately) trained US Navy doctor. He spent months in a blood-drenched field hospital, A Medical Co., 3rd Medical Bn., 3rd Marine Div. near Phu Bai.

The bed of a large truck is overflowing with a jumbled pile of bodies — desperate, terrified Marines had heaved the dead and wounded together in a heap without battle dressings, tourniquets, splints or first aid of any kind. Corpsmen and other doctors are already sorting through the pile in the bed of the truck, untangling the living from the dead, and lowering them into liters.... The vomiting Marine stops moving and is no longer breathing. I start to resuscitate him and then see brains matted in his black hair. I let him go. My hands are slippery with blood, and I have his brains under my fingernails.

I never again saw members of our survey team and don't know what happened to them. Adams, a combat engineer friend from Dong Ha, somehow heard of my plight and stopped by to visit me just before I left Phu Bai. His unit had moved south, and he updated me on the sad fate of a few Marines from my earlier outfit. Adams had been wounded in an attack while helping a seriously wounded lieutenant and had been flown to Okinawa to recover. From Okinawa, Adams had been patched up and returned to the war.

Recently, I got reliving all this and realized that I had spent just two nights in Phu Bai. The first night following the convoy from Dong Ha before going to Gia Le, and the second in a hellish casualty tent after being medevaced.

I don't recall the flight, but a letter I wrote to Cheryl while in a Danang military hospital said that the facility at Phu Bai was full past capacity with combat casualties and sickness. From the field tent overflow described above I was loaded onto a truck with several other casualties. We were stacked on shelf-like structures where we stayed for a couple hours waiting for a plane to take us to a big military hospital in Danang. My letter says that the flight from Phu Bai to Danang was "a real rough airplane ride."

I awoke from sedation at the Danang tarmac. They loaded the wounded on a medical transit bus and put on built-in cots (more like shelves), which ran along both sides. Our destination was the Naval hospital. However, it was filled to capacity with casualties, so they admitted us to the Air Force wing. As I was wheeled through the ward door, I noticed a crudely scrawled cardboard sign that read, "The Marine Corps Builds Oswalds," a repugnant take-off on the old USMC recruiting slogan "The Marine Corps Builds Men" with a foul twist relating to President Kennedy's assassin, who had been a Marine.

The spacious hospital ward was loaded with patients. It was clean and the overworked medical attendants treated us well. I became aware that some of my personal items had been recovered and placed in olive drab cloth Patient's Effects bags. One day I heard the name LaFortune called, and I remembered that name from my Parris Island platoon. Amazingly, he lay in a bed close to mine with shrapnel wounds from a mortar round. All casualties in this ward had physical wounds. Other areas housed victims stricken with diseases, such as malaria, dengue fever, Rocky Mountain spotted fever, and serious cases of jungle rot, dysentery, and dehydration.

At first during my short stay in Danang, I was unaware of the severity of my injuries though my left leg, ankle and foot looked hideous. A hard half-cast encased the underside of my left foot and ran up to my knee. My distorted foot and ankle were severely swelled and had taken on a deep blackish-purple color. My grossly swelled flesh draped over the sides of the half-cast. Instead of being supportive, the cast felt too tight due to the swelling. Huge blisters had formed on my foot and ran up my shank. There was a hole on the inside of my left foot and ugly veins extended up through my ankle. My right foot ached, but nothing like the left one.

My head still throbbed and rang nonstop. My lower body hurt intensely. Time passed slowly as I writhed in excruciating pain. I was informed that my left foot above the ankle would likely require amputation, and that I would be flown to a hospital in the Philippines. In the chaos of so many casualties needing attention, the half-cast remained on my leg until I was admitted to the hospital at Clark Air Base. Little did I know that I would be dealing with nerve damage and pain of varying intensity from the wounds for the rest of my life. But I'm fortunate that I survived the war and feel that fate did me a big favor. I could easily have become another name inscribed on the black granite Wall in DC.

Reliving this experience each year as February approaches, I think back to my mindset during those few days that we surveyed the landscape at Gia Le. I had no concern or guilty feelings about intruding onto the countryside of the Vietnamese people, heavily armed and with survey equipment. Marine Corps indoctrination, war-instilled anger and hatred prevented such thoughts. The Seabee's hungry rock crusher and heavy equipment inside the big concertina wire enclosure tore up the land. Uninvited, our survey squad mapped out the terrain far outside the wire where a sprawling US military base would eventually be located. Everything associated with war cast its tragic spell on the common people and the very land where they lived. Where their ancestors had also lived for centuries.

With these thoughts ever-present, I'm painfully reminded of how Native Americans felt during the mid-1800s when white Americans shamelessly broke treaties and intruded on their ancestral territories with guns and survey equipment in hand to plot routes for the Transcontinental Railroad. Tracks were laid across Indian lands, and by 1869 steam locomotives pulled trains from coast to coast. The advent of cross-country rail travel (called "Thieves' Road" by Indians) led to near extinction of massive buffalo herds, greedy exploits for gold, and the catastrophic end to the indigenous people's way of life.

I feel deep shame that our country's military decimated indigenous populations and involuntarily forced tribes to live on squalid reservations. Ongoing dark sides of US history countrywide. We all need to gaze into a mirror and contemplate. It's no wonder that Native Americans fiercely resisted, and I wish they had prevailed for eternity.

Getting hit generated varied feelings. I was damn glad to be out of the fighting part of the war. Yet there was the uncertain anxiety of what my future would hold. Not knowing the fate of my buddies created a strange feeling of guilt akin to abandonment. Relatively minor wounds or sickness often meant recuperation on the *USS Repose* hospital ship (nicknamed "Angel of the Orient") which floated offshore in the South China Sea, or at an in-country hospital such as at Cam Ranh Bay before being tossed back into the fray. Serious casualties could result in an eventual flight back to the "World" (USA), followed by a possible discharge from the military. Visions of going home kept flitting through my head, yet I hardly dared think such thoughts for fear of being let down. Those who were blind, horribly burned, paralyzed, or suffering multiple amputations had a much grimmer mixture of feelings.

HOMEWARD BOUND

A plane full of casualties landed at Clark Air Base on the Philippines Island of Luzon. There, I was admitted into an amputee ward. Distinct visions of the pain and anguish I witnessed at Clark are forever etched in my brain: seemingly endless rows of legless young men having bandaged stumps tethered down to bed frames with plastic cords. Some had lost arms and legs. Most amputees had serious fragmentation wounds and burns. Bed after bed held kids my age and younger —some eighteen and nineteen years old— hideously maimed. Not only did the amputees have pain from the trauma of limb loss, they also suffered phantom pain... sensing pain from a limb no longer there due to the severe nerve damage that resulted. Also in the ward were a few South Korean ROK (Republic of Korea) Marines with similar wounds.

The hospital at Clark and other such infirmaries on the journey were not facilities for extended care, but rather fairly brief drop-off points. They were sort of way stations to stateside hospitals having more specialized and intensive capabilities. The survival rate of Viet Nam war casualties was much greater than in any earlier war, mainly because of the availability of medevac helicopters and the proximity of life-saving medical facilities. Advanced hospital technology and improved medications also helped keep tens of thousands alive who would have previously died in the field. The most horrendously wounded may have been better off if they hadn't pulled through. Though my experience with branches of the military other than the Marine Corps was limited, it became evident that the USAF had the best living conditions and the finest facilities. We were provided the highest quality treatment possible under extremely demanding circumstances.

At Clark, I learned that I would be transferred to a hospital in the US. I was allowed a brief phone call to Cheryl, compliments of the American Red Cross — our first conversation since I'd left California months before. Uniformed Marines had visited Cheryl at work in Concord with news that I was WIA (wounded in action). The unexpected visit was especially troubling, since it was well known that uniformed military personnel commonly showed up to inform that a family member had been KIA (killed in action). Cheryl also received a brief ill-defined telegram from the Corps about my status, as did my parents. In later years, Mom expressed her lament upon receiving the telegram, especially the vagueness of details. The telegram's reference to my head wound caused Mom to worry that possibly shrapnel had blinded me. A telegraph message is extremely antiquated considering the world of today.

My flight toward home from Clark Air Base was aboard an Air Force C-141 Starlifter jet. C-141s were long-haul troop and cargo carriers. They also transported caskets containing KIAs to Dover AFB in Delaware, our military's largest mortuary. The one I left Clark on had been modified as a hospital ship with narrow beds stacked one above another down both sides of the huge fuselage. We landed at the US Navy Base in Yokosuka, Japan for refueling.

Months later, I learned that Pittsfield native Dave Robinson spent time in the Yokosuka Naval Hospital after being shot November 1, 1967 near Gio Linh. Davey, a Marine corporal, was eventually sent to the US to recover in the Chelsea Naval Hospital in Massachusetts.

High in the air soon after departing Yokosuka, I witnessed a deeply distressing incident that has haunted me all the years since. In a bed below mine, nurses and doctors began working on a young Marine who was in crisis. He had lost both legs, one at mid-thigh and the other at about crotch level. He was bleeding heavily through thick bandages below his waist. I watched as this half-person was unwrapped by nurses, frantically working to stop his bleeding. In the confusion, we casualties aboard were unaware that the C-141 had released enough fuel over the ocean to allow a safe return landing at Yokosuka. We had no idea of what was happening.

Back on the ground, attendants wheeled a cot carrying the young kid down the length of the aircraft. He was conscious, managing a weak wave, as he rolled out of sight. I don't recall his name, but it seems that he was from Rhode Island. This scene continues to be a recurrent nightmare.

The jet continued on to Elmendorf AFB in Anchorage, Alaska for a brief stop before reaching our destination at Andrews AFB in Maryland. My hospitalization at Andrews was similar to my experiences in Da Nang and at Clark, only more extensive in casualty count.

They gave me a choice for long-term care at either Chelsea Naval Hospital or at the Navy's hospital on the Portsmouth Naval Shipyard. My decision was easy since Cheryl lived with her Tasker grandparents in Northwood at the time, and connections with other family members and friends were relatively close.

I flew from Andrews AFB to Pease AFB, where I was driven by ambulance to the Naval hospital in Portsmouth. The trip from Pease over familiar roads was short, and my emotions were building from the reality of making it home. I passed through the main gate of the base where Dad stood guard in 1945, a short distance from the Naval clinic where I was born on June 15th of that year.

What an unimaginable return nearly twenty-two years later! I was elated to be close to my roots but disquieted by the unknowns about my future as a Marine or as a civilian… and feeling like neither.

Hospital on Portsmouth Naval Shipyard

First to visit me at the hospital was Cheryl, followed by Mom and Dad. My emotions leading to their arrival were of immense joy and excitement. To a lesser degree crept uneasy feelings of apprehension. Months had passed during which I experienced unspeakable horror, anger and hatred. The war had generated confusion, doubts and disillusionment in my psyche as to why the US was fighting in Viet Nam. I felt betrayed by my country, that it had betrayed us all. Hospitalization provided time for me to ponder the extent to which I had changed. I wondered if maybe I was blind to changes that others would see and feel about me, especially loved ones. I worried that maybe Cheryl had also changed and that we might be strangers to each other. Similar questions were most likely swirling around in Cheryl's head too. Her consistently sweet letters during the time I had been gone were lovingly reassuring. Still, apprehension hung suspended in the air.

As it turned out our reunion was heartwarming and wonderful, though in an awkward setting with an open ward full of so many sick and wounded serviceman. I recall laying there listening to her footsteps coming close, leading to our first hospital visit. Cheryl came to see me as often as possible, and we attempted to make plans for our future. Immediate plans were tempered by the fact that I was badly injured and still property of the Marine Corps. We had no clue as to what would happen next.

High school friends Jean Stimmell and Mike Wade, who were by then out of the service, came to visit. Also, my friend Rip Perrino and others… faces and embraces I came close to never sensing again.

One day soon after being admitted to the hospital, I was interviewed by the editor of the small Pittsfield newspaper about my experiences in Viet Nam. When I saw the article in print, I was dismayed that much of my criticism of the war was missing or watered down. Had I known more about this right-wing editor I would have refused his interview.

Easily visible from the hospital loomed "The Castle" (the Portsmouth Naval Prison), another post where my dad stood guard in 1944-1945. Some knew this prison on the Seavey Island Shipyard as "Alcatraz of the East." Through hospital windows we patients occasionally saw gangs of inmates in prison garb chained together marching somewhere under the watchful eyes of shotgun-toting Marine guards. Early morning sea mist rose from the channel and made the prison appear as the ghastly, forbidden fortress that it was. Its appearance matched its reputation. The prison was occupied until 1974, when it was closed down and abandoned. It now stands in stark disrepair. I have some historic publications about the shipyard and the prison's history.

One hospital ward (Ward D, as I remember) was barred off for sick or injured prisoners. Other wards contained mostly Navy personnel, from a cancerous lifer to a freshly circumcised seaman apprentice temporarily relieved from submarine duty. The hospital also provided services to Marines stationed at the Shipyard's Marine Barracks.

The Marines I was in the company of were hospitalized with diverse war wounds from Viet Nam. I don't recall all the names of those who were hospitalized during my time there, but I remember some of the wounds they suffered. The following paragraphs describe a couple.

One with a mangled leg contracted a nasty staph infection. He was placed in isolation where the bacteria wouldn't spread to others. Last I knew, the infection had spread within the Marine's leg, which had been amputated close to his crotch.

Another Marine had been terribly wounded as he raised his rifle to shoot at an NVA soldier who was also firing his rifle. The enemy's bullet had traveled down the length of the Marine's rifle barrel, tearing away his thumb, forefinger and part of his hand. The round continued on and split his jaw. A fragment caused the loss of an eye. While at a previous hospital, this Marine's jaw had been wired together and some surgical work had been done on his scarred face. I recall that this kid was from Vermont and, like so many casualties, he was most likely under 20 years old.

We Nam vets formed a tight brotherhood, joking and pulling warped pranks over each other's disabilities. For example, while sitting outside the orthopedic clinic awaiting my appointment, I found that my crutches had been sneakily sent by elevator to the upper floor, leaving me immobile. Another Marine who had lost an eye occasionally removed his patch, exposing his empty socket while he awaited delivery of a false eye. Another had been shot in the butt and was teased for having two assholes. Despite such pranks, we diligently looked out for one another. My closest wounded Marine brothers during this hospitalization were Don Rollman and Bob Lonergan, both also from New

Hampshire.

Doctors regularly removed bandaging and used silver nitrate sticks to cauterize the sizable hole on the inner side of my left foot below the ankle bone, eventually getting it to close and heal. Other flesh wounds from the mine explosion were healed. The orthopedic surgeon, after viewing X-rays and examining my lower left extremity, determined that due to the severe destruction of my left foot and ankle an operation was not an option. The bones were too obliterated to reconstruct. His decision was that long-duration casting would allow natural fusing of the smashed areas. Therefore, my left leg remained in a cast from foot to knee. Once, when a replacement cast was being fitted, the Navy technician accidentally cut my leg. He was trimming the cast at the inside knee bend location when his scalpel slipped and went deep into my leg. Blood ran steadily down into the cast before the technician got the wound bandaged tight. This cast stayed on for weeks, blood and all. During the lengthy casting period, all but my big toe became considerably hammered and distorted.

I also had significant nerve damage at portions of my left foot and along the back side of my lower leg which nothing could be done to improve. Parts of my foot were numb to feeling sensations, while other parts were the opposite, as if being shocked by electrical current. The shock sensation ran from the sole of my left foot up the Achilles tendon to the underside of my knee. Other nerve-related sensations up my leg felt as though insects were crawling along it when there were no insects present.

In early May, I was told by Marine higher-ups that I would be attending a ceremony at the National Guard Armory in Manchester, at which I would receive the Purple Heart medal. This event turned out to be a publicity farce. Commandant of the Marine Corps, General Wallace M. Greene, Jr. was to speak at a Veteran's Forum at the armory. Another lance corporal and

I were summoned to the event as an added attraction for the audience and local media. We were driven to the armory and General Greene pinned the medals on our shirts as we stood at attention. I was supported by crutches during the medals ceremony.

As part of his speech, the Commandant said that America was winning the Viet Nam War, "and I say that without any doubt whatsoever." What bullshit! It would have been much more meaningful had he had simply visited us at the hospital. I received a letter of acknowledgement as a recipient of the Purple Heart from then US Senator Thomas McIntyre of NH dated May 17, 1967.

Regarding medals and ribbons: Having served in a war that doesn't make me proud, I have no adoration for the medals and ribbons presented to me. For all these years I've kept them under cover, only bringing them into the light at antiwar protests when I've pinned them on my old jungle shirt or field jacket. For the sake of descendants who may be interested, I'll list them here and note that they're kept in a cardboard box with my dog tags inside the old Cate family trunk. Some medals have corresponding ribbons and certain ribbons authorized have no associated medal.

Purple Heart Medal, Combat Action Ribbon (CAR), Presidential Unit Citation Ribbon (PUC), Vietnam Service Medal, Republic of Vietnam Campaign Medal, National Defense Service Medal, Republic of Vietnam Gallantry Cross Medal with Palm, Republic of Vietnam Civil Actions Medal with Palm. The CAR and PUC ribbons have no associated medal.

TOM McINTYRE
NEW HAMPSHIRE

United States Senate

WASHINGTON, D.C.

May 17, 1967

L/C Paul B. Nichols
c/o Portsmouth Naval Hospital
Portsmouth, New Hampshire

Dear Corporal Nichols:

I was pleased to learn that you had been presented with the Purple Heart medal.

I know that this must have been a proud moment for you and certainly a very deserved honor and recognition of your outstanding and courageous conduct in Viet Nam.

If I may ever be of assistance to you, please do not hesitate to contact me.

With best wishes and warm regards,

Sincerely,

Tom McIntyre
U.S. Senator

TM/grl

NH Senator McIntyre's letter

Incidentally, often times rightfully earned military medals and ribbons fell through the cracks and were never issued. The *Combat Action Ribbon*, recognizing an individual's combat encounter as opposed to that of a unit battle, is a common example of this. My dad was understandably proud of his service during WWII but hadn't received this ribbon. I helped him submit the records to substantiate issuance of the ribbon, and he received it a few years prior to his death. I now have Dad's CAR somewhere in my files.

One day, some warped military lifer on the Naval base thought it would be entertaining for those hospitalized Marines among us who were somewhat mobile to tour The Castle. We all abruptly turned down the invitation, having no desire to be paraded through the cell blocks gazing at military prisoners.

The nasty war in Viet Nam played on the hospital TVs with each newscast. During early June, television broadcasts also covered the "Six-Day War" between Israel and the Arabic countries of Egypt, Syria and Jordan. For the first few days of news coverage, those of us hospitalized from war in Southeast Asia wondered if the US would engage in that war too.

In big cities across the US (notably San Francisco), and in Canada and Europe, the summer of 1967 was known as "The Summer of Love." These were high times for the hippie counterculture movement and all it brought on. For those of us isolated and ensnared in the Viet Nam quagmire, this love and peace concept was difficult to fathom. But most of us devoured the psychedelic music, which had rapidly progressed by American, Canadian, and British rock groups during the time we had been stifled in the war zone.

Several new bands had emerged while I was away and others, like *The Beatles* and *Pink Floyd*, had transitioned into psychedelia. West Coast hippie bands such as the *Grateful Dead, Quicksilver Messenger Service, The Jimi Hendrix Experience, Janice Joplin with Big Brother and the Holding*

Company, *Jefferson Airplane*, and *Country Joe and the Fish* generated a huge fan base with their fantastic music. Rock/blues groups like *The Rolling Stones*, *Neil Young and Crazy Horse*, *The Doors, Cream, Fleetwood Mac, The Who, John Mayall and the Bluesbreakers, Savoy Brown, and Canned Heat* electrified the Sixties generation. Among less widely known psychedelic rock bands were *Moby Grape, Strawberry Alarm Clock, The Electric Prunes* and *Iron Butterfly.* Such great creative bands and related artwork were prolific during the mid-1960s into the 1970s. This music coincided perfectly with the fervor of the times. Creedence Clearwater Revival released their first terrific rock album in 1968, with more to follow. A group called *The Grass Roots* played a popular song titled "Let's Live for Today" which exemplified our thinking. And the psychedelic artwork on album covers and concert posters was vividly colorful and abstract. I have a great book of art illustrations titled *High Societies: Psychedelic Rock Posters of Haight-Ashbury.*

In 1967, a nationwide veterans' organization called "Vietnam Veterans Against the War (VVAW)" was founded in New York City. As its name implies, this group was made up of servicemen and women returning in strong opposition to the war they had been fighting. Membership quickly expanded. Chapters grew as the war surged in unpopularity and even included active duty troops serving in Viet Nam. Underground antiwar newspapers were printed and circulated within active military outfits. I have been a member for VVAW for many years.

A major VVAW antiwar demonstration took place in Washington, DC called Operation Dewey Canyon III from April 18 to April 23, 1971. Hundreds of Vietnam veterans and Gold Star parents marched from Arlington National Cemetery to the US Capital. An encampment was set up on the Mall behind the Capital building. On the final day of the demonstration, vets approached the Capital fence one at a time, passionately announced their names and military units and made statements against the war before throwing their medals, discharge papers, etc. over the fence. This profound event added increased fervor to the many monumental antiwar demonstrations in DC and all across the country.

On Friday May 29, 1992, Vietnam veterans Steve Fowle, John Jones, Jean Stimmell and I traveled to New York City in Steve's VW Rabbit. Our objective was to attend the 25th anniversary celebration of the Vietnam Veterans Against the War organization. Through VVAW contacts we rented a quad room for the weekend at the Vista Hotel, 3 World Trade Center. Nam vet Dave Connolly from South Boston joined us at the eventful gathering along with many other vets and their partners from across the country. A generous reception was held at a nearby restaurant for attendees that night.

The next morning VVAW veterans visited the NYC Vietnam Veterans Memorial, then marched to Battery Park where a rally took place. Later that day there were many prominent activist speakers, including Daniel Ellsberg, David Dellinger, Bobby Muller, and music by Country Joe McDonald. We partied and listened to great rock music well into the night at a downtown club called The Wetlands Preserve. The four of us skipped the more formal business sessions on Sunday and returned home tired from all the festivities.

The World Trade Center was bombed in late February 1993 by terrorists angered at US support of Israel. A van loaded with a massive bomb exploded in one of the Vista Hotel's parking garages causing extensive damage to the complex and injuries to several. The Center was destroyed with thousands of casualties during a terrorist attack in 2001.

My sea bag with uniforms and related belongings were eventually shipped to the hospital from Okinawa where they had been left in storage at the time of our departure for Viet Nam.

NH Vietnam veterans Steve Fowle, Jean Stimmell, Paul Nichols and John Jones at Battery Park, NYC at VVAW 25-year celebration

Later, some of my stuff from Gia Le arrived, including my Bowie knife and a few things that had been in my tent that fateful morning of the mine explosion. (I have since given the knife to son Shawn.)

I was disappointed to find that they had not returned some items, including a few American greenbacks, my camouflaged boonie hat, my camera, a new bayonet, and a crude handmade bamboo-handled sickle I had taken from a smoldering Cam Lo hamlet. The extra bayonet had been given to me by friends in supply at Dong Ha. I planned to mail it and the sickle home as souvenirs from the war but hesitated due to warnings from the Corps. Mailings of any type of weaponry were prohibited, and we were told that suspicious items were X-rayed by postal personnel. Big trouble for offenders they said. I had mailed home one complete C ration meal and the tire tread sandals described earlier. I had sent a couple pairs of worn jungle boots and new jungle utilities home from Okinawa. I have some of these things to this day.

The few of us who were hospitalized but ambulatory were allowed short trips to downtown Portsmouth if we did limited chores inside the hospital. My job was receptionist duty at the dentist office. This was a strange experience. There must have been a shortage of Novocain resulting in audible patient groaning! Time downtown was mainly spent in bars, which were numerous and seedy. The city was very blue-collar and was in no way the upscale tourist mecca that it has become in the years since. Taxi drivers seemed to enjoy our rowdy company as they drove us back to the hospital.

Hospital officials had prohibited me from driving since my lower left leg was in a cast. But one night while on weekend leave, I caroused to excess in Pittsfield with my high school friend Mike Wade. It was late when I headed for Northwood in our 1965 VW. These bugs had four-speed manual transmissions, and the foot control space was cramped. I attempted to depress the clutch with my cumbersome left leg to downshift, while traveling far too fast. I missed a sweeping curve in Chichester on Rt. 28 and rolled the car over several times down over a steep roadside embankment into the shallows of the Suncook River. The VW landed upright on all four tires, still running with tailpipes at water level bubbling the surface as it purred. Unhurt and not realizing the car was in the river, I stepped out into nearly knee-deep water. My soaked cast turned to soggy paste. I grabbed my crutches, turned off the car's lights and ignition, and hitchhiked to Pittsfield. I got to Rip Perrino's house where a raucous party was in full swing. He and a few partygoers drove me back to my VW. The hour was so late and the car was so far below road level that no one, cops included, had seen or reported the accident. I started the VW up and the boys pushed me out of the water, getting soaked in the process from my spinning rear wheels.

I drove diagonally up over the steep embankment onto Rt. 28 and managed to limp the severely crippled rig to Northwood where I parked it at Cheryl's grandparents' place. The Seacoast Volkswagen dealership declared our car a total wreck but offered us a small value towards a new one. Due to the circumstances, I hadn't reported the accident to our insurance company, so we took quite a monetary loss. We bought a brand-new light blue 1967 VW bug under a payment plan at a cost of approximately $1,800.00. Back at the Navy hospital I explained my ruined cast to my perplexed doctor as a brook trout fishing mishap, and a replacement was applied.

By mid-summer of 1967, Portsmouth Naval Hospital's orthopedic department was phased out. I was still in a lower leg cast getting around on crutches. To our surprise, Don Rollman and I were released from the hospital and were assigned limited duty at the Shipyard's Marine Corps Barracks (the same place where Dad had been assigned to in 1944). Mostly, he and I answered telephones and tried to stay out of the way. The petty spit and polish regimentation at the Barracks proved to be beyond adjustment after all Don and I had been through. Before long they offered me leave, allowing me to live with Cheryl at her grandparents' home in Northwood. Don went home to Lebanon, NH. We assumed a medical discharge would soon be forthcoming. (In 1987 this Barracks detachment became a thing of the past, as Marine outfits left the Shipyard ending 174 years of continuous service, leaving security to Department of Defense police.)

While on leave in anticipation of becoming a civilian, I bought a classy low-budget 1951 Mercury with an eight-cylinder flat head engine and standard shift with overdrive. I have photos of this chariot. My leave status changed, and instead of a discharge I received orders to report to Camp Lejeune, NC, not later than August 26. Don Rollman received the same set of orders. With this turn of events, I sold the Mercury to Dad.

Cheryl quit her job and we prepared to return to North Carolina. Unexpectedly, we were invited to attend Don and his girlfriend Martha's wedding in Lebanon. I applied for and was granted a five-day leave extension. We had a good time at the wedding and soon began our drive to Camp Lejeune. We traveled together — Don and Marty in their snazzy Ford Mustang, Cheryl and me in our new VW Beetle. We arrived at Lejeune on August 31st and applied for base housing at Tarawa Terrace. Don's rank was corporal, and I was one rank down from that, a lance corporal. As an NCO (noncommissioned officer), Don qualified for much improved quarters than me. He and Marty moved into their Midway Park abode, while Cheryl and I settled in at Knox Trailer Park, the same maze of dull silver cans we had lived in the year before. This time our rental was trailer #931. Cheryl was a little more than three months pregnant carrying Shawn.

I was assigned limited duty in Headquarters Company and shuffled into what was called a "Casualty Platoon." This platoon had no productive function. It was merely a warehouse of dejection and rejection. It was a catch basin — a dumping ground for mostly black, low ranked, angry and demoralized Viet Nam returnees. It was a product of the upheaval brought on by the unprincipled war. The platoon consisted of Marines in three categories: those having minor unresolved disciplinary charges, those with physical disabilities, and "short-timers" (those with little time left in the Corps) who were denied the decency of an "early out." We were of no value to the Marine Corps and likewise, the "Crotch" was of no value to us. Rejection at both ends! We just wanted out, to regain our civilian lives and try to forget the rotten war.

Our shitbird attitudes reflected the demeaning nature of the outfit and our unmotivated state of mind. The common feeling was that we were just so many pieces of shit in a shitbird platoon catching every shit detail that came along from the Black sergeant in charge. We mostly hung around the darkened barracks. A Marine among us whose balls had been blown off in the Nam had been engaged to be married. He had learned that his plans for marriage were null and void. He was majorly dispirited about his future. Occasionally we would lose someone whose discharge came around. Spaces were filled by others marking time in limbo.

One day, I witnessed a Black private summoned outside our barracks where he received a less-than-honorable discharge. A formation was ordered facing the private. The formation was ordered to do an about-face, turning all backs on the private while his undesirable discharge was read. I don't know the reasons prompting his discharge, but this crude ceremony is unforgettable. "Bad paper" discharges were common and often unwarranted due to PTSD issues, minor disciplinary charges and deep racism.

Much has been said and written about the extremely vile treatment many servicemen got from antiwar civilians upon their return to the US. The warehousing experience I've described in the casualty platoon at Camp Lejeune is in ways more degrading than the hurtful actions and inactions of the general public. More on action and inaction later.

I left the barracks at night to be with Cheryl, my source of love and sanity. Military life wasn't easy for Cheryl either, and her sacrifice from normalcy was significant. Mornings I returned to the barracks. I had most weekends off, so Cheryl and I often left the base and took the Governor Cherry Ferry to the beach on Emerald Isle. Topsail Beach was another of our favorite getaways. We had little money for entertainment or anything else, but the beach provided a brief escape from all things military. We also spent time with Don, Marty and other friends based at Camp Lejeune. Our common bond was lower-ranked military status, rather than from geographic, cultural, religious or political standpoints. On September 17, 1967, as I drove toward the main gate, I heard on our car radio that there had been an accident on Mt. Washington's Cog Railway in the NH White Mountains. Eight people were reported killed and at least seventy-four injured when an excursion car broke loose and crashed into a gorge below.

While stationed at Lejeune, I thought it would be a good idea to have my four wisdom teeth removed, as they had grown in crooked and were bothering at times. It would cost me nothing while still in the Corps. I made an appointment at a Naval dental clinic to have the most troublesome tooth yanked… and yanked it was! The line awaiting the clinic was long when I arrived. Most of those leaving ahead of me came out holding a gauze pad to their jaw. Hurriedly, the dentist stuck my gums with Novocain. He began prying and pulling on my tooth with various tools before the anesthetic took hold, tearing the corner of my mouth in the process. As soon as he got the tooth out and the gaping hole crammed with wadding, I was out of the clinic in a flash, holding my bruised, swollen jaw as bloody drool oozed down my wrist. I never returned to have the remaining three as much as looked at.

Recalling my military dentist experience brings to mind a story Dad told of getting an aching molar filled on a South Pacific Island sometime prior to his Bougainville landing during World War II. The dentist's crude drill was foot-treadle powered, sort of like an old-fashioned sewing machine. I heard of Dad's uncomfortable makeshift slow-grind ordeal on several occasions over the years.

Intermittently, I was ordered to the Naval Hospital at Camp Lejeune for physical tests, X-rays and evaluations. After considerable hurrying up and waiting during these occasions, they sent me back to the barracks. Finally, in mid-November 1967 I appeared before the Physical Evaluation Board. As a result of this formal exercise, consistent with the typical ration of USMC bullshit, I agreed to a 40 percent disability rating: "Loss of use of left foot." I decided not to rebut the relatively low rating, which would have required putting up with prolonged appeals. Cheryl and I wanted out. Shamefully, procedures to obtain the lowest possible rating were historically common throughout the military, but they were magnified during the Viet Nam War era. In hindsight, as with thousands of others, I should have contested the rating.

Throughout my travels from that gruesome field tent to the hospitals that followed, I'll never forget the incredible multitudes of mangled young servicemen. America's youth, hideously maimed partial people stuck with tubes and drains hanging on by feedings of blood, antiseptics and morphine — many lethally poisoned by Agent Orange, though not yet knowing it. A myriad of forever altered lives whose plight was sealed by our country's culturally ignorant, arrogant, selfish, misguided leaders. Images that will remain seared in my visions, my thoughts, my dreams, my DNA until I'm dust. Such a needless, senseless waste.

Early on December 18th, Cheryl and I stopped at Camp Lejeune's main gate for the last time. I used a USMC "Red Devil" putty knife borrowed from the gate attendant to scrape off the base sticker from our VW's bumper. I threw the tool into our car, which was packed from floor to roof. Cheryl was 7 1/2 months pregnant as we headed toward New Hampshire in cramped bucket seats. We reached my Mom and Dad's house in Chichester at 3:30 AM on the 19th.

As of January 2, 1968, I was placed on the Corps' Temporary Disability Retired List (TDRL) and released from active duty.

Assigned this status, I was ordered to appear for further medical evaluations in eighteen-month intervals at the Portsmouth Naval Hospital to determine whether or not my physical condition had changed. I was unable to sever ties to Portsmouth Naval. After undergoing these periodic evaluations, it was determined that my disability was rated permanent at a 30 percent level. This reduced rating is another that I should have appealed, but I wanted no more bureaucratic hassles from the military. Based on the experiences of other wounded vets, it's likely that this was the military's devious strategy! I was placed on the Permanent Disability Retired List (PDRL) on January 1, 1973, ending my military path.

Paul's USMC retired ID card

Several years later my friend Ed Tasker, who had lost a lower leg to a Viet Cong booby trap, encouraged me to obtain a rating from the Veterans Administration (VA). I, like many Vietnam vets, had stayed clear of the VA, but Ed said I'd probably receive a more favorable compensation rating from VA adjudicators. The military's system for compensation was based on time in service and rank, neither of which I had much of. I took Ed's advice and found that his suggestion was valid. I waived the ridiculous military retirement compensation rating and opted for the VA system, which based rating determinations on an individual's service-connected disability, regardless of years of service and rank. However, the VA had its own unsavory and corrupt elements also, as I will address further on.

During my initial evaluations at the Manchester VA hospital, I was asked if I had served in areas affected by our military's spraying of Agent Orange and other defoliants. It was obvious to me that I had. The VA had a big map of Viet Nam with vast areas of the country shaded orange where the heaviest spraying had taken place. Locations where I had operated were identified, mostly colored orange. With this documented, my name was added to the VA's Agent Orange Registry. Ever since then, I've received the Agent Orange newsletter containing updates on the various diseases recognized by the VA for compensation purposes due to chemical exposure.

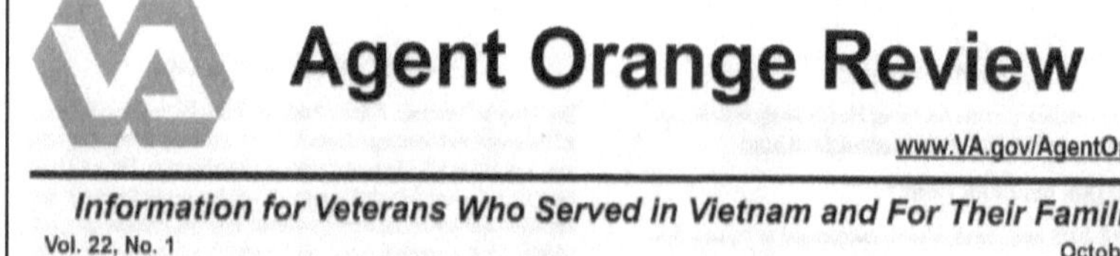

VA's Agent Orange newsletter heading

So far, I've lucked out, having none of the many diseases linked to herbicide spraying. Sometimes, I feel fortunate to have been wounded severely enough to be flown out of Vietnam fairly early on in my 13-month tour of duty. Had I stayed for the duration, it's likely that my hearing loss and tinnitus would be worse, and I would have been at a greater health risk from Agent Orange exposure. Also, the longer I stayed in dangerous I Corps, the chances of being killed or more severely wounded would have been far more likely. Staying far from the war in the first place would have been the best scenario.

WHAT A LONG, STRANGE JOURNEY

Shawn Eric Nichols was born at Concord Hospital on February 5, 1968. Needless to say, Cheryl and I were delighted to have our healthy newborn son, bringing exuberant expectations of a happy future together. I did my best to stay away from all news about the war, but it was impossible. The late January Viet Cong and NVA surprise attacks of the 1968 Tet Offensive raged throughout South Vietnam. Reports of the intense fighting, mounting US casualties and a surging nationwide antiwar movement cranked steadily across all media forms. Near constant pain from my injuries kept the war close despite attempts to bury it and transition into my new civilian status. Shawn's birth added positive dimensions to Cheryl's and my life.

The war's most fierce fighting took place throughout South Vietnam during the '68 Tet Offensive, at which time the Viet Cong were seriously decimated by US and ARVN forces. The NVA remained strong, despite huge troop losses. From a strategic standpoint, the Offensive was triumphant. It proved that there was no "light at the end of the tunnel," the lie our military and political hawks kept telling the American public. Our citizenry became evermore disheartened about the misbegotten war, as were returning veterans and deployed troops. Increasingly, the war was viewed as a futile no-win venture by a widening cross section of Americans, including many from older generations, religious leaders, teachers, concerned parents and a small but growing number of journalists and elected officials. Yet, our country remained majorly fractured with angry us-and-them divisions, even within families.

Toward the end of his first elected term, President Lyndon B. Johnson became demoralized by the war's ongoing carnage. He withdrew from the Democratic presidential race in March of 1968. The Democratic National Convention held in Chicago in late August of 1968 turned chaotic and violent, with massive antiwar protests and angry calls for changes in the country's political system. The rebellious convention led to the November election of Republican Richard M. Nixon over Democratic candidate Vice President Hubert Humphrey, and to long-lasting calamity for the Democratic Party. Decades later, documents reveal that candidate Nixon had covertly sabotaged Johnson's peace negotiations between South and North Vietnam to gain popular support in the 1968 presidential election.

Regretfully, I didn't vote in that chaotic election. After my experiences in the war, I wanted to stay as far away from US politics as possible. It was the first election I was old enough to vote in, and it turned out being one of the closest in US history. The Tet offensive, the tragic assassinations of Dr. Martin Luther King, Jr. and Bobby Kennedy and other traumatic happenings during 1968 cranked up the divisiveness and tumult to explosive levels from coast to coast. Prior era's culture was erupting. Our country was on the brink of revolution!

I needed employment, so I inquired about the ASCS County Office Manager trainee position that I came close to taking with the USDA agency back in 1965. Luckily, there was an opening, and I was hired in February 1968. The prospect of administering federally legislated agricultural programs at the county level was appealing, as there was minimal regimentation and relative job freedom. Salary and benefits seemed quite good for the times. Once hired for a permanent position, the job entailed a combination of office responsibilities and traveling throughout the county I was employed in. Although many of the programs administered by ASCS were geared to huge farming communities in parts of the US producing commodities not applicable to New England, a few important natural resource-related programs were a perfect fit.

The pioneering soil conservation programs developed by President Franklin D. Roosevelt's administration during the Great Depression and the dustbowl tragedy of the early 1930s had been continued. And they had been refined and expanded to address serious current-day problems. The early programs were certainly ahead of their time, especially when considering the steadily declining state of the natural environment in subsequent decades. Soil and water conservation, forest improvement, wildlife and endangered plant species preservation, pollution abatement and prevention, energy conservation and other resource stewardship programs were of great interest to me. Based on my past work on farms, with the NH State Parks Division and with SCS, the position with ASCS seemed fitting and rewarding.

The training program was New England-wide. In late February I began travelling to various ASCS offices within New Hampshire, Massachusetts and Maine. Cheryl and I rented an apartment on Earl's Beach Road at Northwood Lake, where she and Shawn remained while I was away in training. I returned each weekend, leaving for my assigned work locations either late Sunday nights or very early Monday mornings. Though I was fortunate to have a meaningful, suitable paying job, the distant periods of separation from Cheryl and Shawn were difficult on the three of us. This was not a positive situation for Cheryl and me following the eventful twists and turns in our lives since my draft notice arrived in 1965.

For US World War II veterans of both theatres, their mission was crystal clear; our country was unified, and everyone sacrificed for the cause, the outcome was victorious, and the world was grateful. Heightened pride and patriotism were natural hallmarks of all who lived through those menacing war years. The GI Bill was signed into law providing a wide array of benefits for returning WW II vets. Coming home from Vietnam was totally different.

Earlier in this memoir, when describing my experiences in the casualty platoon at Camp Lejeune prior to being discharged, I briefly mentioned Vietnam veterans' homecoming from the war and the public's reception. More needs to be recorded about this, so now I will digress.

At Dad's suggestion, I joined the "Veterans of Foreign Wars" organization. His belief was that veterans would always look out for veterans, which could be handy if I needed help while on the road with my trainee job. Being lonesome and bored, I stopped at a couple VFW clubs during my out-of-state travels. The atmosphere was far different than I expected. The members in the bars were mostly red-faced, pebble-nosed World War II vets. I saw no other Vietnam vets, and a quiet but harsh alienation filled the air. Instead of camaraderie I felt rejection and isolation. My final visit to a VFW post occurred when a blindly patriotic hard-ass scoffed that we hadn't won our war yet, further stating that his generation would have whipped the gooks asses by now. Some VFW and American Legion member vets downplayed the Vietnam War as even being a real war! Imagine the resentment we who came home broken felt about such attitudes. They fanned the flames of bitterness.

Throughout subsequent decades, until recent years, the disrespect and hostility from VFW and American Legion chapters toward Vietnam vets has been nearly universal. It is for these and other reasons that Vietnam veteran membership in such organizations remained very scant. Particularly since the arrival of the current millennium, World War II and Korean War veterans are dying in massive numbers. Vietnam veterans and those who follow are now welcome with open arms in order to keep these outfits afloat.

Much has been said and written about the vile treatment of returning Vietnam vets by the civilian population, particularly from college students and antiwar protesters. I personally know vets who have spoken of the hateful reactions they received upon coming home to the US and the emotional and physical pain experienced as a result. There are stories that returning vets were advised by the military not to wear their service uniform on their flight home so as not to enflame civilians at airports and public establishments. I believe that many of the repulsive actions by those opposed to the war did in fact happen. Tragically, the most readily available targets of public wrath about the war were returning veterans. However, I also think that the broad scope of such behavior has been appreciably exaggerated.

Coming home as a casualty, I didn't witness outright public disrespect. My surroundings were mainly in hospitals among military doctors, nurses, attendants and other hospitalized veterans. My visitors were family members and friends. My travels outside the hospitals were quite limited until after I was discharged from the Marines. Once outside the hospitals I wore civilian clothes, except for my field jacket. My seabag and uniform were closeted away where they remain to this day.

No vets that I knew craved gala fanfare or parades or to be treated as courageous heroes. Most of us knew the war was wrong, but our brothers were bleeding in it with no choices. Even in the absence of overt disrespect, we were greeted with an air of public indifference. Americans were sick of the damned war and wanted it swept under the red-white-and-blue rug. As a result, most vets fell deeper into isolation and kept all aspects the war bottled-up inside. At a tragic cost.

Jean Stimmell reminded me of feelings along these lines with the following quote from a Vietnam veteran in the book by David J. Morris titled *The Evil Hours*: "The war had hurt me. I wanted the country to feel some of that hurt." Yet, at home, he could barely begin to describe what he had experienced because no one in America was listening. The vet continued: "I realized that the problem wasn't just that they didn't understand the war but that they didn't want to understand it.

What I had to say was not only inconvenient to their peace of mind but a tangible threat to it."

Of course, Cheryl (and years later, Mary and family members) definitely knew that I served in Vietnam and that I had been wounded, but that was about the extent of it. My letters home to Cheryl and my parents kept details of scary experiences and their dangers pretty much void of detail. Several photos showed me smiling, not revealing my true feelings. I didn't want undue worry to occupy their days and nights, especially since there was nothing they could do about the situation. I bitched a lot in my letters about shitty living conditions and about the Vietnamese, and I expressed dreams of coming home. I tried to omit heavier things.

I recall the first time anyone graciously acknowledged my participation in the atrocious war. It happened sometime during the 1990s as I was leaving a Concord quick-lube garage. It took me totally by surprise, and I didn't know quite how to feel or how to respond. The young mechanic noticed a VVA (Vietnam Veterans of America) decal on the rear window of my pickup truck as I was slowly driving out through the garage doors. The kid thanked me for my service, innocently wanting to show his well-intentioned respect. This just blew me away because nothing like that had happened in all the years prior. He was about the age of so many of the war's hellish casualties, and he reminded me of the mangled teenagers I saw in amputee wards. I was, on one hand, appreciative of the young man's gesture, but I wasn't proud of my participation in the war. This made the occurrence quite surreal, and I drifted down Loudon Road in a tearful daze.

During the turbulent war years, the news media focused on and exploited isolated occasions of disrespectful activities perpetrated by opponents of the war. Incidents have been recorded where undercover FBI agents, CIA goons, and cops secretly joined large peaceful antiwar demonstrations, blending in with the crowd for the purpose of inciting violent, anarchistic behavior. They also contrived fake drug busts to further denigrate protesting masses. This discredited legitimate protests and strengthened the prevalent "us and them" divisions of the times.

Late in the 1960s, early 70s, radical groups such as Students for a Democratic Society (SDS), the Weather Underground and the Black Panthers went overboard in legitimate antiwar activism causing violence and destruction, mostly on college campuses and in big cities. Many of their activities hurt the image of peaceful protests and undermined a measure of public support for the antiwar movement that was sweeping the land. The Black Panther Party promoted many peaceful community social programs, however, centered around food accessibility, health clinics and educational fairness for the underprivileged class. Another focus of Black Panther activity was the reduction of police brutality against African Americans.

The tragic student killings during May of 1970 at Kent State University by Ohio National Guard soldiers followed by needless student deaths by police at Mississippi's Jackson State University magnified the unrest to explosive levels. Revolutionary sentiment was quite widespread, primarily among America's youth.

Another unfortunate consequence of the war was the reluctance of some employers to hire Vietnam veterans. A stigma had developed about vets coming home with undesirable traits such as anxiety, depression, temperament swings, violent behavior, drunkenness and drug addiction. The trauma of the war plus the harmful reception back home had destructive life-altering affects. Homelessness, restlessness, broken relationships with family and friends, substance abuse, incarceration and suicides took a heavy toll. Several factors influenced how well or poorly veterans made the transition from war to home. A major stressor was the intensity of the trauma experienced. There were considerable variations, such as branch of military, location and length of service in the war zone, a person's MOS (Military Occupational Specialty) and other circumstances. Everyone's personal experience varied. Pre-war traumatic events intensified war trauma. Multiple factors had cumulative effects. This said, adjustment to civilian life after the war came easier for many vets, who merged into society and moved on to happy, productive lives.

The VA (Veterans Administration) had shabby, inadequate facilities that offered little to returning Vietnam veterans. Many VA doctors, therapists and the administrative personnel took a distant or antagonistic approach to dealing with Vietnam vets needing help. Dispensing copious pills of all descriptions was the VA way of treating problems, mental and physical. Claims for deserved benefits were stonewalled by VA officials and became ensnared in ridiculous bureaucracy. I vividly recall the disdainful attitude toward me by a woman in charge of Records Release at the Manchester VA hospital. I rightfully requested some of my records, and her reluctant mannerism was maddening to me. VA claims denial led to a long, arduous appeal process, which was degrading and often had a negative outcome. One of the VA's favorite, most widely used reasons for the denial of disability compensation for PTSD was their determination that the vet had a Personality Disorder. By relying on catch-all Personality Disorder findings, the VA justified denial of veterans' claims.

Throughout the decades following the war I have had extensive dealings with the VA. In recent years, I have experienced major improvements in various functions of the Department, particularly in the quality of health care, both mental and physical. Administrative personnel are more helpful and respectful. My health care providers are conscientious, competent and more open to alternative treatment methods instead of or in addition to meds. Facilities have been upgraded and the clinics have been modernized. The VA's Vet Centers, first established in 1979, have proven invaluable to traumatized veterans and their family members through professional counseling programs and outreach referral services.

Military discharges other than "honorable" were quite common during the war. There were various lesser levels of discharges (called "bad paper"), which had a profoundly negative impact on a veteran's life, including ineligibility for VA benefits and federal employment and a diminished overall standing in society. Through the years, cases have been proven where less than honorable discharges were wrongfully delivered, often instigated by PTSD. Discharge upgrades are possible but are mentally exhausting and difficult to obtain.

The Vietnam Veterans of America organization's September/October 2014 magazine (*The VVA Veteran*) featured an extensive article titled "Gold Star Mothers: The Awful Price of Membership." A Gold Star Mother designates the mother of a son or daughter killed in battle while serving the USA during wartime. A national association called the American Gold Star Mothers (AGSM) was formed by mothers of servicemen killed during World War I. The organization serves as a powerful support group to mothers shouldering the grief of a common loss. AGSM members volunteer at hospitals helping wounded veterans and advocate for veterans' well-being. They also stand together at ceremonies honoring veterans.

The above-mentioned article states that some World War II Gold Star Mothers didn't welcome mothers of Vietnam-era casualties. To some WW II mothers, the Vietnam War wasn't regarded as a real war, so the moms of those killed in Vietnam were considered unworthy of being Gold Star Mothers. According to a former AGSM president from the Vietnam-era, sons and daughters killed in Iraq and Afghanistan are considered heroes. Recognition of such losses generally received far more public sympathy. Eventually, during the decades following the Vietnam War, mothers of the dead have received the respect they long deserved by the organization.

Inscribed in the black granite wall of the Vietnam Veterans Memorial (The Wall) in Washington, DC are the names of more than 58,000 men and women killed during that needless war. Each tragic casualty had a Gold Star Mother.

My sister Nancy married Michael Wilson in the spring of 1968. A former Marine, Mike had recently returned from combat in Vietnam. Nan was attending nursing school in Hanover, NH when she met Mike, who was a Vermonter. Together they had a son named Benjamin, but the marriage was short lived. Mike often became violent and took his anger out on Nan, hitting her and dragging her across the floor by her hair. During occasional visits, Mom noticed that Nan had been bruised and scraped, but Nan was quick to come up with dubious stories as to the cause.

The divorce came when Nan could withstand no more brutalization. Mike abandoned all fatherly responsibilities, and Ben grew up not knowing him. Mike died of cancer in February 2015.

In the decade following her divorce, Nan had a tough time bringing Ben up as a single parent maintaining a full-time nursing job. Mom and Dad helped with the situation all they could. Nan became involved in a few tenuous relationships, none of which worked out until she met Alan Pollard of Danbury, NH. She and Alan were married at Mom's and Dad's house in Chichester on June 27, 1981.

A couple brief humorous recollections: Nan used to always hold family birthday celebrations for Ben, often at Newfound Lake but some years at different locations. One such party took place in Danbury at the old farm where Alan grew up and where his father still lived. On a rise of ground behind the house was a small field where Alan had some magnificent marijuana plants flourishing to a height of six or seven feet and with full top greenery close to the flowering stage.

Mary, Nan, Alan, Dad, and I happened upon these plants during a casual walk about. Unsuspecting, Dad was unfamiliar with what marijuana plants looked like. He mistook them as being sumac, which appeared somewhat like pot plants. Sumac has a similar compound leave structure with similar deep green color, and the top growth of early season sumac wouldn't have formed its colorful conical clusters. Dad disliked sumac due to its invasive nature, and he figured we all must feel likewise. Dad walked up to one of the biggest plants, bent it over enough to grasp it firmly and began to yank up on it with vigor. My dad was in his 70s and rugged for his age, but the roots of the plant held until he finally gave up. The plant was a weed alright, just not the useless weed Dad thought it was! He would have been appalled if he had known that the plant was the illegal marijuana, but he never found out. Alan, Nan, Mary, and I stood there thunderstruck but snickering as the scene played out. The plant stood somewhat bent among the others but survived until harvest.

Alan owned a full-grown Alaskan Malamute dog at the time. Unbeknownst to Alan, the dog had grabbed his leather wallet with all its contents, wandered off and buried it. After searching for a spot of freshly disturbed ground in the yard, the wallet was recovered.

Nan and Alan's marriage lasted for a decade or so but ended in divorce mainly due to Alan's heavy drinking. Following the divorce, Nan became immersed in the Seventh-day Advent religion with all the wacko ideas that cult adheres to. Alan remained a loyal father figure to Ben until his death in late 2015 in Maine, where he had lived alone for years in his remote cabin.

In the early hours of January 14, 2011, Mom, Ben, Mary, and I sat at Nan's bedside at Concord Hospital's ICU facility, where she died from cancer-related complications. She had been battling colon cancer for the past few years and had recently retired from her long career as a registered nurse. During Nan's career she worked as an attending hospital nurse, in ICUs, in emergency rooms, in hospice, and in elder care facilities. In retirement, she was looking forward to doing non-profit volunteer work, expanded church activities and caring for Mom. Nan was 63 years old when she passed. Her ashes are buried in the Nichols plot at the Loudon Ridge Cemetery.

During the late spring and summer of 1968 my training assignments took place in various counties in Maine. I vividly recall learning of the assassination of Robert F. Kennedy in early June while I was having breakfast at Helen's Restaurant in the seaside town of Machias, Maine. As a county office trainee, I was running the Washington County office while the manager was on vacation.

In July, I was required to become the Acting County Office Manager of Piscataquis County, Maine for an indefinite assignment until a vacancy could be filled for a permanent manager. I worked out of Dover-Foxcroft, the county seat of a very large and remote northwesterly, mostly forested, economically impoverished, sparsely populated county.

Each week I roomed with a nice elderly couple in their old backwoods farmhouse in Monson, two towns northwest of the office. Living quarters here were very bare-bones.

I was very unhappy to be stuck in that county. The drive to Northwood and back each weekend was long and arduous. Agency leaders within Maine assumed that I would become the full-time manager of that county operation. I stalled on making a decision, hoping that a better option would open up elsewhere. I couldn't imagine settling down with my family in Piscataquis County. Manager positions were few and far between, and I really needed an alternative.

Finally, the chance came about for a move to Franklin County, Maine, located southwest of Piscataquis County. I was hired as County Office Manager in mid-January of 1969, with my office in the county seat town of Farmington. This was another remote inland area, but there was a small college in town, a movie theater and some decent places to shop. A major ski resort (Sugarloaf) was located in the county, and the city of Waterville was within reasonable driving distance. Plus, it was somewhat closer to New Hampshire where our family and friends lived. Cheryl and I considered this location a positive option until a more preferable opportunity arose. We three moved out of Northwood and rented a new duplex apartment with a long uphill driveway in the little rural town of Industry, a few miles from Farmington.

The snowiest winter of our lives happened that winter. We were snowed in for days at one point. We became close friends with the family that shared our duplex apartment, Glen and Barbara Haskell and their young daughter, Keelie. We met other friends and had some wild times. We attended a few memorable parties at a big run-down mansion. Joe Pardoe is the person that comes to mind who owned the old estate. We took occasional trips to the city of Waterville with friends. There we visited a few "head shops" and hung out in bars. I bought some record albums and several cultish comic books filled with zany stories having bizarre illustrations done by R. Crumb and others. These comics had titles like *Zap Comix, Mr. Natural, Uncle Sham, Big Ass Comics* and *The Fabulous Furry Freak Brothers*. There were similar books of various titles from 60s culture. I still have a few of these crazy magazines stored away in a box. I wonder if they'll be valuable years from now!

One snowy winter night, Cheryl left a party nearby to check on Shawn. He was being cared for at our apartment by a babysitter who was fairly new to us. On the way, she rolled our light blue 1967 VW bug onto its side. Cheryl was unhurt, but the car was heavily damaged. We bought a brand new 1970 Ford XL at the dealership in Farmington, where Cheryl had taken a bookkeeping job. Because she got a great deal, we bought a car that we never could have otherwise afforded.

In the early spring of 1969, I bought a new Harley-Davidson XLCH Sportster at the Concord dealership. Often on weekends I drove the bike back and forth between Maine and NH, while Cheryl and Shawn followed along in our car. These earliest motorcycle trips were freezing cold with snow still visible along the highway shoulders. My bike had no windshield or fairing, and I nearly froze during the four-hour ride to and fro.

The new cult-like film, *Easy Rider*, was wildly popular with nearly everyone in our generation. The movie centered on many things that were going on of a rebellious and bigoted redneck nature during the Sixties and early Seventies. The film's music score fit perfectly throughout, and I watched the movie several times. Having a Harley motorcycle added powerful connections to the storyline and made the *Easy Rider* freedom compelling to me. A restless longing that fostered an unrealistic fantasy.

A few friends in Maine had motorcycles also and needless to say many wild adventures ensued. Winding road bike jaunts to Carrabassett Valley's Sugarloaf ski resort and beer drinking at the Red Stallion Inn were especially fun. Cheryl's brother Buzz also had a Harley Sportster, creating additional rowdy motorcycle escapades in both NH and at our place in Maine.

A couple friends and I drove our bikes from Maine to attend the annual motorcycle weekend race event in the Loudon/Laconia area. We didn't attend the race, but we exuberantly enjoyed the non-stop partying that took place during that wild, unruly weekend. Our bike spent the 1969-70 winter months standing stately in our apartment behind the living room couch, with a big poster of "Captain America" (from *Easy Rider*) on his chopper tacked to the wall behind it.

Sixties culture continued. Our barber friend Gary bought a new bright yellow Oldsmobile 442 (this in addition to his Triumph Bonneville motorcycle), which we friends referred to as "The Yellow Submarine," after The Beatles' song title. This car was a sporty, racy model. Several of us male friends piled into the Yellow Submarine accompanied by oodles of beer and marijuana joints. Gary drove us to the little rural town of New Vineyard, where a unique cable-suspended bridge with a wooden planked floor spanned the river a considerable distance below. Traffic crossing the bridge was rare. The psychedelic music of Jimi Hendrix, Janice Joplin, Blind Faith, The Doors, Traffic, The Beatles, Pink Floyd, Cream and others blasted on the car radio.

With the windows rolled up and the inside air blue with pot smoke, Gary gunned the 442 to about midway of the bridge, then slammed on his brakes bringing the rig to an abrupt halt. This drastic activity caused the bridge to slowly undulate up and down as the suspension cables stretched and rebounded. The influence of marijuana added fun distortion to the motion of the bridge. The merriment continued as we repeated this exploit over and over again, stoned and laughing with the psychedelic music blaring. Such memories are golden!

Despite my job, our friends and our satisfactory living conditions, Cheryl and I longed to return to New Hampshire. Many a weekend we three drove back and visited local friends, my folks in Chichester, Mary and Carroll Bailey (Cheryl's mother and stepfather) in Northwood and Charlie Noyes and Maxine (Cheryl's dad and stepmother) in Deerfield. We got along wonderfully with them all and spent the overnight at one place or another. I notified the NH State ASCS Executive Director of my interest in applying for any comparable position whenever an opening became available within the state. Eventually this contact brought about our desired move.

Two local NH Marines had been killed in Viet Nam. My high school classmate's brother, LCpl. Walt Murzin, was KIA by small arms fire in early October 1966 in Quang Nam Province. In April 1968, Cpl. Richard Brooks, son of a poor Pittsfield family was killed. Hushed rumors had it that Brooksie got fragged, but I don't know any details of what actually happened to him other than that he died of non-hostile action in Quang Tri Province. Other local kids were seriously wounded. Ed Tasker from Barnstead lost a lower leg to a booby trap while serving in the Army. Dave Robinson, a Pittsfield Marine, was shot three times in an NVA ambush. More on Davey later.

Two Marines from nearby towns ended their lives by suicide shortly after returning from the war. Wayne Campbell, who had married a family relative, went on a scary AWOL (Absent Without Leave) rampage following his tour of duty in Viet Nam. Wayne, Sarah and their baby daughter hid out with Cheryl and me in our Maine apartment for a few crazy, unforgettable days while MPs (military police) and civilian cops scoured Wayne's hometown area in NH. Wayne's unhinged stalking of his young family became more threatening, and a violent outcome seemed assured. Following a terrorizing family ordeal at a house where Sarah and her daughter were staying, Wayne became trapped by police and shot himself in early 1970 as a final escape.

Unable to cope with his Marine Recon experiences, Gordon James of Center Barnstead violently ended his life. Years later, after hours in a Pittsfield bar, I had a conversation with Gordon's older brother about this tragic loss. Gordon was another tragic casualty of the war.

Another friend from Barnstead, Donald Lines was AWOL from the Army after serving in Viet Nam. One night in Tennessee during the summer of 1967 he got into a fight at a teen club and shot a young man to death during the scuffle. Don was sentenced to 2nd degree murder and jailed in a maximum security prison in Nashville. In May 1971 he escaped and spent years on the run before returning to Barnstead. His story is long and involved. Early in 1997, he was arrested and sent back to Tennessee to finish his sentence, plus an additional 6 months for his escape. While he was in jail, I made several music cassettes and sent them to Don with letters. He wrote me letters back. I also wrote letters to Tennessee state officials in an attempt to get him released. Many Barnstead folks also attempted to gain Donald's freedom. He finished his jail time and returned to Barnstead in 2000. Don died at home of Agent Orange caused cancer in 2012.

In Gloria Emerson's book, *Winners and Losers*, is a letter written February 27, 1970 by a nineteen year old man from NY to his parents just prior to his tour of duty in Vietnam. Before leaving, he asked his parents to read the letter only if he was killed in the war. That May he was killed in Cambodia across the border from Vietnam. The letter, opened after his death, stated that he died in vain, and that the war was an immoral, unlawful atrocity. He asked that his parents inform Americans of the lack of sound judgment in Washington, DC's war-mongering policies.

In late June 1970 I was hired for a management position in Laconia, NH where the separate ASCS operations of Belknap and Carroll Counties were to be combined. Prior to this new combined county arrangement, individual audits had discovered serious problems in both county operations which had to be corrected. Addressing the many areas of dysfunction cited became a major undertaking. For the first month and a half at my new job, I had no office help, and the workload was hectic.

Overall, the job at the county level was ideal for me. My immediate bosses were two farmer-elected committees, and my position required office work and travel throughout both counties. Supervision and assistance was provided from supportive ASCS State Office personnel. The conservation programs I administered were dear to my heart and were carried out in coordination with technical consultants from sister-agencies. The farmers and forest owners I worked with were, for the most part, congenial and appreciative. Within bounds, I ran this little operation as I saw fit. Years later, these positive features turned negative.

Cheryl, Shawn and I moved from Maine into a downstairs

apartment on North Main Street, Laconia, that July. Over the past year Cheryl and I had become somewhat distant, and our marriage slowly drifted downhill. This was very unexpected, because prior to our separation caused by military service, especially the war, plus my months of out-of-state training, our relationship seemed harmonious and well-suited. We hadn't seriously discussed this situation, thinking that our return to NH would revive our once strong feelings toward one another.

Significant changes had taken place as to what was important in our lives and what we wanted for the future. Cheryl had become much more conservative, while I had grown quite liberal. Our differences gradually magnified. In thinking back, if Cheryl and I had waited until I returned from Vietnam to be married, it is very doubtful that we would have wed. I think we would have taken separate paths in life. As it turned out, our lifestyle paths veered drastically. It was at about this time when Uncle Don Jenkins and Aunt Hilda were divorcing.

Throughout the years following my active military service, America's war in Vietnam raged on with grossly mounting destruction, deaths and maiming on all sides. Antiwar sentiment vastly intensified across the US, Europe and elsewhere. It had become starkly evident to me long before that those of us who got sucked into the morass had been fed a shit sandwich by a succession of lying American elected, appointed, and military officials. Not only were they deceitful, they were also incredibly arrogant and culturally ignorant.

I strived to keep my cascading emotions, opinions and nightmares to myself in a deep state of denial, pretending that none of it really mattered. I stored my medals out of sight in a box, and some of my military clothing hung in a closet. Other stuff remained crammed in my locked seabag. I rarely even spoke of Vietnam or my experiences there. Despite attempts to move on, near constant physical pain in my shattered left foot and ankle, injury-affected upper extremity, ringing ears and headaches kept the war close to the surface. Hair-trigger temper flashes and angry arguments got the best of me at times, often under unexpected and ordinarily insignificant circumstances. I self-medicated far too much with alcohol and dope.

The phenomenal era of the Sixties counterculture movement continued nonstop, with social movements on several fronts. Women began vocalizing their need and desire for equality in the male-dominated society, leading to the Women's Liberation Movement. Native American activism ramped up in their quest for justice, forming the American Indian Movement. As previously mentioned, The Black Panther Party became active mainly in big cities, promoting social justice, racial equality, and antiwar endeavors. The Gay Liberation Movement became active in reducing the societal stigma associated with gender identification and sexual choice. The Environmental Movement brought to the forefront the essential necessity to protect, conserve and sustain our country's natural resources.

Another phenomenon was the Back-to-the-Land Movement. It involved a migration mostly of Sixties generation youth, sometimes from affluent families and generally from cities and suburban areas, to the rural countryside where they took up varied forms of homesteading. The goal was to live in a simplified manner, to have sustainable lives free of rampant materialism and away from the mainstream American lifestyle. Communes sometimes developed, and the pioneering spirit flourished well into the 1970s. I have a copy of *The Foxfire Book* from this period offering information on hog dressing, log cabin building, mountain crafts and foods, planting by the signs, snake lore, moonshining, and other stuff about plain living.

Another handy reference on homesteading was the *Whole Earth Catalogue*. Having grown up in the country with parental farming lineage, having worked on farms, and having studied natural resource conservation during my two years at UNH, I was already a back-to-the-lander at heart. No adjustments were needed for me to fit right into the emerging lifestyle.

My office for the newly combined county ASCS operation was located in the Forestry Building on Main Street, Laconia. The transition required long hours of work and considerable traveling between counties. Being happy to leave interior Maine and enthusiastic about my new position, I didn't mind the extra work. I advertised locally for a Program Assistant to help with the heavy workload. Among several applicants, I hired Mary Piper who began working for me on August 11th, her 19th birthday. Mary, her husband Carroll and their young son Corey D. Piper (born June 14, 1970) lived in Laconia. My ambition and connections to agriculture and forestry coupled with Mary's congenial personality and keen office abilities made our dual county operation excel.

Early in the spring of 1971, I had our Harley customized at a South Weymouth, Massachusetts chopper shop. The transformed bike was costly and beautiful, with a 12-inch extended front end, black enamel teardrop gas tank, custom seat with tall chrome sissy bar, fat rear tire, a bobbed rear fender, no front fender and additional chrome parts. The pipes were very loud. Like my first Harley, there was no electric start option. Harley's were famous for starting hard. When exhaustive kick-start attempts failed, I rolled it downhill and jump-started it.

All that summer I had wild and wonderful rides on that tiger of a machine. I craved the exhilarating rebellious sensation of speed and freedom while on that bike. Deep and silently within, I felt as if I could outrun the war that persistently gnawed at my body and soul. My hair was growing longer, and my sideburns nearly met at the chin. Among the fun trips Cheryl and I took on the bike were a ride across the Kancamagus Highway, stopping at Lake Chocorua for photos, and to a reunion with Don and Martha Rollman, friends from our USMC days who lived in West Lebanon, NH. During winter months the Harley was stored in our living room, as it had been in Maine.

1969 Harley XLCH Sportster customized 1971

Cheryl with 1969 Harley XLCH Labor Day Weekend 1971

My cousin Judy (Uncle Don and Aunt Hilda's daughter) was married to David Buzzell. They built a geodesic dome home on the Tan Road in South Pittsfield, which I often helped Dave with during construction. Dave was a fantastic acoustic and electric guitar player. We had many great times in the dome with his dwarf brother Jimmy from NYC and friends drinking, smoking pot and listening to rock music. David played lead guitar in a band that performed at a Portsmouth bar called the PRA Club. Portsmouth wasn't the glitzy city it has become, and the PRA was kind of a dive. Judy, Cheryl and I went there a few nights while Dave's band played. With certain songs, Judy joined the band adding great vocals. I recall a fun moonlight toboggan party that Cheryl and I went to at the dome. Stuck in the snow at the top of the steep toboggan run sat a bottle of Southern Comfort. Sliders took a swig from the bottle before venturing down over hill. The ride was fast and got faster. Partying continued inside the dome after each toboggan run.

In time, an unintended, unanticipated romantic relationship blossomed between Mary and me. As our initial infatuation flourished, it gradually grew into deeper and deeper intimate affection for one another. The strength of our shared attraction and passionate emotional connection continued with intensity. The guilt and confusion we felt, both being married and having young sons, weighed heavily. Spousal relationships at our respective homes grew increasingly complex, disjointed and difficult to mask, as our mutual feelings deepened into attachments of true love. Not knowing in which direction to turn, we continued our secret relationship while our deteriorating marriages grew increasingly incompatible. Neither of us knew where all this would lead, but our impassioned bonds toward one another carried forth.

Cheryl and I decided to buy a house and began checking out affordable possibilities with local realtors. I sold our Harley in the late fall of 1971 in order to have a down payment on a house. Cheryl became pregnant that November as our marriage continued to disintegrate. The big house at the North Main Street flower enterprise was sold, and the new owners no longer offered our apartment for rent. In the spring of 1972, we three moved to a second-rate apartment on South Main Street, thinking this would be a temporary stay until we could buy a house. Our second beautiful son, Travis Dylan Nichols, was born on August 2, 1972, at Concord Hospital. Maybe, I thought, this wonderful new addition to our family would level out our troubled relationship.

In mid-October that year Cheryl and I put a deposit on approximately 22 acres of land extending from Route 106 up the hill on the NE side of Loudon Ridge Road in Loudon. This parcel was part of a much larger farm that had been abandoned long ago. Although our names were both on the deed our hearts were fractured, and our love had faded beyond reclamation. Buying the land was for the most part an act of desperation. Nevertheless, we began cutting some pines and gray birch for access to the general area where a house might be built.

During my years in Maine, my political inclinations had solidified in support of the Democratic Party. I regretted that I had sat out the 1968 election, when my political energy was nil. Throughout President Nixon's first term my left-leaning viewpoints intensified. I felt strongly that "Tricky Dick" had to be stopped from winning a second term. My first ever vote was in the 1972 election. I voted for Democratic Senator George McGovern, a highly decorated WWII pilot and staunch antiwar candidate. He lost to Nixon in a landslide.

As the war in Vietnam wore on, Nixon ordered the invasion of Laos in 1971, causing massive death and destruction in that adjoining country. Bob Woodward, investigative reporter for *The Washington Post,* documents in his 2015 book *The Last of the President's Men* that in January 1972, Nixon confided to his ruthless National Security Adviser, Henry Kissinger, that all the years of US bombing in Southeast Asia had been a failure. That it achieved "zilch" in Nixon's own handwritten words. However, that February Nixon ordered more intensive and sustained escalation in the bombing. The murderous failure continued.

The infamous Watergate burglary began coming to light during the late summer of 1972, and the scandal continued to heighten. The protracted turmoil within government deepened at all levels as the plot thickened. Among his many immoral and criminal acts, Nixon ordered the 1972 Christmas carpet-bombing of Hanoi. For twelve days, beginning on December 18th, an armada of B-52 Stratofortress bombers killed more than 1600 civilians, some of which were children at an elementary school. Many other deaths took place on December 22nd when US bombs mistakenly hit the innocent Bac Mai hospital. They also bombed the port city of Haiphong during this operation (Operation Linebacker II). This intensive bombing episode reflected Nixon's "madman" tactic. He thought the North Vietnamese leaders would seek peace if they believed their main adversary was crazed. Nixon crowed, "Peace is at hand." But it wasn't!

President Nixon went whole hog that Christmas in other ways also! With a stroke of his pen while Congress was on Christmas break in 1972, Nixon terminated the Agricultural Conservation Program, by far the major program administered by ASCS in New England. With no new funding and no future program authorization, it threw our agency into disarray. Seasoned employees were let go or displaced in the upheaval, including Mary who took a position in the Strafford County ASCS Office in Rochester. It was later ruled that Nixon had abused his authority in ending the program. Congress eventually reinstated the 1973 program concurrently with 1974's.

In the early spring of 1973 divorce proceedings were underway between Cheryl and me on the grounds of

"Irreconcilable Differences," a justification for no-fault marriage dissolution. Cheryl was involved in a romantic relationship with Paul Fitzgerald of Laconia, who later became her husband. Mary and Carroll were also in the process of divorce. Mary and I spent time together whenever possible.

Being separated and in dire financial straits from all that had transpired, I moved to Epsom where Jean Stimmell lived with his girlfriend Suzy in his tiny old house trailer on a small plot of land. Jean, my best friend since high school, was very generous to let me move into his already tight quarters. My living space there, including my few possessions, was minute, but we managed quite well. I contributed food and beer and shared our utility costs. Mary sometimes visited me at the trailer. I traveled back and forth to work in Laconia in my Ford pickup truck.

We had a wild summer with frequent visits to Nip Moak's secluded Northwood "manor" where various friends often hung out. The Stone Church in Newmarket usually had good weekend music venues, including bands called *Lunch at the Dump* and *Last Chance Oasis*. Jean, Suzy and I often ventured to Newmarket for the music and also for the tasty family-style Sunday brunches featured at the Stone Church. We patronized various bars and joined raucous gatherings with friends in the area. Radios were constantly set to the WBCN-FM station out of Boston. This unorthodox station was like no other in many ways. It promoted social activism and uniquely covered the rock music scene, President Nixon's downfall, and broadcasts of wild humorous programs. One of our favorites was on Charles Laquidara's shift called *The Big Mattress* with the continuing adventures of "Duane Glasscock." WBCN also broadcast regular astronomical reports from "The Cosmic Muffin," Darrell Martinie. There's a great documentary film covering WBCN titled *WBCN and the American Revolution*.

I spent parts of each weekend, holidays and school vacations with Shawn and Travis, often at my Loudon property or at Mom and Dad's place in Chichester. The kids and I frequently got together with Mary and Corey, and the three boys got along splendidly. Three peas in a pod, each two years apart in age!

A couple times earlier in this memoir I have mentioned Davey Robinson. During the demise of my marriage, he and I had become close friends with common military connections. Davey had been badly wounded November 1st, 1967, while with the 3rd Marine Division in Vietnam's I Corps region and was disability-retired as a result. Davey had spent time recovering from gunshot wounds at the US Navy hospital in Yokosuka, Japan. He and I had mutual feelings about the worthless war we somehow survived.

Davey had married my cousin Judy Cate (Uncle Earle and Aunt Betty Cate's first offspring). Davey and Judy had two young daughters and were in the throes of divorce. Mary and I often visited Davey at his home in Pittsfield, NH, during this crazy period. Davey's place was popular with party-minded friends.

The spate of divorces continued with the separation of David and Judy Buzzell. Davey Robinson and my cousin Judy (Jenkins) Buzzell had renewed their high school romance while their respective divorces were in process. Mary and I continued our romantic relationship, though necessarily from a distance. We had lots of fun-filled adventures with Davey and Judy during this time period and long after those two eventually split up.

By this time, Uncle Don Jenkins and Aunt Hilda were divorced. Hilda had moved to Florida, and Don retained their home in Pittsfield. Uncle Don's companion, Phyllis, was also divorced, and they were later married. Phyllis had three children by her first marriage. Hilda remarried. She and husband Fred moved to Georgia, then later to South Carolina. After Fred's death in 2021, Aunt Hilda died at their SC home the morning of September 6, 2021. She and my mom were both 97-years-old when they died. Hilda passed 1-year and about 20 hours following Mom's passing (more about Mom in later pages). The death of Aunt Hilda marked the last of a generation on my side of our family.

With considerable traveling between Northwood, my office in Laconia and work throughout Belknap and Carroll Counties, I needed an economical car. Using my credit card to come up with the required down payment, I took out a loan and bought a new bright orange 1973 Volkswagen Super Beetle. At about that time, Mary bought a new yellow Volkswagen Beetle. In early summer 1973 she was placed in charge of the Strafford County ASCS Office. Mary drove to and from work in Rochester from her Gilford Avenue home in Laconia.

Cheryl and I became legally divorced on July 3, 1973, following 7½ years of marriage. We were independent that Independence Day, but the untethering had taken a heavy toll on us both and on our families. I retained the Loudon property and the payments that went with it, my old Ford pickup truck, our vinyl record collection, some family things, my military stuff, plus a few ragtag personal belongings. I also got nearly all the letters I had sent and those received from family and friends during my time in the Marines. I highly regard them to this day and marvel at the constant expressions of deep unwavering love and passion for one another that Cheryl and I had. All that went down the drain as we had both become different people. Cheryl got the rest of what we had, including the swanky Ford XL we had bought in Maine.

I moved from Jean's trailer to a first-floor apartment on Main Street, Laconia in the fall of 1973. This low-rent apartment was adequate but sparsely furnished. I had an air mattress for a couch and my two old hydroplane boat cushions for living room chairs. I had a dilapidated double bed and desk from years back when I lived with my parents, and cardboard boxes for bureaus. The apartment was directly across the Forestry Building's parking lot, so I walked to my office.

Mary and I regularly hung out with a wild crowd of couples

from Laconia. A few were from Mary's high school days, and one married couple (the husband, a Vietnam veteran) lived in the apartment next door to mine. There were many parties and lengthy visits at our favorite pub known as the "Sportsman's Den." Not far away was another local hang-out called "The Hidden Cove." Mary and I were together as often as possible, considering all that had been happening in our lives.

In spare time during that fall and winter I cut Gray Birch clumps, Poplar and weevil-damaged White Pine from the former field on my land. Over many years the area had grown up to scrub trees. I hooked a chain to the big, scattered junipers and pulled them out of the ground roots and all with my pickup truck. Dad helped me burn brush many times that winter, often long after darkness set in. To vent my rage, the burning brush piles became pretend representations of the repulsive Richard M. Nixon as they diminished to smoldering piles of ash.

The next spring, I had a plot tilled in the cleared field by a farmer up the road, and I planted several rows of potatoes. Bob, the Vietnam vet who lived in the apartment next to mine, planted potatoes in rows beside mine. I bought a Lange cast iron wood stove at a Concord boutique called Isis & Rasputin. The stove sat idle in the living room of my apartment in anticipation of building on my Loudon property.

Unable to make full payments on my land, I had two contiguous 5+ acre tracts surveyed for subdivision on the Rt. 106 end. Scattered bent and rusting on the first of the two lots were an old sap pan, numerous dilapidated sap buckets, and the remains of a brick arch. Only the tips of metal sap spiles showed from several old Sugar Maple trees in the area. Like the abandoned farm itself, the spiles had never been removed when maple season ended in the distant past. The trees' girth had nearly enveloped the spiles. This was so unusual that one day I took close-up photos of a few of these trees.

By December 1973 I had sold both lots to Grant Avery, who

was in the process of divorce. Grant built an impressive log cabin home on the property and married Diana, who had also become divorced. Grant and Diana were good neighbors. This left me with the adjoining 11.3-acre piece at the top of the hill. Though just raw land, the acreage I retained was by far the most desirable parcel. Many hikes had convinced me that my land had great potential.

In February 1974, Merrimack County was added to my Belknap and Carroll County ASCS operation with a separate office in Concord's Federal Building. Now, with a three-county responsibility, I had two offices, two assistants, three committees and a big area to cover. This combination was further fallout from the 1972 Nixon surprise. The added workload was extremely hectic and exhausting. It required lots more traveling, more meetings, and more agency personnel and landowners to deal with. Administering the various programs within the counties was nearly more than I could handle. I spent long hours of extra night work in my apartment.

That March I applied for a building permit and began clearing the big pines at the site of my future home. At the approximate site where our house stands, remnants of a small farm dump were visible, including the metal headboard of a bed. Such dumping areas were common on farms of bygone times. Shawn, Travis, Mary and Corey were often with me on the land during weekend visits. Uncle Don Jenkins brought his small dozer and helped me skid the logs to the landing in the field.

At Royal Page's mill in Loudon, I had our logs sawn into one-inch thick boards, 6544 Bd. Ft. The following month Jean, Suzy, Mary and I stuck the lumber at the end of a field up the Ridge Road operated by dairy farmer Emerson Moore. I hired Bob Hibbard, a nearby farmer to plow and harrow the remainder of my field that May.

Despite all President Nixon's skulduggery with his extensive cast of henchmen, his administration struggled on as the

Watergate hearings heated up. His detestable, corrupt Vice President Spiro Agnew had been forced to resign in October 1973. By August 1974, the Nixon scandal had more fully come to light, and it forced him to resign from office to avoid inevitable impeachment and jail. Vice President Gerald Ford took over as president and soon issued a pardon to Nixon. Ford said that the pardon was for the good of our country.

In the spring of 1975, a new director was hired in the Merrimack County ASCS Office, easing my routine back to Belknap and Carroll Counties out of the Laconia office. (I was flown to Washington, DC in March 1976 for a three-day awards ceremony in acknowledgement of handling the three-county operation.)

The reduced workload allowed time to prepare for my move from the city apartment to my land. In May 1975 I acquired a loan from the Northeast Federal Credit Union and had the cellar hole excavated by John Thompson. During early summer, a 32-by 36-foot concrete foundation was poured by my friend Denny Gray. I hired a carpenter to do the basic framing work, closing the place in. I capped off the top with rolls of double coverage asphalt roofing. Uncle Don dug the trench for the underground electrical line from the road through the field to my homesite. He also installed the septic system for my cellar bathroom, dug a shallow well, the water line and did backfilling and grading. I worked with Don on all these projects. Close friends provided very basic plumbing and electrical work at very low cost. I bought a second-hand toilet and used appliances needed to make my underground bunker livable. I insulated between each of the joists with thick fiberglass batting. Jean Stimmell helped me run Metalbestos chimney pipe through the roof, then I hooked up the Lange wood stove at a central location of the abode. I stacked cordwood that I had cut and cured inside and outside of the doorway.

Travis at Loudon Ridge cellar dwelling December 21, 1975

I moved out of Laconia for the last time in early fall of 1975 and into my secluded cellar hole residence. Houses on this end of the road were few and far between, and cars seldom passed by the end of my long driveway. Life was remote in the bunker, particularly that winter surrounded by deep snow and snuggled next to the wood stove. In ways, I lived like a hermit. With few windows, daylight was in short supply.

I had a dilapidated World War II-era Jeep (we named Jerry the Jeep) with a manually operated plow that I used to plow the snow from the long driveway. When the Jeep wouldn't start, which was often, I left my car at the end of the driveway and walked the 400-foot distance through the snow to my abode.

Mary's divorce had been finalized in early March of 1974. Though she retained her house in Laconia through divorce and thereafter, she and Corey spent an increasing amount of time on the Ridge. A strong brotherhood continued to grow between Shawn, Corey and Travis. The boys built snow forts, tree houses and had numerous outside adventures when together on the Ridge. They reluctantly helped us with our big vegetable gardens and stocking cordwood supplies. We five had many warmly memorable times in our crude underground dwelling, and we took hair-raising trips down the steep snowy sliding hill. Christmas, Thanksgiving and birthday celebrations took place from a unique below ground perspective.

Annual Easter hunts were held outside amongst the trees unless foul weather forced the tradition inside. Mary made the kids creative Halloween costumes each year and we drove them up and down the road trick-or-treating. The homemade costumes cost nearly nothing and were wonderful. Friends from local towns often stopped by, and there was considerable rowdy partying inside our bunker, known to them as "The Hole" and in the outside surroundings.

Mary inside Loudon Ridge cellar dwelling January 1, 1976

Our cellar dwelling was mostly an open area with only a couple rooms walled off: a crude bathroom and a root cellar. The three boys' beds were lined up side-by-side at an opposing wall from Mary's and my bed, with racks of clothing scattered about. In anticipation of building a house, I had pine lumber that had been milled from our trees piled on stickings to dry along one inside cellar wall. This, in addition to stacks of cordwood, basic household furnishings, the woodstove, kids' toys, my tools, etc. made the place quite crowded. The limited kitchen area where Mary prepared meals was extremely rudimentary. Cookware, dishes and other kitchen utensils were stacked at random.

Thinking back all these years later, the cellar years were definitely an unusual pioneering sort of living. The conditions were humbling and crude, but I wouldn't trade the experience over more standard living quarters. It is doubtful that due to today's more restrictive zoning laws a cellar hole residence would be allowed, though I didn't inquire prior to moving underground. We have a few photos from those times, but I wish we had taken more.

Mary and I were married beneath the pines near our homesite in a simple ceremony on September 18, 1976. Our marriage certificate lists the few who were present: Shawn, Corey, Travis, Jean, Judy (formerly Jenkins and Buzzell) and her son Aaron Buzzell. Loudon JP Mary Maxfield presided. Only two photos were taken, both soon after vows were said. One is a group photo of all in the wedding party, and the other is of Mary and me in our rope hammock strung between two pines near the "lion rock." We had a big yard sale in Laconia at Mary's house just before she sold it. She, Corey and I spent the winter underground in Loudon. Shawn and Travis were with us whenever possible.

In the spring of 1977, Neil English, a Vietnam veteran, began building the house which we had designed by Magnus

McLetchie. The summer months were unusually rainy, making living conditions less than ideal in our cellar dwelling. One day when Mom and Dad came to visit Mary and me, we decided to play a game of cards. As the four of us sat playing at our old maple table, a couple 9-inch thick, four-foot lengths of water-saturated fiberglass batts let loose from the floor joists above soaking us and the things around us. We laughed, though it wasn't really funny! The wet mess grew as more soaked fiberglass bats sagged and fell to the floor. Water seeped in all directions. Furniture and other belongings got badly damaged by continual moisture. By then it was time for us to vacate the cellar.

Mary, Corey and I (and Shawn and Travis too on weekends) slept out back in our big Mariposa tent in the pines behind the house. After the framing and roofing were completed, we moved back into the cellar.

Neil and a helper worked steadily on the house throughout the year. Loudon residents Bruce Yeaton, and his mason tender Joe Merrill, built our massive three-flue fieldstone chimney. As a condition for taking on the chimney project I had agreed to supply the rocks. I took vacation time off from work and collected angular, flat-faced rocks from wherever I could find them and spread them out under the pines near the house. I was glad to have my 3/4-ton Ford pickup truck during this time. Assembling the stones on the ground allowed Bruce to choose the ones that best fit into the artistic scheme of his towering structure.

At just above eye-level in our living room, on the left face of chimney is a sparkly stone fragment from the bottom of our dug well, and just below the stove thimble on the right is a big rock nabbed that summer from the summit of Mt. Washington. We had taken a trip up the auto road with our three boys in my VW bug. Wrestling the rock into the VW was quite a feat, and Mary sat astride it all the way home. Hoisting the rock out onto the ground at home created another challenge. Bruce and Joe were both very rugged and set the rock in place among so many others.

Plans called for a big fieldstone fireplace with a rocked-in wood storage area adjacent to it. We decided to eliminate the fireplace idea in the interest of a more efficient heat source. Instead, we installed a Vermont Castings Defiant parlor stove and used the recessed nook beside it for music components. We piped the wood stove into the center flue of our chimney and stood on a big slab of bluestone.

That year we also had a big Logwood hot air furnace piped into a separate flue with ductwork installed from the cellar. Registers placed throughout the house brought heat somewhat uniformly into each room. Our Lange stove was piped into the third flue facing the dining area.

We bought the11.5-acre wooded lot adjoining our south boundary in May 1977. I cleared the trees on an area of the lot which had been a field years ago, and we burned the brush. The remains of a sawdust pile created by a lumber mill was evident at a location now unrecognizable. One day when discussing our property with Uncle Bob Nichols I was surprised that he knew of the sawdust pile. He recalled working at the sawmill that had operated there in his younger days prior to joining the Marines. The additional land gave us desired protection from others building close by. It also provided us with more forest for logs, cordwood, garden space and recreation. Plus, the extra area increased our prospects for construction of a pond.

Neil worked steadily on our house well into the fall of 1978, when we were finally able to move upstairs from the cellar. We all welcomed our new living conditions after the extended underground experience. Neil returned in the spring of 1981 to do custom finish work.

Mary and I hosted an exuberant July 4th party at our place in 1979 and again in 1981. Many friends from Pittsfield and

Barnstead attended, as did our kids. Plenty of tasty food was prepared by Mary and party goers, and we consumed quantities of keg beer. We bought the kegs in advance of our parties. To keep them cold, we tied them with a long rope and rolled them into our pond in the deepest spot fed by springs. On party day we hauled on the ropes and loaded the kegs into our Ford tractor bucket. The bucket worked well because ice was added, and the bucket was raised to a perfect height for serving beer after the kegs were tapped. Our wheelbarrow was filled with block ice to keep bottled and canned drinks cold. We hired Trigger Cook's band to play during one of the holiday events. Band members became drunk during breaks on slices of vodka-laced watermelon. Toward the ending music set, they smashed their instruments and jumped from Jean's lowbed trailer where they performed into their drum set. It was at one of these parties when the top of our biggest nearby sugar maple tree got its top blown off by Danny Ladd's cannon fired from the tailgate of his pickup truck. This added to the rowdy celebrations along with a big array of firecrackers and rockets. Wild times!

Decades later the maple stands by the wall with its massive spreading reach above the main trunk with a vast array of entangled limbs. We call it "The fairy tale tree" due to its magical shape and "The mother tree". When tapped in springtime, the magnificent tree shares plenty of sap with us.

Over Labor Day weekend 1979 Mary and I joined several of our friends from Barnstead and Pittsfield at a fantastic 2-day outdoor music festival at the Waumbek Village in Jefferson, NH. Bob Ellis, Teresa Taylor, Mary I rode to Jefferson in the back of Mike Stone's new Ford pickup truck. The night of September 1 we listened to the Dave Bromberg Band, followed the next day by an afternoon concert by Taj Mahal and his band. Mary was barely pregnant with Jessie at the time. Corey stayed in Laconia with Mary's sister Cindy and her then-husband Steve. The ride home from the festival in the back of Stone's truck was very scary, as he drove like a crazy man. We stopped to piss near Lake Chocorua and demanded that Stone slow down on the rest of the drive back home. We made it home unscathed!

That fall we hired John Thompson with his D-6 dozer to dig a small pond in one end of our meadow, which collected water from springs and an intermittent brook. I had worked at the site off and on for weeks cutting the trees (mostly swamp maples), piling the cordwood, and burning the brush. We had purchased a used 2-wheel drive Ford tractor, which helped us tend the land, haul cordwood and plow snow. The troublesome Jerry the Jeep had been sold years before. To help with our homesteading, I bought a plow, harrow, and brush hog. I had a wood-hauling wagon and 3-point hitch counterweight built by a Belmont farmer.

Though Shawn and Travis were in Cheryl's custody and resided in Laconia, our family maintained close relationships and spent wonderful weekends, school breaks, holidays and family trips together. Cheryl was quite reasonable in sharing time spent with our two kids, though she took a much more conservative and regimented approach toward raising them than me. Mary and I did our best to treat all of our kids equally and with fairness. We shared the occasional hassles with ex-spouses common to most separated families, but we strived to keep our children free of our domestic entanglements.

Until our kids were fully grown and on their own, Mary and I never took a travel vacation without them. During the late Seventies, Mary, our three boys and I took a journey in my Ford truck. We borrowed our friend Stone's truck cap and clamped it onto our truck. Beneath the cap was the boys' hideout as we set off for Vermont, New York and Canada. Each night we all camped in our big Mariposa tent, except for the last night. By then, our tent had fallen apart so we stayed in a hotel. This was the tent that we camped in while our house was in the early construction stages, so it is no wonder that the Mariposa fell into disrepair.

The spring and summer of 1980 were very eventful. Our beautiful daughter Jessica Cate Nichols was born May 5, 1980, at Concord Hospital, making us a family of six. Mary and I were delighted to have a daughter in addition to our beloved sons. As it turned out over the years, our four kids are loving siblings to each other. Mary and I are most fortunate for this.

During an earlier selective timber harvest at our property, our biggest white pine was cut down. The butt log, gnarly with big knots from stump up several feet, was of no use to the loggers. I asked that they haul it with their skidder up near our house, which they did. On the first of June 1980, the Ladd boys brought their dual chainsaw-powered Alaskan Mill rig to our place. We set the machine up and ripped several wide 3-inch-thick planks down the length of the log. Neil English made one plank into our magnificent one-of-a-kind trestle table, which still sets in our home's dining area. Jean Stimmell helped me mount the remainder of the log atop two big boulders in a yard area close to our house. For decades the flat-topped log has functioned as a serving table at gatherings we've hosted. It has been referred to as "The table where dancing girls perform," though none ever has to my knowledge!

We bought a brand new 1980 light gray Oldsmobile Cutlass wagon (We named it "the Gray Ghost"). My precious orange 1973 VW Super Beetle was too small for our family of six, so we sold it. That month Mary and I joined friends at Temple Mountain Ski Area where we attended an outdoor music concert. NH folk singers Tom Rush and Bill Morrissey performed, followed by great blues music from Bonnie Raitt. Doc and Merle Watson also performed that day, just five years prior to Merle's death from a tractor accident.

In early August 1980 we hired John Thompson back to enlarge our pond. While he was here, he cleared the stonewall separating our two lots, removed stumps, and bog harrowed the cleared ground with the monstrous harrow which he pulled with his dozer. With this, our field was extended. He also roughed out some woods roads to provide better access to our property.

On September 6th, Mary and I took the Gray Ghost to the Lewiston Fairgrounds in Maine to attend a Grateful Dead concert. We met up there with several friends from Pittsfield and Barnstead.

When we got to the gate carrying huge quantities of beer in bottles, we were denied entrance with the beer. Beer was ok, just no drinks in glass bottles. The crew at the gate were making everyone with glass leave it behind. We had a big cooler with us, and there were no objections to us hauling in bulk beer. So that's what we did. We opened all our beer bottles and dumped the beer into the cooler. Two of us grabbed opposite handles on the cooler, and away we walked into the concert area with beer sloshing erratically. The weather was gorgeous, so beer became somewhat warm and stale as time went on. But we didn't mind.

The tantalizing fragrance of pot wafted through the air. A guy on horseback meandered amongst the massive crowd hawking "black beauties" and other drugs. The Dead played for several hours and were really on top of their music. One of the best concerts I ever witnessed. Roy Buchanan also performed, as did Levon Helm with members of The Band. News coverage of the concert estimated that there were 30,000 spectators at the event. Mom and Dad looked after Corey and Jess until we returned home at about 2:00 am.

That fall some friends and I built our three-sided woodshed, which provided a convenient dry place for cordwood storage and our farming implements. During springtime of the mid-Eighties, we bought brook and rainbow trout for our pond. They thrived quite well, but we lost most through the culvert and down the brook toward Rocky Pond during storms of heavy rain and with spring's snowmelt. We decided not to restock our pond.

In early October 1983 we drove to Washington, DC in the Gray Ghost with our three boys. Jessie stayed with Mom and Dad while we were gone. We visited various memorials, Smithsonian Museums, the White House, the US Capitol, the Washington Monument and Arlington Cemetery. I sat on the sod embankment in tears as Mary, Shawn, Corey and Travis walked through Constitution Gardens to view the Vietnam Veterans Memorial (the Wall). Facing the black granite wall engraved with the names of those service members killed in the war overwhelmed my emotions.

During the mid-1980s, Jessie was having stomach problems. Mary and I had her condition evaluated by her pediatrician with no acceptable diagnosis. At the doctor's direction, we tried various remedies, but none alleviated her symptoms. Flashbacks from my brother's ordeal with stomach cancer haunted. My worries intensified Mary's worries. We brought Jessie to the hospital at Dartmouth-Hitchcock in Lebanon, NH for a sonogram and further evaluation. It was determined that anxiety was causing her tummy troubles, which thankfully later went away.

On December 31, 1986, Mary and I held a fun New Year's Eve party attended by many of our close friends from nearby towns. Mary prepared lots of tasty food, and drinks flowed with enthusiastic gusto. Both men and women played unstructured pool games down cellar on our dilapidated old pool table from Mary's childhood home that her parents had given us. We used to claim that "Ridge Rules" meant no rules at all! The table wasn't exactly level, and the pockets which should have caught sunken pool balls were worn out, causing balls to bounce and roll astray on the concrete floor. The wayward balls were gathered and racked up for the next game. For several years we had raucous pool games at that table. Sometimes when there were only three players, we played a game called "Fuck Your Buddy," which required three players. We termed the game "Pop Your Pal" depending on who was present.

Mary, Jessie and I flew to Washington, DC in October 1990, where we took in most of the attractions from our earlier trip with the three boys. On this journey we three visited the Wall. We found the names of several men I knew who had been killed in Vietnam.

Below is a poem I wrote in honor of my Black brother Buckner Crump, Jr. killed in Thua Thien Province:

Two Buckners

Two Buckners graced our outfit —
One's first name,
Dizzy's soul mate.
One's last,
nicknamed "Lightning."

Young skin,
ebony and ash,
clad in jungle green.
Twins of fate,
brothers in arms . . .
two of many.

We partied hard on Okinawa,
whooped: "Eat the apple, fuck the Corps."
Bonds of lambs tightened.

Landed scared at Cua Viet,
asked: "What are we doing here?"
Bloom of youth faded
as the shit came down.

Lost track of one near the Zone,
many monsoons past.
I've visited the other,
his address doesn't change —
Panel 21E, Line 66.

*Buckner Crump's name engraved on the Wall,
with reflections of Paul, Mary and Jessie*

At some point during the 1980s decade, Mary and I got tired of heating our house entirely with cordwood. Our choices were to stoke or freeze! This became too confining, especially when we wanted to go away for an overnight, take a family vacation, or to attend a work conference together. Referenced earlier when describing our chimney, the furnace was hungry and consumed big chunks of wood. It could only be used in times of extremely cold weather when the draft could be opened occasionally to prevent creosote problems. Upstairs in the living room sat our Defiant wood stove. Its front doors could be opened to function like a fireplace or closed making it an efficient heater. In the dining area stood our Danish Lange wood stove, the one I had stored in my apartment while living in Laconia, and the one that had later provided heat while living in the cellar. Most of the time the Lange alone did a good job in keeping our house comfortable.

Feeding the rigs in spring, fall and winter consumed 5-6 cords of wood each year, which I cut, split with a heavy mall and steel wedges, hauled from our woods and piled. The wood harvesting operation greatly worsened pains from my war injuries, more so as I aged. When possible, I summoned our young boys to help with the wood gathering project.

Our solution to this heating dilemma was the installation of a propane furnace piggybacked to our wood furnace. This gave us the option to heat with wood or not. Or sometimes both. After heating primarily with wood for 39 years, we eventually switched to a pellet stove for a few years, then just propane in 2020. Our Defiant remains in place but is now seldom used. The Lange rests cold in the cellar, and we sold the wood furnace.

In writing this memoir there have been subjects that I've dreaded recounting more than others. The following few paragraphs present a struggle so deeply personal and difficult to adequately describe that I've skipped over it time and time again. However, the impact on me and our family has been powerful and long lasting. The subject I'm reluctantly delving into is PTSD, post-traumatic stress disorder and related "moral injury."

More recently, afflictions resulting from explosions during US wars in Afghanistan and Iraq, traumatic brain injury (TBI) have been recognized, and serious mental and physical conditions are disability compensable by the Veterans Administration.

Head injuries from football, soccer and other violent experiences are also known to be causes of TBI. There is a wealth of research documenting these conditions. PTSD, moral injury and TBI sometimes run together as consequences of wars.

Some PTSD symptoms can be passed down from parents, known as secondhand PTSD. Major stressors from a person's earlier years often worsen the impact of tragedies that happen later in life. My little brother Larry's agonizing, life-ending ordeal with cancer and the excruciating protracted mental pain that siege passed to us family members is an example. People who have been fortunate during their life not to experience dire personal tragedies may have trouble fathoming the damaging extent of this. But it has been proven factual. PTSD is not only a war-based problem, but is commonly prevalent in cases of domestic assault, transportation crashes, natural disaster survival and any number of other traumatic causes.

Each issue of the VVA (Vietnam Veterans of America) magazine includes a locater section. Many of the inquiries are profound. From the May/June 2021 issue I clipped a query from a woman who had been searching for her brother for 26 years, a Marine who served in Vietnam and suffered from severe PTSD. She stated that her father had looked for his son all his life following the war.

For me, it is impossible to pinpoint a specific year because there wasn't one. Sometime from the Seventies into the Eighties, the submerged psychological trauma from my Vietnam experiences surfaced, extending its long winding tentacles. Hair trigger anger bouts joined restlessness, startle response, heightened vigilance, nightmares, guilt, moral injury, the need to control, and other symptoms of PTSD such as a lack of trust. Pride and trust in our government's leaders during our fathers' admirable service in WWII, then being lied to and betrayed by the need to invade Vietnam magnified other complications.

Often after awakening from gut-wrenching nightmares, I

walked around outside in the darkness to convince myself that I was at home on the ridge and not far away in the war.

Nighttime was especially fraught with danger during the war. Identifying familiar features in the peaceful moonlight was reassuring. As denial faded, the PTS beast became unleashed, intruded, and began its foray into my serenity. The haunting intensity of it all stealthily crept up, hooked on, and wouldn't let go. I'm including one of my lengthy journal entries which accentuates the trauma I kept reliving:

Endless War

I'm soaked to the skin, cold, muddy, and pissed off. Just relieved myself of daybreak patrol. Spring is late this year—everything's behind schedule except the perpetual enemy— that unrelenting, illusive culprit I must hunt down and kill. The body count rises, yet they still they come. This fucking war drags on year after year.

A windswept rain plagues the morning ambush. Mist rises from the distant swamp as I descend from higher ground, consciously placing each foot to avoid snapping twigs and booby traps. Signs are clear; they were here again last night. They prefer to do their dirty work in darkness. Water runs down the barrel of my shotgun — a 12-gauge pump-action, loaded to the max with OO buckshot magnum loads… *much like the point-man carried. Can't get the ones full of nasty little darts, but these pellets kill good.*

I scan the narrow trail, look down, and stealthily advance. My head spins: *Are there trip wires leading to a mine shrouded by vegetation? Maybe a grenade lashed to a tree limb overhead, spoon ready to fly at the slightest nudge? Or is some motherfucker lurking in the brush, gleefully waiting to trigger the blast?* Erratic breath joins surging pulse. I squint through downpour, sniff the air, listen for anything. *Stop! This is bullshit, a different situation. What am I, fuckin' crazy? But I almost got killed before I almost got killed. Yeah, but that was then and there... I'm here and now. Aren't I?*

Reached the edge of the sprawling meadow. It has that musty odor of decay and stagnant water. Grass that will be head-high in two months now flops, tangled and brown as if sprayed with Agent Orange. I gaze across, check the tree line closely. Ominously visible off to the right, the dike beckons—*paddy dikes were often mined, I'll avoid the temptation of using it to cross the marsh. Good place to wait though, crouched and ready, thumb on the safety, wishing the streams of water would spare me at least an unblurred pathway down my glasses lens... the sighting one.* I hear a trickle through the dike. Birds' intimate calls. Frogs or bugs in the spongy bog, croaking—peeping. Dying trees creak—too deep in water, agitated by gusting winds. Last year's leaves lie quiet. My mind wanders, *was there a movement in the alders? Or is it just me, anxious for revenge, seeing things that don't exist. I'll move on—have a few more points to check.* There's no bamboo, but punji stakes pierce my brain. I glance back in case a spider trap was missed. There are none today, of course.

The patrol is over until next time. The enemy will live another day, attack another night. In a strange way I'm glad. I have no heart for hunting. I hate to kill and maim. I don't even like guns. It's amazing how relative things are — how situational fate can be — how something far away is really near.

The beaver will persist in flooding the lowlands, mucking our pond, burrowing its embankments, clogging the outlet, feeding on prized saplings, and drowning trees with misplaced backwater. Pacification is unrealistic. Forced relocation is ineffective. Diplomatic negotiations don't apply. Hamlets purged reappear. Search-and-destroy missions will continue long after any threat is gone. My firepower is mechanical and calculated. Theirs is instinctual, driven by a natural will to survive in the only environment they know. That haunting question stabs again, *hasn't this happened throughout time, in different places, ravaging other lives?* Its answer drips like blood.

Tethered fast, yet drifting into the quagmire, I sip coffee and dry off.

I don't recall the year or the triggering situation, but an incidence of my flashing anger, most likely under the influence of too much alcohol, happened late one night many years back. Enraged, I forcefully punched the ornate glass Tiffany light which hung above our dining area table, sending shards across the floor and leaving the fixture dangling. Another time, in a fit of temper I threw a cement block across our kitchen floor creating a permanent gouge in the new Armstrong flooring. I never became physically violent toward a family member, but occasionally my outbursts of anger were damaging to objects.

Pain in my left foot and ankle had been a constant to deal with ever since the explosion. Each day it subtly reminded me of where I'd been.

As I lay in bed, I dreaded stepping onto the floor, well aware of the unwanted physical response that was sure to follow. It was accepted in a strange way because there was no turning back the time to pre-Vietnam. But other feelings, those in my head, heart and guts were different. They went beyond nagging physical pain, and certainly beyond mere acceptance. They stuck and wouldn't be shrugged off; they couldn't be drunk nor drugged away; they sometimes persisted day and night; they intruded into all senses. In public, I seldom mentioned that I was a veteran.

As time went on, I found that I wasn't alone. Tens of thousands of Nam vets were experiencing this lonely steadily creeping PTSD monster. I wrote this dark poem about PTSD years ago not to complain, but to explain:

In the Clutches of the Beast

Prowling, seething
fangs and talons bared
The silent marauder lunges

Like a dull jackknife across knuckles

when that one trusted cog
fails
when that one solid keeper
abandons
when basic faith
vaporizes
The cloaked deception mangles

Like a dildo lashed to a pervert

intruding
emerging
unrelenting violation
Bend over — touch toes
Stand straight — evoke attention
Sit and relax for a spell
Attempt a daydream — try sleeping
The rape is perpetual

Vintage scars streak the surface
veiled as bygone pain
Raised, sunken, bridging holes
none is superficial

Parasitic demons lurk fathoms deep
Name them, the shaman says
Occupying forces, latent impostors
eluding nomenclature
Unleashed, the predator stirs

Creeping malignance
surging hunger
familiar quarry
The Beast pulsates to be nourished

Increasingly, I spent hours drinking with friends at Pittsfield's Country Pub, at the Foxglove (Bear Jenisch and Carol's pub), at friends' houses and at home. Various illegal drugs were readily available, and I ingested them with quantities of alcohol. My substance abuse intensified the post-traumatic stress I was unknowingly trying to fend off. Self-medication wasn't working. This irresponsible behavior was negatively affecting my job and my immediate family. Mary put up with my excesses for years, but eventually she became exasperated. Her caring attempts to moderate my extremes fell by the wayside. We both grew angrier, depressed and less connected as our marriage began to disintegrate.

By 1990 our future together was in free fall, and Mary was forced to plan for our separation. She urged me to get help through mental therapy as a last chance possibility of rescuing our troubled relationship and the family we both loved. In desperation, I paid a visit to my friend Peter Baldwin at his home in Gilmanton. Peter was a renowned doctor of hypnotherapy and was a professor of psychology at Antioch College in Keene. He led me to his "cupboard," the cozy little building separate from his house, where he met with deeply distressed clients. I have a couple tape recordings of our visits, which Peter felt could be valuable in his lectures at Antioch College. During one visit, Peter lined me up with Dr. Linda Zollo, a trusted female therapist who had extensive experience with PTSD patients in Palo Alto, California. Initially, I was hesitant to open up about my problems to a shrink, but as time went on, I became more willing to cooperate. My visits with Dr. Zollo continued from that June until late November 1991. By then I had a clearer understanding of the stressors I was struggling with, and family life had improved. Dr. Zollo helped me greatly, and I gained unlimited respect for her.

At 6:00 pm on Veterans Day, 1991 I turned on our television to get the local news. I was immediately stunned by the lead story about a Vietnam veteran from Gilmanton who had shot his wife and three others to death in Kentucky. That veteran was Robert Daigneau, who later that day killed himself. This was the Bob Daigneau who I had traveled to Parris Island with via train from Manchester, the guy I mentioned earlier in this memoir when describing our boot camp platoon. The news of the killings blasted me back to the war that Bob and I both had wounds from, in body and mind. I fumbled through my platoon yearbook, and Bob's stern photo stared from a sea of stern photos, including mine. Bob and I had reminisced in Laconia over coffee many years after the war. He suffered nonstop from the serious physical wounds and raging PTSD. He had been involved in minor scrapes with the local cops and had been recently admitted at the Togus VA Hospital in Augusta, Maine, for treatment of his physical and psychological problems. I was deeply affected by his rampage in Kentucky, and I wrote an emotional essay soon after the incident which was published in local newspapers. I also wrote a poem reflecting on the horror of it all titled "6:00 PM Veterans Day 1991, Five Casualties of War."

I knew Bob's parents through my USDA work with farmers in the Gilmanton area. The Daigneau farm was located on Smith

Meetinghouse Road off from Frisky Hill. Bob's mother made the best tasting elderberry wine, and she shared a glass or two with me when I stopped by the farm. I recall talking with Arthur (Bob's father) who was seriously ailing with kidney disease. He was a veteran of WW II and was known for his hard work in running the farm. One time, when telling me stories of his early healthier days, he prefaced the conversation with this humorous lament, "Back when my cock stayed as hard as a hemlock knot...." Over the years I've snickered at Arthur's plain-spoken introductory regret about his energetic past. Memories of his Marine son Bob have stayed with me.

As part of a nationwide effort to downsize specific federal agencies, a limited "buy-out" quota was authorized for qualifying employees. Fulfillment in my job had greatly diminished as key USDA conservation programs were negatively altered and automation was taking hold through lousy computer systems. Also, strong political influences increased making my job far less appealing. I had an "Abolish Dogshit" stamp made and affixed the expression in bold red ink on certain reports to supervisors. It was time for me to move on.

After much deliberation and consultations with Mary, I volunteered for early retirement. I was the sole volunteer in the state at my pay grade, and my application was accepted. My last day working for ASCS was November 3, 1994.

Our decision required a reduced retirement annuity, 2% for each year under age 55. I was thrilled for the opportunity to be free of my job after 26 years. However, I was at loose ends having no idea what the future might hold, and the unknowns added tension to my deeper stressors.

My best friend Jean Stimmell began studying for his master's degree in psychology at Antioch NE Graduate School in the January 1994 term. Later, as part of his internship requirement, he worked at the Manchester Vet Center, an arm of the Veterans Administration charged with readjustment counseling services for veterans.

Jean recognized my continuing battle with war stress and suggested that I make an appointment at the Vet Center. Trusting Jean's judgement, I began weekly one-on-one counseling sessions in November 1994 with Vet Center therapist John Brock, a Vietnam War combat veteran. He and I delved into my war experiences and the relationship troubles I was having, including issues of control. John noted the cultural concern prevalent in our society regarding control, particularly among men, and that he found it especially problematic with most of the vets he counseled. He suggested that part of veterans' urges to control was because everything about the Vietnam War was so damned out of control. Resulting from this grew the strong impetuous to control life events.

Occasionally I met with the Center's Team Leader, Caryl Ahern, a thoughtful and competent therapist who further helped me sort things out. After finishing his degree at Antioch, Jean went on to become Team Leader at the Vet Center in Sanford, Maine.

In 1988, my Vietnam vet brother John Jones (Jonesy) had returned to the Central Highlands of Vietnam where he had served as a medic in a Green Beret A-Team early during the war. He was an active member of our Veterans for Peace chapter, and I got to know and respect him greatly. He encouraged me to consider revisiting Vietnam, to see the country's beauty, to sense its peacefulness, and to most likely soothe my troubled soul. At a veterans' meeting I attended, Jonesy showed slides of his return and spoke poetically about the experience. The trip had helped him a lot in dealing with his severe PTS, he said.

President Bill Clinton, a 1960s antiwar protester and draft evader, lifted the US trade embargo against Vietnam in February 1994. This act made travel from the USA less complicated than when Jonesy returned in 1988. The following year, Clinton established full diplomatic relations with Vietnam. By then, many

American vets were returning to the country.

During January 1995, with Mary's total support, I began planning for a solo journey back to Vietnam. Saying I was apprehensive would be an understatement. In fact, I was very scared despite Jonesy's inspiration. Too much of me had never left Vietnam, and nightmares often tormented. The thought of returning made my guts churn, yet I felt that I needed to go. Getting my visa, passport, flight arrangements, shots at the travel clinic, and arranging for someone to meet me at Tan Son Nhut Airport in Ho Chi Minh City (formally Saigon), was time consuming. I bought a couple Vietnam travel books to help put my trip together.

On March 10th, 1995, I flew out of Logan Airport and landed at Los Angeles International Airport, where it was raining hard. LAX was a monstrous airport swarming with people of all races and languages heading in all directions of the globe. I had no suitcase, only a backpack, two cameras and canvas shoulder bag. It was very confusing to get to my gate at the China Airlines terminal, but I made it in time to catch the flight to Taipei, Taiwan.

While in Taipei, sitting in the modern terminal awaiting my next flight, a big color TV screen warned women about the dangers of breast cancer. Attractive women were demonstrating self-diagnosis of tumors by feeling their bare breasts. I had never seen anything as explicit on US TVs. Men, women and kids sitting in the terminal watched attentively, but no one swooned or joked at seeing bare breasts. This was a lesson to me about Asian cultural differences. It was as though such public presentations were to be expected.

After a short wait time in Taipei, I flew to Ho Chi Minh City where my emotional sojourn through much of Vietnam commenced. Visible as we landed were tufts of grass growing up through cracks in the runway. The plane came to a stop quite a distance from the terminal, so passengers boarded extremely hot and crowded shuttles which took us to the terminal. There, I scanned the sea of excited Vietnamese people of all ages who were waiting to greet family members and associates from the plane. I looked for a man named Mr. Vu, who would help me through customs and take me to a hotel in the city. I had no idea of how to identify Mr. Vu nor did he know the appearance of who he was picking up. I was sure glad when amongst the crowd I saw Mr. Vu holding a cardboard sign with my name boldly hand-printed on it. I don't know what I would have done if he hadn't showed up!

Mr. Vu was also assisting another American Vietnam veteran, Taylor Hallman from NY City. Mr. Vu brought me to the Vien Dong Hotel, where rooms were priced from $12 to $50 per night. There were several French people and travelers from other countries at the hotel, and the only available rooms were the shabby 6th floor ones at the $12 rate.

In the lobby I met Taylor. He, Mr. Vu and I had lunch and Tiger beers in the hotel's restaurant. Taylor's war service had been mostly in the more southern district areas, so that's where he was interested in returning to. My interests were north toward the former DMZ. That first night I got little sleep because I was wakened by rats running close to my head, across my backpack and all around the room. My journal notes depict a vivid portrayal of that night's experience and a graphic description of the $12 room. For the second night I was able to get much nicer $32 room on the 5th floor, free of rats!

After spending a couple days in Ho Chi Minh City, I flew on Vietnam Airlines to Danang. There I connected with my Vietnamese guide, Mr. Tra, who I met at the Pacific Hotel where I was staying. Mr. Vu had lined up this connection for me.

For several days I traveled with Mr. Tra and Mr. Long (the driver) to old battle sites in provinces of the former I Corps region. An enduring friendship grew with Mr. Tra as a result of this chance encounter.

While we were traveling the countryside, we also stopped at various city locations. I was able to send and receive occasional fax messages with family members and the Manchester Vet Center through my hotel lobby. Jessie, at age 15, lived at home so she included little messages along with Mary's faxes. That was our only available mode of communication during my period in Vietnam, and it was wonderful to have the option. As I got dressed each morning and went to put on my socks, I discovered a loving hand-written note from Mary folded into each pair. All these handwritten connections were invaluable to me, and my fax messages also comforted folks back home.

I'll spare readers of this memoir most details of my two-week journey. I took lots of hand-scribbled notes in a journal and scads of photographs and 35mm slides as I traveled. After returning home I wrote an account of my trip with photos, which was published as a major feature in the April 30, 1995, Sunday edition of the *Concord Monitor* and a photo essay in the June 1995 edition of the *New Hampshire Premier* magazine. April 30 was a significant date to the Vietnamese because it marked the 20th anniversary of the war's end. I recall asking about the many brisk Vietnamese national flags prominently visible all along the roads as we traveled. The flags were in recognition of the country's reunification, similar to the 4th of July celebrations in the USA. The former DMZ was no more.

In Danang, I had a conversation with Le Duc Nhan outside his tailor shop. Through broken English, I told him that I had been wounded during the war, and he answered my questions about how to travel to Gia Le. Mr. Tra, our driver, and I traveled north to Phu Bai, crossed the railroad tracks west of Highway 1 and drove through Gia Le Thoung village. Along the narrow road leading into the countryside, we stopped several times where Mr. Tra spoke to local people for specific directions toward where I was wounded. The locals were kind and helpful, though land features had changed over the many years. I was unable to locate the exact spot where the land mine had exploded, but my bodily quivers and streams of tears related that I was close enough. Ghosts from the past haunted.

On the day my column appeared in the *Sunday Monitor*, I received phone calls from two local men who had served in the Phu Bai area during the war. They were appreciative to learn of my return. A third call I got that day was from a guy from Boscawen who had spent years in the Marines and later joined the Seabees. He had worked operating a rock crusher in 1967 during his Vietnam tour and was familiar with places I had been in the Gia Le area. He noted that mines were a huge problem there, as were rocket and artillery attacks. Many had been killed during his time in Gia Le. He mentioned that his outfit had welded a long steel roller extension onto the front of a bulldozer to help find land mines in the roads. He also mentioned booby traps found having grenades inside C-ration cans with pins pulled ready to explode when slightly moved. Much of this was very familiar to me from years gone by.

I wrote a poem titled "Toward Convergence" chronicling the voyage. Copies of all these are in my files, though nothing could adequately describe the power of the experience, the reconciliation, the validation and the inner peace I gained. The journey was good for my head. But throughout my travels, I felt sad and guilty seeing my huge country's destruction still so evident throughout this tiny country's borders. That and tragic stories I was told while visiting. All of this stays with me.

Backing up a bit, the following experience has never been included in any of my writings: In late 1966, the combat engineers and grunts (infantrymen) I was with entered the smoldering remains of a hamlet on the outskirts of Cam Lo suspected of being occupied by a cadre of Viet Cong. An American gunship had attacked the hamlet prior to our arrival, setting it ablaze and causing serious casualties among the inhabitants. Our corpsman did what he could for some of the living victims. What was left of the thatched hooches appeared like those typical of the poor peasant farming villages throughout the vicinity. After cautiously searching the area, surviving dogs, pigs, ducks and chickens were killed, villagers' provisions were destroyed, and still-standing dwellings were set aflame. A grenade was lobbed into at least one suspicious-looking hooch. No one walked out. The ARVNs among us hauled off survivors to some location deemed pacified. This was one of many infamous search and destroy missions conducted by US troops during the long nasty war. It was in these ruins where I picked up a homemade bamboo-handled sickle that I hoped to send home — the implement that I never saw again after getting wounded.

Nightmare: *Nights leading up to my 1995 trip to Vietnam I had several recurring nightmares. In one such dream I had returned to the Cam Lo area and searched to find the site of the destroyed hamlet. I came across what I felt was the location. Vivid in my dreams was a hamlet of perfectly intact hooches, with lush little gardens nearby amongst banana trees and bamboo thickets. The scene was sunny and peaceful. Quiet except for the sounds of birds. No animals. Moving closer, I saw villagers. Women and children only. They stood staring at me in terrified shock. Seeing an American! I wanted to stand among them or sit beside them and talk. I wanted to express genuine regret for my part in the horrible war against their people. I wanted to apologize for what my country did to their people and to their country. I wanted to tell them that the war's sad legacy also continues to cause pain and loss in America. As I stepped toward a small group of villagers they dissipated right before my eyes. I turned and moved slowly forward. But in whichever direction I stepped, the person ahead would vaporize. One after another they vanished into nothingness. I stood alone, weeping in the silent empty hamlet.*

Each time the dream haunted, my reaction was just as bleakly realistic. I awoke drenched in sweat, convinced that I wasn't deserving of these peoples' presence. Not worthy of finding solace or reconciliation in their sacred land. Denied the chance to even make peace with myself. This was an aspect of moral injury, among others.

Mercifully, my 1995 journey to Vietnam didn't resemble my dream. I met and interacted with so many wonderful people over the two-week period. I experienced a country at peace, its peasant majority was poor but seemingly content.

Paul with Vietnamese family in Cam Lo vicinity March 17, 1995

I continue to communicate with Mr. Tra, who as a child had grown up in a village southwest of Danang that was sympathetic to the Viet Cong. The village was attacked by US troops in 1968, and a massacre ensued. Another of many smaller My Lai tragedies. The experience was gruesome and difficult to hear recounted. I also with kept in contact Pham Duc Phong, an artist in Hanoi who had fought as an NVA soldier during the war.

On my drive to work on May 12, 1994, the radio announced the death of Lewis B. Puller, Jr. He was the son of famous Marine Corps General "Chesty" Puller, the most highly decorated veteran in USMC history for his valor during WW II and the Korean War.

In 1968, recently married, expecting a child, and serving as a Marine in the I Corps region of Vietnam, Puller, Jr. tripped a booby-trapped howitzer round while hurrying along a narrow trail. The horrendous blast caused hideous wounds to his body, loss of both legs, loss of massive portions of both buttocks, a split scrotum, loss of his right thumb and little finger and loss of his left hand except for his thumb and half of his forefinger. Obviously, blood loss was tremendous. He suffered charred flesh from the explosion and a ruptured eardrum. His upper body was peppered by shell fragments. Puller was medevacked to a triage center in Danang, then on to Yokosuka, Japan and from there to Andrews Air Force Base in Maryland. Somehow Puller managed to survive.

During the 1980s and into the early 1990s Puller battled rage, depression, addiction to pain killers and alcoholism. He and his wife separated in 1991. That same year his Pulitzer Prize winning autobiography, *Fortunate Son* was published. The book's title was taken from Creedence Clearwater Revival's song by the same title. On May 11, 1994, Puller ended his life by suicide.

Before his death, Lewis became very involved in The Vietnam

Children's Fund, an ambitious project to fund and construct a series of elementary schools throughout Vietnam in the spirit of peace and reconciliation. During my return to Dong Ha in March of 1995, Mr. Tra, brought me to the site where the first school was under construction. I have photos taken that day. The school, known as the Lewis B. Puller, Jr. Elementary School was dedicated in April that year, marking the 20th anniversary of the end of the war.

I didn't know Lewis Puller personally, but I met him a couple times when he was in NH campaigning for Democratic Nebraska Senator Bob Kerrey's 1992 presidential run (Kerrey lost the primary to Bill Clinton). Kerrey had been a Navy SEAL squad leader during the Vietnam War, where he was seriously wounded in body and soul. In 1970, and with the loss of a lower leg, he became a reluctant Congressional Medal of Honor recipient.

The reason I'm relating these particular war experiences in Lewis Puller's life is because they exemplify what nearly became Tello's and my fate that day in Gia Le. Earlier in this memoir I described hiking along a remote narrow trail in an area infested with booby traps and land mines. Still, my mind remains haunted by the serendipity of not being physically blown away by that howitzer round lashed to a tripwire strung across the trail.

For my 50th birthday on June 15, 1995, Mary gave me tickets for Grateful Dead and Bob Dylan concerts at the Franklin County Airport in Highgate, Vermont. Driving north toward Highgate, a steady train of cars full of folks headed for the music extravaganza accompanied us. Cars were adorned with artful psychedelic Grateful Dead creations as we passed one another, and joyous fans waved out the windows. We had a homemade poster taped to the back window of our Toyota which read "Deadgate Vermont — June '95" accented with a crudely sketched flower and peace sign.

Newspaper clipping and concert ticket stub

Pandemonium ensued before the bands took to the stage, and it was wild amongst the 90,000 of us that were there. At some point the immense mass of concertgoers got out of hand and stormed the snow fence barrier meant to enclose only those having tickets. Bob Dylan and his red-hot band opened the event with a fantastic performance. The Dead's music wasn't quite as mesmerizing as the 1980 concert we had attended, due to the debilitating effects of Jerry Garcia's serious drug addiction. But both performances were thrilling gifts not to be missed. Mary and I slept in our small tent next to our car on the concert grounds in the company of thousands of other "Deadheads."

We were shocked and saddened to learn of Jerry Garcia's death at age 53 on August 9th, nearly two months after we had seen him in concert at Highgate. He died of a heart attack while in a California rehabilitation clinic. The Grateful Dead was an icon of the 1960s. With Jerry and his guitar gone the band could never be resurrected, though members went on producing music.

I worked a few days a week for Uncle Don, but I knew that could only be temporary due to increased pain from the physical demands of construction jobs. I floundered throughout that summer, checking out other part time employment opportunities. Discouraged at the prospects, I entered studies under a VA program at the College for Lifelong Learning (later named Granite State College) based in Bow. Beginning with the 1995 fall semester, I enrolled in a wide-ranging self-design course of study centering on writing and sociocultural issues. The course structure and timing led me to classes at UNH, Portsmouth and Manchester in addition to Bow.

During a two-week period in June 1996, I attended an excellent writers' workshop, which was run annually by The William Joiner Center, University of MA in Boston. Many skilled writers, including Vietnam Veteran friends Gary Rafferty and Pauline Hebert also attended along with around 100 others. The workshops featured classes in poetry, fiction and non-fiction and were taught by acclaimed writers from across the country.

In conjunction with my college degree, I took two excellent self-design contract courses guided by my brilliant mentor, Denis Kenny, an Australian living in Vermont. These courses were titled *East/West Thought Convergence* and *War, Morality and Reconciliation*. The latter, a 9-credit course, met my degree's "integrative experience" requirement.

A major component of the integrative course was a return to Vietnam with a humanitarian organization called "PeaceTrees Vietnam" based in the state of Washington. The group's main objective was the removal of land mines and other unexploded ordnance left over from the US war in Quang Tri Province. These latent munitions are still causing casualties to Vietnamese kids, farmers and others throughout the country.

Designated portions of land were cleared of explosives, and in their place indigenous species of trees were planted. A land mine awareness center was another focus of the PeaceTrees mission. A third purpose was a continuation of improved relations with the Vietnamese people and their leaders. All this helped us Americans deal with our past also.

Following my 1995 trip to Vietnam I knew I would return someday, and this benevolent effort appealed to me. Travel arrangements were coordinated with the West Coast PeaceTrees folks.

Unexploded ordnance near Con Thien firebase March 1995

Prosthetics Outreach Foundation at Hanoi clinic March 1998

I flew out of Boston on February 27, 1998, 31 years from the date I had been wounded, bound for JFK International Airport. From NY, I flew to Vancouver, BC, where I connected with the PeaceTrees group of eight coming from Seattle. We had a short time to get acquainted before boarding a Cathay Pacific plane to Hong Kong. Our group spent several hours touring this busy city before flying on to Hanoi.

This trip with an organization was different from my 1995 solo journey. It involved a fairly tight schedule of planned events, with free time in between. However, like in 1995, powerful emotional experiences were certain to take a toll. To and from connections through faxes with family members and the Vet Center were comforting.

On March 2nd I contacted Phong, the esteemed Vietnamese artist I first met in 1995. We had a wonderful reunion at his

Hanoi home, with friendly conversations somewhat broken by language barriers. We had fun sharing simple lessons relative to our respective languages.

After attending several PeaceTrees events in and around Hanoi, I flew to Danang on March 6. There I met Mr. Tra, my guide from 1995. He brought me to several historic and cultural sites in Danang and Hoi An. We had friendly conversations as the hours moved on.

During my travels with Mr. Tra, we hiked to one of the five Marble Mountains in the Danang area. Hanging on our living room wall is a framed color photo that I took from the mountaintop. The photo depicts a beautiful agrarian scene with intensive cropping patterns, farmers tending their crops and bomb craters from the past, now serving as irrigation ponds. Each time I look at the photo I'm reminded of the serenity of the country where war caused untold death and destruction. For a time, peace and beauty replaces my mind's images of the ruination I witnessed so long ago.

The next day Mr. Tra drove me to various locations in Quang Nam Province, including the sacred My Son Holy Land and his remote childhood village.

While there, I met survivors of the 1968 attack and villagers too young for such tragic memories. An elderly woman, whose parents were killed by our soldiers, totally lost control. She screamed with grief and anger when she saw me, the only American she had seen since the war. Mr. Tra helped her up from the corn stubbled ground, where she had thrown herself in uncontrollable dismay. He led her to a quiet shaded spot where he calmed her emotions by assuring her that I was now a friend, not a foe. In time, they returned to where I stood in traumatized shock, wiping away tears and hoping my heart would remain in my chest, not knowing what would happen next.

Serene view from atop one of five Marble Mountains outside of Danang during Nichols' 1998 revisit

Vietnamese elder and Paul with conical hat gift March 1998

The day was sunny and extremely hot. To my amazement, the old woman took the conical bamboo hat from her head and gave it to me for protection from the blazing sun.

Young villagers giggled at the sight of me with long hair and full beard wearing their traditional hat. Words cannot adequately recount this powerful encounter, but I have photos and memories that will forever remain with me. And I still have that precious conical hat.

It was in this vicinity that we visited a memorial to Nguyen Van Troi, a national Viet Cong hero who was publicly executed in Saigon by South Vietnamese forces in 1964. Van Troi attempted to assassinate US Secretary of Defense Robert McNamara during his visit to Saigon that year. Mr. Tra and I both burned incense sticks as offerings to his sacrifice.

That evening, Mr. Tra drove me on his motorbike from my hotel to his home in Danang City. There I met his family and enjoyed vodka drinks and a wonderful traditional Vietnamese dinner prepared by his wife, Mrs. Hue. I was honored to be so warmly welcomed.

I had to rejoin the PeaceTrees group on March 8th for several days of ceremonies and meetings in Dong Ha. Mr. Tra lined me up with a Vietnamese driver who took me north on Highway 1 to Hue, through Quang Tri and on to Dong Ha. In Quang Tri town, the driver stopped so I could photograph the war-torn remains of a Buddhist high school left standing as graphic evidence of the terrible war years.

Back in Hanoi on March 12th, I packed for the long flights home, which were the reverse order of those from Boston to Hanoi. At that point, PeaceTrees members were separating and traveling in different directions, including My Lai village, for a longer stay in Vietnam. I reached Loudon Ridge fatigued and grateful on March 14, 1998. Along the way I had written copious journal notes, taken photos and collected printed information. From these sources and my vivid recollections, I wrote an essay as a component of my college course with Denis Kenny. Years later, I had many 35mm slides copied onto compact disks and established a computer album from this trip's images in addition to those from my 1995 return.

War damaged Buddhist high school in Quang Tri March 1998

Another aspect of the course evaluation was the development of an art exhibit and oral presentations, taking into account my war background and subsequent returns to Vietnam. I put together an extensive 35mm slide exhibition covering my Vietnam adventures from 1995 and 1998. By the time my course with Denis closed that June, I had spoken at several high schools and colleges covering the war and my journeys back. These occasions were in the company of other local veterans. None of us sought such events, they seemed to find us. I earned my BS degree (Summa Cum Laude) in June 1998 but decided not to attend graduation.

After my 1998 return to Vietnam, a Vietnam combat veteran friend, Dick, who worked for the US Forest Service, visited me a few times inquiring about my two journeys back. He wondered about the toll emotions took as I traveled, the reception I received from the Vietnamese people, the arrangements I made beforehand and during my trips, specific locations I visited while there, and who was my guide to various locations. These were the very concerns that I had when I was making my plans to return, and I was happy to discuss them with him.

As time went on, Dick came to the realization that he needed to travel back to Vietnam. I helped him contact my Vietnamese friend Mr. Tra about hiring a guide. Dick returned to Vietnam and traveled with Mr. Tra to locations in the Central Highlands area where he had served long ago during the war. This revisit was a very positive experience, and it helped Dick deal with past trauma.

Back in the US, Dick and I reminisced about our respective travels and our friendly associations with Mr. Tra. We were amused by the cultural Vietnamese reference to Dick as Mr. Dick. I am glad to have helped Dick in finding his way back.

My earliest invitation to speak publicly was with UNH students at a Vietnam History course in October, 1987. Jean Stimmell, John Jones, and Randy Zoll addressed that class also. Next, in 1988, I spoke with a Quaker high school class at The Meeting School in Rindge, NH. As time went on through the 1990s and well into the 2000s, they often asked several of us Vietnam veterans to address high school and college classes. We most always made sure not to attempt presentations alone due to the exhausting emotional heaviness of the subject matter. Usually several of us joined together. We spoke with classes covering Vietnam War history, literature, political science, and US foreign policy. Also, with classes studying the turbulent 1960s. Poetry readings, photography and personal memorabilia pertinent to the course of study were brought to the class. Students generally sat spellbound during these sessions. They were mostly very respectful, attentive, and asked appropriate questions. Correspondence from many students following the classes was impressive and gratifying.

One of my most emotionally draining talks was at the Merrimack Valley High School. It was especially difficult standing before a class and seeing daughter Jessica and her best friends, Suzie, and Sondra, looking back at me.

Following my 1995 trip to Vietnam I developed a display of captioned photo enlargements. Vet Centers in Manchester and Sanford, Maine, had begun holding veterans' art exhibitions in conjunction with Memorial Day and Veterans Day. Jean Stimmell organized these Vet Center events. Art creations of many forms were featured, including sculpture, pottery, paintings, photography, and poetry. Poetry readings were a common attraction on opening day. I participated in some of these events, the last of which was in 2001.

Nearly every year from 1994 through 2001, several of us vets were invited to address a Vietnam history class at Boston College. Usually there were 8 to 12 vets who joined the discussion in the big amphitheater classroom.

Though there were differences among some of us regarding certain aspects of the war, we all expressed our distain for the lies and senselessness of that tragic fiasco. It was agreed that we were fed a shit sandwich by our government, and we expressed those opinions to each class.

During October 2001, following veterans' presentations, the BC professor invited Mary, Kathy Carney (Martin's wife) and their daughter Katie to address her class. The professor understood the value of her students learning about wives' and a daughter's perspectives on what living with a Vietnam veteran was like. Mary obliged and rode to Boston with Kathy and Katie. Mary has often spoken of that deeply emotional afternoon experience.

Beginning in 1995, on scheduled appointments through

1999, I had sessions with psychiatrist Dr. Perla Kissmeyer on the 6th floor of the Manchester VA Hospital (jokingly termed "The Flight Deck" by us vets). Over the years I spent as her client, she evaluated my PTSD and prescribed a series of drugs to treat depression, anxiety and insomnia. Dr. Kissmeyer was a Filipino American woman who had experienced unthinkable horrors when the Japanese invaded and occupied the Philippine Islands early during World War II. For some reason, Dr. Kissmeyer felt comfortable telling me many traumatic stories of life as an adolescent in Manila under Japanese occupation. Her dad was a medical doctor, in high demand from Japanese officials, who had to be extremely careful about his loyalty to his Filipino clients and to his country, because he was forced to treat Japanese enemy troops. This, and the dangers to his family, caused a menacing threat that they had to secretly live with each day. I suggested that she write of these powerful stories for her family's benefit and for their historic value. She said she intended to after her retirement from the VA. Dr. Kissmeyer retired years ago and I haven't seen her since.

I continued with individual counseling visits regularly at the Manchester Vet Center until mid-May 1997, when I joined the Center's combat veterans counseling group run by Caryl Ahern and John Brock. This group met weekly from 6:30 pm to 8:00 and was known as the Monday night group. All in the group had survived combat in Vietnam except for one elder member, a former Marine who had been wounded during the invasion of Okinawa in the spring of 1945. Over the four years I was in the group, numbers and composition varied. Membership included vets from all branches of the military, but most had served in the USMC or Army. On average, ten to twelve of us were in attendance each week. Sometimes more, sometimes less.

Conversations were very emotional and often heated. Members had endured varying experiences and wounds during the war, but we all had serious PTSD problems affecting our lives and our relationships with others. Some of us also suffered chronic physical pain. One member's son committed suicide during the years I was in the group. Therapists Caryl and John showed professional expertise in keeping our group's discussions within positive, helpful bounds. This was challenging and required keen understanding and compassion.

Late in April 2001, Mary and I held a veteran's brunch at our place. We called it "The year of the Snake Quake," named for the Vietnamese zodiac sign of Tet for that year. Several vets from the therapy group attended in addition to other veteran friends and their partners. Twenty-nine joined us that sunny spring morning for Mary's delicious brunch creations.

By the time I exited the group in May 2001, I was burned out. Group meetings were feeling nearly as stressful as they were helpful. There were times when I stopped to meditate for a few minutes in the plaza by the Hooksett tolls on the way to the Vet Center. Then, following the meeting, I stopped on the return drive home to calm my emotions. I usually had a stowed away beer to sip as I sat for a spell in our darkened car. I left the group on respectful, brotherly terms. I love them all and wish them well, but after four years I needed space. Some members kept in contact with me through phone calls, email messages, and even a couple personal visits to the ridge.

With a BS degree added to my resume, I began checking into the job market during the summer of 1998. I was receiving a reduced monthly federal retirement check due to the early-out I had opted for. That, plus monthly VA compensation payments, allowed me to seek only part-time employment. Several job openings of interest required at least a master's degree, which wasn't in the cards for me.

I decided to try substitute teaching and was hired by the Concord School District. I was called to the middle and high schools a few times in late 1998. The pay was pathetic and the openings for a substitute were sporadic. I found this position very stressful, especially at the middle school level. Not surprising, when I recall how disrespectfully we treated substitutes during my school days! It wasn't long before I quit as a substitute.

In January 1999, I began part-time work at Nancy Carlisle Interior Plantings based in Concord. I was responsible for plant maintenance and replacement at several NCIP contracts with area banks, law offices, insurance agencies, industrial offices, inn lobbies, etc. This job required that I work from ladders at many locations. With numbness in my left leg and increased pain from war wounds, the limited money I made wasn't incentive enough to continue long term. I quit that September. By then it was evident that my reclusive lifestyle wasn't compatible with the outside establishment's world. Mary and I decided that we could make ends meet financially if I stayed home and tended to our little subsistence farm. That's what I did. Keeping up with our many gardens, the huge area we mowed, maintaining our woods roads and pond, and tending to projects in the house had been increasingly demanding as age crept along. Winters brought the varied undertakings of country living.

By 1999, Mary and I were tired of our original dug-type well threatening to go dry during droughty periods. Especially back when our kids were here, we had to be very careful not to use much water for showers, toilet flushing, laundry, watering plants and daily needs. Regarding toilet flushing during dry times, our adage was "If it's yellow let it mellow. If it's brown flush it down." Buckets of water from our pond helped with toilet flushing. We also hauled water from the pond for outdoor plants and flowers. In checking one summer, we had only 1 1/2 feet of water, and the recovery rate was insufficient. I dowsed and staked a spot in the vicinity of our vehicle turnaround that seemed to be an ideal location for a drilled well. We contacted Capital Well Company, Inc., and that winter we had a 420-foot deep well drilled yielding 25 gallons of water per minute. The water tests were favorable, and no filters were required. Wally from Capital Well told Mary that our well was a "sweetheart." We've never again worried about water use.

Somehow, in October 1999, a graduate student from Vermont got wind that I had returned to Vietnam after serving during the war. Julee Allen was working on a research project toward her master's degree. A major component was interviewing American veterans about their war experiences and the aftermath of their returns. Julee limited her interviews to vets who had returned to do humanitarian work in Vietnam. She arranged numerous interviews individually with several vets, none of whom I ever met. She assigned us fake names (I was Jack), and she made transcripts of her interviews, which she skillfully worked into her extensive project.

Julee was very interested in PTSD aspects and our reactions to revisiting the war-torn country. During my discussion with her about war stress, she asked about "closure" — if I found closure by going back. It was during this conversation when I told her of my beliefs that true closure to PTSD is impossible to attain... that the "circle" never fully closes. I described my preferred term, "dilution," rather than closure and spoke of the metaphor of a puddle of piss. I related it to a bucket of fresh water being thrown into a nasty mud puddle, or a puddle of piss. Dilution occurs as some of the filthy water washes out. But then later some condition happens which washes some of the piss back into the puddle. And on it continues.

Julee wrote about my metaphor as part of her in-depth research project, which she finished in May 2000. I have a complete copy of her excellent narrative in my files.

Previously described endeavors to dilute my PTSD proved positive, and continued efforts in this regard have been an ongoing process. The support and understanding that Mary, Jessica, and my mom provided has been invaluable, as well as that of veteran brothers, sisters, and close friends. Writing in journals, authoring occasional opinion articles for newspapers, composing poetry, and even years of intermittent work on this memoir have helped me sort out life experiences and understand the hand of destiny. Lots of reading has been beneficial, as was the course I took on alternative health and healing. Regular stretching and strengthening exercises combined with meditation have been invaluable both physically and mentally.

In troubled times, I've arranged counseling sessions with hypnotherapist Peter Baldwin and psychologist Roger Poire. I also had an illuminating meeting with an amazing Peruvian shaman.

Discussions at schools and other public forums, though stressful, have been beneficial in strange ways. I worked with Portsmouth author Katherine Towler on her fictional island trilogy and am named in the acknowledgement pages of the 2nd and 3rd books of the trilogy. A couple NH Public Radio interviews in the company of John Jones also helped with dilution. Mind and body interactions are real and powerful. Therefore, activities that help one can likely help the other.

I've had numerous consultations at VA clinics and with private pain, orthopedic and neurological specialists in NH and MA. During a December 2014 visit with a highly respected orthopedic surgeon in Concord, it was recommended that I undergo a lower-leg amputation as my only option other than continuing with the pain I've lived with all these years. Strange, because decades ago I came very close to left leg amputation in military hospitals. At the Concord surgeon's urging, Mary and I had a two-hour consultation at a "First Step" prosthetics laboratory in Manchester. This was a very impressive visit where we saw several newly developed prosthetics and learned of the possibilities and expectations following limb loss. I gave amputation serious consideration but decided not to rush into such a drastic option. Alternatively, I've had acupuncture treatments, massages, and Sound Assisted Soft Tissue Mobilization (SASTM) therapy. In some cases, this has helped with PTSD as well as with physical pain.

Again, I must recognize the spiritual uplift I got from my two returns to Vietnam during the 1990s. For the most part, experiencing the peacefulness and beauty of the countryside plus the friendliness of the people toward me was forgiving. Totally different views and feelings from wartime. But feelings of sadness and guilt remain with me, especially after seeing the widespread waste of human lives in the scattered graveyards, the still-lingering wounds of survivors, and the damage to ancient heritage and natural resources from US bombing, artillery, and Agent Orange spraying. Personal stories from Vietnamese survivors I met add to the moral injury aspect of PTSD. Those survivors remain haunted by PTSD.

In reflecting on my time in the USMC, from being drafted through medical discharge, I realize how fortunate I have been and how fortunate I currently am. Considering the Marines' 13-month tour of duty in Vietnam, I very likely could have been killed. My wounds were inflicted months earlier than if I had remained for the full period. Though painful and lifelong, my injuries could have been far worse. I thank my flak jacket and the brave medevac personnel who rescued five of us who were most seriously wounded. Being wounded severely enough to be sent to the US and later admitted to the Portsmouth Naval Hospital was fortunate in obvious ways. For months after reaching the US, my day-to-day association was with corpsmen, military doctors, other wounded or sick troops and, eventually with family members and friends. I had little contact with the general civilian population, so I was spared contact with opponents of the war who may have been disrespectful. To date, I have no apparent health effects from being exposed to Agent Orange, which had been sprayed heavily in the areas where I served. Had I remained in country months longer, the nasty herbicide would have had more time to poison me.

Living on this beautiful Loudon Ridge acreage has been a godsend for Mary, our four cherished kids and their spouses, our six precious grandkids and me. It has been much appreciated by our parents also. Mom was especially pleased that we have this place on the ridge. It's at the opposite end of the country road from the farm where she was born, grew up and was married at, but her nostalgia was clear each time she visited us. Our land here has no physical connection to present or past Cate family property, so nothing was bequeathed to us.

Living here means far more than the house we dwell in. To us, the view is beautiful no matter which direction we look toward. The features experienced each day, like fine art, lie in the eyes of the beholder. There is a special magic to this piece of Mother Earth in all its wonderful qualities. Owning and paying taxes on it is temporary, we know, since we won't live forever. We are merely stewards of the land for a short period of time. And for that very reason we've done our best to maintain, improve and protect it as we enjoy its special features. It's vital that we continue to do the little things to protect our wonderful natural surroundings. Recycling to the extent possible, returning food waste to the earth through composting, using canvas shopping bags instead of plastic, turning off lights when not needed are simple ways to help.

Working the land, producing nutritious food, caring for the forest, walking our woods roads and trails, observing nature's wildlife, flora, fauna, and fungi, relaxing at our pond, and swimming in it, and taking in the beauty of the meadow have added great value to our lives. Many years ago, our property was approved for NH Tree Farm certification. It is known as "Hodgepodge Tree Farm." Ever since we moved on our land, Mary and I have consistently raised big productive vegetable, herb and flower gardens that passersby from the road can readily see. We've also raised raspberries and strawberries and have tended to various fruit trees. We've had all the fresh fruit and vegetables we could eat. We have canned, frozen and dried a sizable portion of the food that our family consumed over winter months. Mary is ideal for this lifestyle, and her adoration of all we have equals mine. Her abilities in several art forms add significant value to our path through life. We are a very loving and compatible couple.

For several years toward the end of local apple season, we put up a barrel of unpasteurized sweet cider purchased at Leavitt's Cider Mill in Pittsfield. The cider cured in our root cellar, and when the cask was tapped a potent good-tasting brew ran through the spigot into our mugs, then into our mouths.

Many years running we made maple syrup setting out as many as 60 taps in our maples and some of neighbors Grant and Diana Avery's trees. Sap was gathered in barrels which were hauled by our tractor. The sap boiled for long hours in two pans on our homemade wood-fired steel framework welded together by our friend Stone. The boiling took place outside in our invisible sap house, a make-believe structure that we jokingly fantasized was real. Family members and friends joined us during the boiling process, which often turned into quite a party. When hydrometer tests indicated syrup grade was close at hand, the hot sap was finished to perfection inside on our Viking 6-burner range.

We've been fortunate for the gifts of wild blueberries, blackberries and mushrooms provided annually free with the joy of harvesting. Gazing at the moon in the darkened star-filled sky adds to our reverence of this place, as do cloud formations during daylight hours. We marvel at the sight of gorgeous sunrises and sunsets. Walks in the woods have always provided solace and wonderment during tranquil and troubled times regardless of the season. Simply having a quiet, remote place to observe nature and reflect provides simple therapy. Even wild seasonal storms produce a sense of awe and respect. Advanced age and associated physical limitations have reduced some of what we can accomplish here, but deep gratitude for all we have remains undiminished. Our top wish is that some family member of a future generation might own this place after we leave, but there's no telling what the future will bring.

Often, folks aware of the subsistence nature of our lifestyle have asked if we raise farm animals or domestic birds to supplement our diet. Our answer has been "no" and continues to be no. Mary and I aren't vegetarians, but we eat limited amounts of meat, and we haven't eaten red meat in many years. Unless vital for survival, we wouldn't own farm animals intended for slaughter. One reason is that we would be tethered to caring for them, which would prohibit us from extended travel adventures. Another reason is because in the process of raising them we would become too attached, like with pets, to have them killed for meat. But mostly it's because I agonize at recollections hearkening back to my experiences described at Uncle Bob's slaughter-house and profound horrors in Vietnam during the war. Returning to those nightmare experiences would be too much for my head and heart to bear. For this reason, I've never had the urge to go hunting since I came back from the war. The necessity of shooting troublesome varmints on our property over the years has been dispiriting enough.

We got a state permit and hired John Booth to dredge sediment from our pond with his big dragline in late August 2000. The dredging caused a mess on the disturbed area near the pond, but when we smoothed and reseeded torn up ground the project proved to be a worthwhile improvement. Water levels pumped down prior to the dragline work were soon replenished and cloudy pond water cleared before long.

Readers of this memoir will likely be perplexed at the following paragraphs, which briefly describe various US interventions in the affairs of sovereign nations in decades following the Vietnam War. Readers may wonder why the hell later military engagements have relevance to the preceding events chronicled in this writing. (Records substantiate each intervention noted below.) Here's why. Anyone who has served in a war, particularly one that was senseless and unnecessary, knows why subsequent wars trigger great anxiety. The historic significance and personal experiences of past wars are ingrained, and they return to the psyche with a vengeance. The past gets commingled with events of the here and now! It's encouraging to know that the Veterans Administration finally realizes and acknowledges this fact and offers ways to help.

The decade of the 1980s began with the election of President Ronald Reagan, a conservative Republican from California. George H. W. Bush, formerly a Texas congressman and CIA Director, became Vice President. Reagan used fearmongering strategies to build massive new offensive weapon systems, along with far-fetched Strategic Defense Initiative ("Star Wars") ideas to defend the US from the "Evil Empire," his term for the Soviet Union, which collapsed in December of 1991.

Reagan brought a huge cast of right-wing ideologues into all departments and at all levels of his administration. Hawkish followers ran the State Department, Pentagon and CIA. Domestic policy positions were filled with archconservatives adhering to Reagan's ideology. A prime example was Interior Department Secretary James Watt, whose greedy tunnel vision policies hastened environmental degradation.

Watt sternly opposed the controversial Vietnam Veterans Wall designed by the young student architect Maya Lin, daughter of Chinese immigrants. Watt initially refused to permit construction. Following heated confrontations over the monument's varying interpretations (especially a design created by a female of Asian descent), a compromise was reached to add a bronze Three Soldiers sculpture and raise an American flag. The Memorial was constructed in Constitutional Gardens on the National Mall in 1982 and dedicated that November. Inscribed on its polished black granite walls are the names of over 58,000 US servicemen and women killed during the long Southeast Asian struggle. The sculpture and flagpole were installed in 1984. The Vietnam Women's Memorial was added at the site in 1993, an unfortunate omission finally corrected.

On October 23,1983, a terrorist suicide bombing of the Marine barracks in Beirut, Lebanon killed 241 US service personnel. 220 were Marines. US troops were part of a multinational peacekeeping effort in that troubled area. Many wondered why we were there.

That same month, a face-saving campaign was immediately arranged with the US invasion of the tiny Caribbean Island of Grenada, codenamed "Operation Urgent Fury." This was really a distraction, lessening publicity of the tragic Beirut debacle. The main justification given for this action was to rescue so-called endangered American students on the island. The operation lasted only a few days with the US claiming victory. Many nations condemned the invasion, including the United Nations Security Council, as "a flagrant violation of international law and of the independence, sovereignty and territorial integrity of that State."

President Reagan ordered US troop withdrawal from Lebanon early in 1984 due to a lack of congressional support for the mission. Investigations into the barracks bombing had been very critical of the flimsy security at the facility.

Among other pursuits reminiscent of US intervention in Southeast Asia were overt and covert meddling in the affairs of Central America, especially Honduras, El Salvador, and Nicaragua during the Reagan years. The public was hearing the same old fearful paranoid shit from the Reaganites about how this time the commies would be crossing our Texas borders. This time they would be Marxist rebels called Sandinistas instead of NVA and Viet Cong. The Sandinistas had overthrown the malevolent dictator Anastasio Somoza in 1979. To repel this imagined threat, our government funded, trained, advised, and armed the corrupt military death-squad dictators of the far right known as Contras. Secret operations run by the CIA were reminiscent of the murderous Phoenix Program in Vietnam, Laos and Cambodia during the 1960s.

By the mid-1980s it became increasingly evident that the US was headed for a rerun of the heinous Vietnam War in Central America. Antiwar demonstrations took place from coast to coast in the US and in several other countries. As the protests became more numerous, they also grew bigger and more dramatic. All were non-violent. The situation was wildly reminiscent of the Johnson/Nixon years, with growing opposition from politicians, journalists, veterans, religious organizations, and the general public. The deceitful activities in Central America reeked of deja vu to thousands of Vietnam veterans across our country and stoked the fires of activism.

At around that time, I listened to a well-attended presentation at UNH by Ralph W. McGehee, a former CIA operative. He discussed his book *Deadly Deceits: My 25 years in the CIA* in which he lays bare the disillusionment he felt after college at Notre Dame, believing his job with the agency would be one of intelligence gathering. Instead, he experienced many years of nasty covert operations in Southeast Asia, mainly in Vietnam. After his presentation, I spoke briefly with him and he autographed my copy of his book. McGehee's book was particularly relevant to ongoing secret activities toward a US war in Central America by the Reagan Administration.

I became increasingly active in peace, social justice, and environmental causes. In 1986, Jean Stimmell and I attended a meeting in Dover, NH, where we joined a newly forming organization called "Veterans for Peace" (VFP) which was based in Portland, Maine. It was at this meeting that we met John Jones (Jonesy), who also joined VFP on the spot. We founded a Merrimack Valley Chapter with several other Vietnam veteran brothers, including John Jones, Steve Fowle, Dwight Graves, and Paul Hague. Some vets from the Korean War and WW II generations also joined our group. Soon our local chapter grew to many members.

In the fall of 1986, four military veterans (three Vietnam War vets and one WW II vet) protested President Reagan's Central American policies by holding a fast on the steps of the US Capitol. One of the Vietnam veterans, Charlie Liteky, had been awarded the Congressional Medal of Honor for his heroism during the war. Just prior to the fast, he renounced his medal in protest, placing it at the Vietnam Veterans Memorial. I traveled to the Capitol with several members of our local VFP chapter to stand with the fasting vets. Thousands of veterans and citizens from across the country also joined the protest, and several prominent Congressmen spoke in solidarity with demonstrators, including Senators Pat Leahy, Ted Kennedy, Tom Harkin and John Kerry, and Congressmen Leon Panetta, David Bonior, and many others. All protest activities at the Capitol were peaceful, with no violence occurring.

Plans took shape in the spring of 1988 for a Veterans Peace Convoy to Nicaragua. VFP chapters across our country established public donation efforts to purchase trucks to be filled with medical supplies, food items and related humanitarian aid. The trucks assembled and formed a convoy with stops in several cities across the US, intending to cross the Texas border into Central America. The trucks were to be gifted in addition to their contents.

Our chapter received substantial donations, enough to buy a used Toyota pickup truck from the Grappone dealership. By the time our truck joined others it was packed full of supplies for the people of Nicaragua. The project's motto was "Feed the Children, Not the War." Jean Stimmell, Karl Bergeron, and Paul Daum volunteered for the journey in NH's truck.

At Laredo, US Customs officials stopped the convoy and refused to allow it to cross into Mexico. A stalemate took place at the border over legal entanglements, which delayed the convoy from reaching Nicaragua. The convoy of trucks and aid they carried finally arrived at its destination.

During July of 1987 and again in 1988, Mary and I hosted weekend VFP parties at our place. The big VFP banner that Mary made was displayed between two trees at the gap in the wall by our house. Vets and their partners attended from adjoining state VFP chapters, including several from Boston's Smedley Butler Brigade chapter. Lots of our local peace-minded friends also came to our parties, as did our kids. A blues rock band featuring Dwight Graves and his group played from Jean Stimmell's low-bed trailer, and tents sat strewn in our field for overnighters.

We rented a big grill and had kegs of beer set handily on our wood wagon. Other houses around us were very few in number, so our parties bothered no one. We have an album of photos taken during the parties.

The widespread antiwar movement, plus heightened media exposure of the illegal "Contragate" scandal by top-level Reagan officials, prevented a US invasion of Nicaragua. Another Vietnam-type fiasco was avoided. The Sandinistas retained control of Nicaragua's government, and the Contras diminished as a violent right-wing threat.

Band at Veterans for Peace party at Nichols' place July 25, 1987

*Dave Robinson and John Jones at Veterans for
Peace party July 25, 1987*

George H. W. Bush won the 1988 presidential election. US warmongering continued, first in Panama. The invasion of Panama, codenamed "Operation Just Cause," began in December 1989. Stated justification for the invasion was to capture that country's brutal dictator, Manuel Noriega, in order to protect Americans living there and to combat drug trafficking. General Noriega had been paid millions as a secret asset to the CIA in the region for over 20 years until his usefulness expired. The invasion lasted only a couple weeks but brought death to untold numbers of innocent peasants and massive devastation to the poorest parts of the country. Noriega was brought to the US and jailed until 2010, when he was extradited to France. He died in a Panamanian prison in May 2017.

Then it was onward to the Persian Gulf to fight the first oil war against Iraq's President Saddam Hussein, yet another brutal dictator that US policies helped create. Both the Reagan and Bush administrations provided Iraq with intelligence and logistical support during Iraq's eight-year war against Iran during the 1980s. Covertly, the US also sold chemicals, live viruses and bacteria to Iraq that could be used in making weapons.

"Operation Desert Shield" was ordered by President Bush in August 1990 in reaction to President Saddam Hussein's invasion of the bordering country of Kuwait. Saddam intended to take control of Kuwait's oil fields, claiming that Kuwait was really part of Iraq from decades ago when the Mid-East was divided up and transformed by Great Britain and France at the beginning of WW I.

Desert Shield amounted to a sizable US military buildup in the Persian Gulf as a muscle flexing threat and preparation for action against Saddam. It was obvious that war lurked ahead. On Veterans Day, 1990, Steve Fowle and I left Loudon Ridge for a big antiwar rally in Boston. My homemade placard read, "How many lives per gallon is it worth?"

*Paul and Steve Fowle prior to antiwar rally
in Boston. November 11, 1990*

Saddam didn't back down and "Operation Desert Storm" began in January, 1991. This war provided a handy life and death test run for US Stealth bombers, "smart bombs" and other new laser-guided hi-tech weaponry. The massive bombardment had devastating effects on Iraqi military and civilian infrastructure. International coalition ground forces then invaded a much weakened and overwhelmed Iraqi army. This war's justification spurred widespread controversies.

I joined others in writing antiwar newspaper letters and attending protests. Such antiwar activities swelled across the US and in many Western countries. Conversely, puffed up right-wingers were all for the war. A new demonstration of US military might was at hand. Support the troops fever also spread across America through a yellow ribbon campaign. The tens of thousands tied around trees, telephone poles and signposts yellow ribbons as a show of support. Vehicles of all types were bedecked with patriotic bumper stickers. One of several slogans from we who opposed the war was "Support the troops, bring them home now!"

In late February 1991, Iraqi troops began a retreat on the major highway from Kuwait toward Iraq's border with a caravan of tanks, trucks and armored vehicles numbering well over a thousand. It was reported that civilians were also traveling in busses on the convoy. Though offering no resistance, the column was unmercifully attacked by US and allied air power. Mangled vehicles and dead Iraqis were spread for miles across the desert in what has been termed the "Highway of Death."

The highway massacre generated attempts for war crimes investigations, but they proved futile. A statement from the late Howard Zinn, Boston University professor, historian, author, and WW II bombardier opined that the shame of killing innocent people couldn't be covered by a flag no matter how big.

Many years after the war, a traumatized special operations soldier who had been involved in the aftermath of these attacks showed me gruesome color photographs he had taken of the death and destruction. Within 100 hours of the ground invasion a ceasefire was ordered. The brutal dictator Saddam Hussein remained in power.

Basking in victory, President George H. W. Bush claimed that a "new world order" was underway, and he ended a speech at the White House on March 1st with, "And, by God, we've kicked the Vietnam syndrome once and for all."

In a radio address the next day Bush said, "The specter of Vietnam has been buried forever in the desert sands of the Arabian Peninsula." These insensitive and erroneous comments enraged traumatized Vietnam vets nationwide. I wrote a long, emotionally painful article about this, which I never sent to a newspaper. It turned out being more of a typed journal entry that served as a means of venting to myself.

I have a memoir by Anthony Swofford titled *Jarhead* which chronicles his experiences and viewpoints as a Marine during this first Gulf War. Swofford writes of doubts he and troops he served with had about the war's devious motives: to bolster and protect US oil reserves in the region and to profit American petroleum companies, some of which President Bush, Defense Secretary Dick Cheney and other officials had direct monetary interests in. Swofford also writes of the atrocities he witnessed along the "Highway of Death."

After one term as president, Democrat Bill Clinton defeated Bush in the 1992 election. Clinton had opposed the Vietnam War and had found ways to avoid military service. This fact stirred up fierce controversy among conservatives and some veterans, but Clinton prevailed. He was reelected for a second term which ended January 20, 2001.

Throughout most of Clinton's presidency the US stayed clear of any extended wars, though military events did occur. In the final weeks of the Bush presidency, US troops had been sent to Somalia on a humanitarian mission which turned violent. During a brief battle in Mogadishu, Somalia, in 1993, several of our servicemen were killed and wounded before a brief surge of sanity prompted troop withdrawal in early 1994, similar to Reagan's troop departure from Beirut, Lebanon a decade earlier.

US embassies in two East African countries were bombed in 1998. Terrorist groups, including al Qaeda, were responsible for the bombings. Clinton ordered missile strikes in Afghanistan and Sudan in attempts to weaken or destroy al-Qaeda leader Osama bin Laden's training camps and weapons arsenals. Al-Qaeda and similar groups became stronger.

During 1999, the US led other NATO countries in a bombing campaign in the border disputed Balkan states formerly known as Yugoslavia. Horrific ethnic cleansing, rape and destruction was taking place between the various republics' ethnic groups. NATO ground troops were not deployed, and eventually the bombing led to a shaky peace accord and further breakup of war-torn Yugoslavia.

Saddam Hussein instigated several threatening pursuits during the 1990s, though not directly against the US homeland. Hussein caused problems over UN economic sanctions that were imposed and resisted UN weapons inspection efforts in Iraq. In response to these and other threats, Clinton ordered bombing missions and missile launches several times during his eight-year presidency.

Clinton was impeached in late 1998 for perjury and obstruction of justice regarding repeated sexual encounters with a White House intern. He was acquitted early the following year and finished his second term in office.

The US presidential election of 2000 between Republican George W. Bush (one of H. W.'s sons) and Vice President Al Gore was hotly contentious and incredibly close. Mary and I supported Gore, who won the country's popular vote. In the end, the electoral college vote came down to Florida's results. After great controversy concerning a recount, the US Supreme Court decided the election by granting Bush the required electoral vote total by a slim margin. Thus, the detestable Dick Cheney became vice president.

If the previous discourse outlining US military entanglements in the affairs of other countries isn't enough, the following paragraphs concerning Afghanistan and Iraq represent the biggest debacles since the shameful US war in Vietnam.

One of the many fine people I met when I traveled with the PeaceTrees organization to Vietnam in 1998 was Mattias Forsberg from Sweden. We became very good friends during that trip and kept in touch by email during the few years that followed. Unexpectedly, Mary and I got invited to his marriage to Nguyen Le Thanh, a Vietnamese student who Mattias met at college in Hanoi.

The wedding was to be held in Uppsala, Sweden on August 18, 2001. Mary and I decided to attend, and flew from Boston on August 13th to Zurich, then on to Stockholm.

We stayed in a hostel in Stockholm where we met and conversed with travelers from various countries. We had a great time seeing the sights in that beautiful city. On the 17th, we took a train to Uppsala and attended the wedding the next day, and a grand wedding it was. During the festivities we met many friendly people, including Thanh's mother and sister from Hanoi and members of Mattias' family. Their friends from England and other European countries also attended the wedding. We spent time with Michiel Pool from the Netherlands, who we became close friends with. (Michiel has visited us in Loudon twice since then, once with his mother)

Mary and I enjoyed this special opportunity to converse and exchange worldviews with folks from other nations. In ways, some were critical of political decisions made in the US and certain aspects of our culture. Mary and I agreed with some of the points they made but realize that no country is flawless in history or culture.

From Stockholm on August 20th, we boarded a Viking Line cruise ship for an overnight voyage to Helsinki, Finland. We had a fun time in Helsinki for a couple days before flying back to Boston on August 23rd. Over the years, Mary and I have recalled how fortunate we were to have made that European journey when traveling was simple and safe. Change lurked ahead.

About two weeks after our return, on September 11, 2001, New York's World Trade Center was attacked by al Qaeda suicide terrorists who intentionally flew two commercial airliners filled with passengers into the Twin Towers. A civilian airliner also crashed into the Pentagon. A fourth aimed toward Washington, DC crashed into a field in Pennsylvania when the hijackers were overtaken by courageous passengers.

Much has been recorded about these coordinated attacks planned by Osama bin Laden and carried out by 19 hijackers. Fifteen of the 9/11 terrorists were Saudi Arabians, as was

Osama bin Laden. One was Egyptian, one was Lebanese and two were from the United Arab Emirates. These attacks killed nearly 3,000 innocent people in addition to the hijackers.

Vague warnings of coming attacks had been received by US intelligence agencies but had not been taken seriously enough by the Bush administration. The September 11th attacks were the deadliest in US history since the Japanese attacked Pearl Harbor in 1941.

These attacks were such tragic, momentous events for our country that I've consulted my journal for notes from that day and from my subsequent entry of September 16th. I'll include a few here: *When the first plane hit the North Tower that morning, Mary was in Concord at work. She immediately phoned me at home and told me to turn on the TV. Within minutes, the second plane crashed into the South Tower. I had been preparing to join Vietnam vets John Jones, Pauline Hebert, and Gary Rafferty for presentations at a literature class at Rivier University in Nashua. The class was shut down and postponed until a later day. Like most everyone, I became glued to television coverage.*

Knowing that Travis was flying home to Austin from a work assignment that day, we were very worried about his safety. At the time of the attacks, he was in the air headed home. No one knew how extensive the terrorist attacks would be or where they might occur. Around noon Trav phoned us to let us know that he had landed safely in San Francisco. Like other flights nationwide, his was grounded. He later got a flight to Dallas, rented a car and drove home, getting to Austin at about 2:00 am.

In another way, our family was very lucky too. In the early summer of 2000, Mary and I traveled to New York City to attend a Bruce Springsteen & the E Street Band concert at Madison Square Garden. Travis was away for work, and we stayed with his wife Dara in their NJ apartment. During a walk around NY City with Dara one afternoon, we stopped at a pier to look across the water toward the World Trade Center Towers. Dara pointed to an office window on the 96 floor of one of the towers where she worked for a financial organization. Within a few months, she and Travis had moved to Texas. Had she still been at work in NYC on September 11, 2001, she would have been killed in the terrorist attacks. Fate had smiled on our family.

The world drastically changed after the 9/11 attacks. Most countries were stunned by the extensive carnage. President Bush launched "Operation Enduring Freedom" on October 7, 2001, ordering air and sea bombardments of terrorist training camps and infrastructure in Afghanistan. Though none of the airline attackers were Afghans, the Islamic fundamentalist Taliban organization controlled the country and provided a safe haven to al Qaeda forces, including Osama bin Laden. He was the key target of US attacks in Afghanistan.

NATO nations soon supported the US cause, adding air power. In time, coalition ground troops joined ground units from the US. Despite heavy fighting, bin Laden and many of his surviving al Qaeda members soon escaped through the mountains into Pakistan with several Taliban fighters. Hundreds of combatants and "high value" suspects were captured and sent to the US detention camp in Guantanamo Bay, Cuba. There they were held for harsh interrogation, including abhorrent torture methods such as waterboarding for certain prisoners. In 2004, a major scandal erupted when torture was disclosed by the *Washington Post* and the *NY Times*. Many detainees have been held at Guantanamo for indefinite periods without trial. Several held have never been charged with a crime.

With consequential parallels to the North Vietnamese strategy during that long American war, the Taliban's operative mindset, as stated by their fighters, had been: "You have the watches, we have the time."

The war in Afghanistan (The country known as "The

Graveyard of Empires") was ongoing, with direct US involvement for nearly 20 years, until all US troops withdrew on August 30, 2021, as ordered by President Joe Biden. The war presented a no-win situation to the US. Finally, the dead-end canyon of nation-building in Afghanistan had been realized at great costs. Similar results as from the Soviet Union's war there throughout the 1980s and from colonizers centuries before. Much controversy ensued from President Biden's decision.

In total, just under 2500 US troops were killed over the 20-year period. Many from allied nations were also killed. Thousands more were wounded in body and soul. Considerable destruction occurred across Afghanistan. Tens of thousands of innocent Afghan lives were lost, plus an untold number of combatants. Millions became internally displaced or refugees abroad. The Afghan government and military collapsed, and their unpopular president fled the country. Those unable to escape were left to the controlling powers' vehemence, including many Afghans who had served as interpreters and in other capacities in the fight against the Taliban. The US and other countries now spend hundreds of millions of dollars in aid to Afghanistan attempting to keep the war-torn country afloat.

President Bush, greatly influenced by Dick Cheney, Defense Secretary Donald Rumsfeld and others of that ilk, exaggerated the threat that Saddam Hussein (America's once favored dictator) of Iraq posed to the US and the world. Simply put, they told lie after lie.

Among the falsehoods, the administration touted that Saddam was directly connected to al Qaeda and the September 11 attacks. He wasn't. However, the major whopper of a lie came from the administration's insistence that Saddam had developed "weapons of mass destruction" (WMD) that could threaten the US and allied countries. The WMD, they claimed, was nuclear, chemical and biological. The British government went along with this Bush fabrication whole hog, while French and some other country's leaders had strong doubts and resisted intervention.

Opposing countries, especially France, were treated as pariahs by right-wingers in the US. French toast was termed "freedom toast" and French fries were called "freedom fries" by US conservatives, including some in Congress. Incredible stupidity!

Another factor in the nation building scheme was control of Iraq's immense oil producing capacity, in which US petroleum corporations had direct interests. The US oil industry would be better served with a friendlier democratic system of government following the removal of Saddam Hussein's brutal authoritarian regime. It was as though they believed, *What's our oil doing under their sand?* The envisioned democratically run government turned out being a ridiculous pipe dream.

In the lead-up to the war, enormous peace protests took place regularly across the globe. A coordinated International Day of Protests occurred on February 15, 2003, in which millions of concerned people from more than 600 cities representing about 60 countries held antiwar demonstrations worldwide. Mary and I joined friends Paul and Chris Hague, Jean Stimmell and Bruce Marriott that day in frigid New York City where hundreds of thousands protested. Locally, protests were substantial and nearly continuous across the state. Jean Stimmell and I attended a demonstration with the Seacoast Peace Response in Portsmouth. I was pictured prominently on the front page of the *Sunday Monitor* while at a big peace demonstration in Concord on March 15th.

Mary Nichols, Paul and Chris Hague, Paul Nichols, Jean Stimmell and Bruce Marriott at an antiwar protest in NYC February 15, 2003

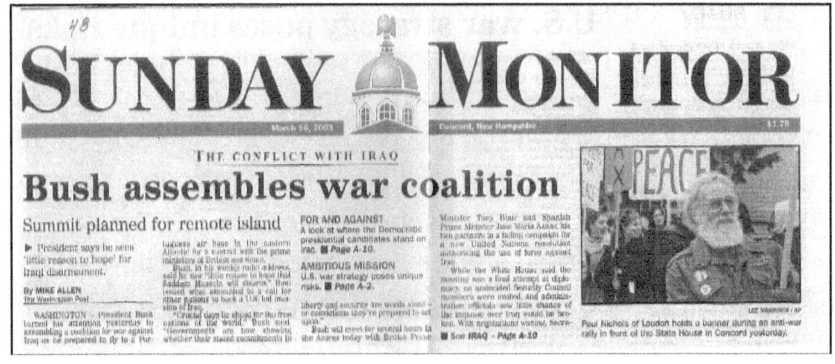

Paul at antiwar demonstration in Concord March 15, 2003

During February 2003, a nationwide online antiwar poetry campaign (*Poets Against the War*) had begun by poet Sam Hamill. There is an interesting story behind the beginnings of this initiative involving First Lady Laura Bush and Hamill. I joined thousands of poets from all across the country submitting poems numbering in the tens of thousands well into the war years. An anthology containing many of the early poems was published in 2003. I have a copy of the anthology titled *Poets Against the War.*

Bush and his neo-con cohorts were determined to oust Saddam. On March 20, 2003, "Shock and Awe" began with a massive bombing campaign carried out by the US, the UK and several allied countries. The horrendous attacks overwhelmed Iraqi forces. US-led coalition ground forces, principally from Britain and Australia, invaded Iraq. Minimal troops from other countries joined the effort.

Shortly after the war began, more huge protests took place in America's cities and in cities around the world. On March 29th, Mary and I marched with friends in a massive peace rally in Boston. I think it was the late Howard Zinn who said that there is no higher form of patriotism than dissent. But, as with the Iraq War of 1991, the antithesis came in the form of blind patriotism by supporters of the war. Yellow ribbon mania and orgasmic flag-waving fervor collided with massive opposition protests. Our stance was to support the troops, not the war!

Since 1973, military service has been on an all-volunteer basis. As a result, the only men and women fighting our country's wars have been those who freely joined. Therefore, a heavy burden has fallen on a widely disproportionate few during the long Iraq and Afghanistan wars, requiring multiple deployments. Had there been a draft from the beginning, the wars may have taken far different paths. Resistance would have been more intense and widespread.

This lack of conscription was not only an important factor

affecting recurrent deployments of US servicemen and women, it also affected the level of public opposition to those wars. Compulsory military service generates dissent, especially when the cause is deemed senseless. The majority of our young men and women breezed along unaffected with their civilian lives, as did their families and the unfazed public. Tying a yellow ribbon to a signpost seemed a safe and patriotic thing to do. But for those obliged to their military enlistments, the burden of redeployment became heavy. Tragically, our troops have paid a tremendous price in mind and body.

The capital city of Baghdad fell in early April 2003 and Saddam fled into hiding in the countryside until being captured that December. He was later hanged in an Iraqi prison. The invasion's mayhem, foreign occupation and internal divisions fueled a potent insurgency.

During the summer of 2004, in light of increased international antiwar fervor, renewed effort was begun to accept poetry online under the title, *Voices in Wartime*. A few of my poems were included with scads of other online submissions. An anthology of some of the poems was published in 2005, followed by the production of a full-length documentary film featuring many excellent poets. My Vietnam veteran poet friend from South Boston, Dave Connolly, is prominently featured in the film. I ordered a DVD copy of the documentary and inquired at Red River Theatres in Concord if they would be interested in sponsoring a public showing. They enthusiastically agreed, and the *Voices in Wartime* film was presented at the NH Technical Institute on February 4, 2006. Public attendance was substantial and included college students.

Beginning in 2003, President Bush authorized heinous forms of torture of high-level captives by CIA and US military police at Abu Ghraib, one of Iraq's most infamous prisons. Water boarding was one of many forms of torture used. Revelations came to light in 2005 of the CIA's greatly expanded practice of "extraordinary rendition," which had very limited use during the Reagan and Clinton administrations. Extraordinary rendition meant that captured combatants were kidnapped and secretly transported to specific colluding countries for extreme interrogation known as "torture by proxy." The use of these covert "black sites" allowed the US to deny that such shameful and illegal acts were taking place.

The war became even more intensely despised. Widespread demonstrations continued during the years following the invasion. Mary and I attended a roadside protest in Northwood with Jean, Russet and folks from town on September 24, 2005. Media sources regularly denounced the war and the malicious falsehoods that instigated it.

During 2006, the Poetry Society of NH published a poetry anthology titled *The Other Side of Sorrow*. The front cover is a photograph of the revolving doors of the World Trade Center taken less than two months before it was destroyed by foreign terrorists. The book contains poetry from many famous poets and others not so famous. Veteran friends Neil English, Dave Connolly and Michael Casey have poems included. Three of mine appear in the book. Following publication, public readings were held at numerous locations to promote sales of the anthology and a more thoughtful, peaceful world.

Fighting continued between Iraqi insurgents and the US-led multinational forces, eventually evolving into a ferocious civil war between the country's religious and sectarian factions. By the spring of 2007 coalition forces, including the British, withdrew at increased levels. Later that year Bush ordered limited US troop withdrawal, expecting the Iraqi army to contain the violence. By then, thousands of US and coalition troops had been wounded or killed in addition to millions of wounded, killed or displaced Iraqis. Extensive destruction had taken a heavy toll on cities, infrastructure and ancient cultural treasures throughout Iraq. Billions of US dollars continued to be poured down the rathole. The disastrous war came to be known as a no-win fiasco to all but the most strident hawks, the majority of whom had intentionally stayed clear of combat themselves. Those of that ilk are rightly termed "chickenhawks," cheerleaders for war perched high on safe branches, drooling as they promote it safely from afar.

Journalistic reporting about the Bush wars in Iraq and Afghanistan was conducted in far more restricted ways than during the Vietnam War. News reporters and camera crews had liberal freedom to travel throughout South Vietnam and to enter ongoing battles as they saw fit. They could freely describe the war they were covering to news outlets in words and images, though considerable editing sometimes took place by our government officials.

This was not the case in Iraq and Afghanistan. Reporters and camera crews were "embedded" with specific military units and under tightly controlled circumstances. Unlike during the Vietnam War, such restrictions prevented the public back home from getting more complete news from the Bush wars. Instead, the news was cherry-picked and purged, thus presenting a distorted view of the savagery inflicted by the war. News coverage of caskets carrying dead US troops arriving at Dover Air Force Base was prohibited in an effort to keep the public sanitized from the war's horrific carnage.

During 2008, lawlessness and factional fighting was mostly confronted by the Iraqi army with support from US troops and heavy war machinery. That September, Mary and I flew to Toronto, Canada to escape the huge NASCAR races at the NH Motor Speedway down the road from our place. While enjoying our visit, we saw a big antiwar parade marching through the city. It was a parade supporting US military war resisters and deserters. The focus was against then conservative Canadian Prime Minister Stephen Harper, who would not allow sanctuary to US resisters fleeing ongoing wars in Iraq and Afghanistan.

Harper's policy was opposite that of the Canadian leadership in the 1960s and early 1970s when US draft evaders, resisters and deserters were openly accepted. Mary and I joined the parade and had encouraging conversations with many in the parade and at the rally that followed.

The US war in Iraq officially ended in late 2011 under the Obama administration. Out of the destabilized chaos of Iraq and a rampant civil war in Syria grew the Islamic fundamentalist group commonly called ISIS (the Islamic State of Iraq and Syria). ISIS expanded and became the most dangerous terrorist scourge confronting the US and Europe. This extremist group, plus al-Qaeda and its splinter groups, have caused continued murderous attacks throughout Iraq and Syria and across the US, Europe, Western Asia, and North Africa.

Returning troops from Afghanistan and Iraq have suffered PTSD symptoms similar to vets of previous wars. Women served in more expanded roles than ever before in the armed forces. They experienced combat stressors like those of men and often had additional trauma from sexual abuse, generally caused by servicemen of higher rank. Overall, 20 or more suicides per day have taken place among Afghanistan and Iraq war veterans. As the severity of this problem became recognized, military units held demobilization sessions with returning troops to help with the transitioning process. When filtering back from war in Vietnam, such debriefings were unheard of.

The VA established crisis centers and hotlines across the country to help Afghanistan and Iraq war veterans address PTSD and moral injury cases. Like in Vietnam, casualties from land mines and booby traps, now referred to as improvised explosive devices (IED), were frequent. Such explosions, in addition to mangling bodies, caused brain damage.

Republican Arizona Senator John McCain launched his 2008 presidential campaign, choosing Alaska Governor Sarah Palin as his vice-presidential running mate. This was a monumental mistake, as she had a nasty Tea Party ideology with the warped right-wing mindset of that political movement. What's more, she was dumb and attracted joke after joke!

McCain, a Vietnam veteran and former POW, rode his "Straight Talk Express" entourage campaigning across the country with a stop in Peterborough, NH on November 2, 2008. My Nam vet brother Jonesy, me and many other veterans, wearing our military jungle shirts (including Charlie Richmond, a former Marine veteran of WW II and a member of the Vet Center therapy group I attended), stood peacefully at the rally with banners in support of Democratic candidate Barack Obama. Our presence intensely angered the McCain supporters, who openly seethed with hostility toward us. The vile, aggressive harassment we endured that day was unimaginable.

At home, still shaken by the experience, I wrote a poem called "Straight Talk Express." While I respect McCain for a few of the positions he took over the years, he was an angry man and far too conservative to my way of thinking. McCain has since died of brain cancer.

While standing quietly at other rallies in support of Obama, our veterans contingent enjoyed lots of positive expressions, and we also withstood many disrespectful slurs from passersby.

I recall a car veering up to the curb where I stood on North Main Street in Concord. The driver rolled the window down and furiously yelled that I was a traitor, then continued down the street.

Another time, in a different NH city, someone shouted from a car window inferring that we were fake veterans by asking where our DD-214 forms were proving our military service. We called back, "Show us yours!" as the car rolled on its way. The us and them divisions in our country are worsening year after year. The attitude is: *If you're not with us, then you're against us!*

Barack Obama was elected US president in 2008. He

inherited the Bush wars and our country's dire financial crisis. Soon after his inauguration in 2009, Obama significantly reduced US troop numbers in Iraq and Afghanistan to mainly transitional and counterterrorism forces. Instead of widespread use of ground troops, Obama opted for deadly drone strikes from strategic US bases against high-valued ISIS leadership targets, the Taliban, al-Qaeda and its offshoots. Though several top-level terrorist leaders were killed, many innocent civilians were also killed in drone attacks. The antiseptic nature of lethal push-button air attacks originating from safe secluded bases on US soil was more palatable to the American public than when our troops' blood was drenching foreign soil. Nevertheless, drone strikes served as a recruiting tool for more terrorists and came far from ending the killings across the globe.

Obama won a second term as president over Republican Senator Mitt Romney in 2012 with Joe Biden as Vice president. One of many key accomplishments during Obama's second term was the May 2, 2011 attack in Pakistan by a Navy Seal team killing Osama bin Laden, mastermind of the September 11, 2001 terrorist attacks on the US.

The recap I've briefly outlined of our country's interventions since its war in Southeast Asia correctly portrays the US as a warring, militaristic country. Our leadership has been arrogant and ignorant of other cultures and their histories. Our front-line soldiers in Iraq have the newest state-of-the-art night vision technologies, but our leaders back home are blind!

Defense contractors, such as Lockheed Martin Corporation and Raytheon Technologies Corporation, and mercenaries (soldiers of fortune) promote warfare across the globe to gain immense profits. Year after year, persuasive lobbying in Congress allows them to suck up high percentages of our country's defense appropriations. So it all amounts to a perpetual money drain through unrestrained military intervention in foreign lands.

Peace-minded veterans and others in the peace movement over the decades hoped our time and efforts toward nonintervention against other countries would be rewarding. But not in support of countries' violent authoritarian leadership. With few exceptions, such as prevention of open-ended US invasions of Central American countries, our hopes were not realized.

In the spring of 2004, I wrote a lengthy poem titled "Fresh on Yesterday's Tracks" linking the folly and ugliness of the Vietnam War with the folly and ugliness of the Iraq War. My poem was published in *The South Boston Literary Gazette*, in an issue of the *VVAW* quarterly and in a few other publications. One of the poem's ending stanzas includes a beautiful lyric written by George Harrison from The Beatles' 1968 song, "While My Guitar Gently Weeps." The lyric I borrowed expresses hope that we learn with every mistake we make. Sadly, since World War II our country has learned very little from its misbegotten wars.

In 2010, I submitted a couple of my war-related poems to Kent State University's Wick Poetry Center in Ohio. The Center was working on a collaborative, international exchange featuring Vietnamese children's paintings coupled with American's poetry. Poems were sought which could be coordinated and paired with the children's art creations. A book titled *Speakpeace* was published highlighting the joint artwork. One of my poems, *Changed Perceptions*, was accepted and paired next to a 13-year-old Vietnamese boy's poignant painting titled *Extermination*. I have copies of the book. The paintings and poetry were displayed in exhibitions all across the US until the fall of 2013, when it traveled to other countries. I believe the exhibit's final destination was at Ho Chi Minh City's War Remnants Museum.

Manchester's Currier Museum of Art held an exhibition called,

Visual Dispatches from the Vietnam War during the fall of 2013, ending on Veterans Day. The exhibit featured photos from local Nam vets as well as by famous photojournalists, poetry and written memorabilia from the war. One of my poems and a graphic photo I took in 1966 were displayed in addition to items from many, many others. Mary and Jessie attended the exhibition, as did several of our friends and folks from near and far. I chose not to go due to the heaviness of emotions it would be certain to bring out, but Mary took some photos of the wall hangings.

A PARTING GLANCE BACK and
A HOPEFUL LOOK FORWARD

During the summer of 2002, Mary and I had a 24-foot by 28-foot barn constructed at the edge of our field. Attached to the north end of the barn we had a 12-foot by 16-foot sap house built. A water line was run from our well, and we installed a yard hydrant in the barn to provide year-round water access.

Mom felt that a barn roof should have a weathervane, and she insisted on paying for one as a gift. Mary and I found a nice blue heron (shitpoke) weathervane in Wells, Maine, and it was installed on the roof ridge of our new barn. This additional construction has been a boon to our small-scale agricultural efforts, especially during our elder years. Having a sap house with a small wood-fired stainless steel Leader evaporator has made the evaporating process easier than in earlier times. In more recent years we've set out a maximum of 25 buckets. In the late winter and early spring of 2021, we made more than six gallons of syrup and had many memorable times with family members as the trees were tapped, the sap gathered, and during the boiling process.

Dad died unexpectedly at home in Chichester on September 2, 2005, just a few days before his 87th birthday. Mary and I were vacationing at Popham Beach and were mostly through our week's rental of cabin #5 at "Kennebec Kottages."

Dad had died in bed sometime overnight very peacefully. Mom rose early that morning and went to the kitchen to make coffee, not knowing that Dad had passed. When she called him for breakfast he didn't respond, and in checking, she found that Dad had died.

All that morning Mom and Nan tried desperately to phone Mary and me but were unable to get through on Mary's cell phone due to the lack of signal on our end. There was no phone at the cabin. At around midday Mary and I walked up the beach trail through the dunes to our cabin where a Phippsburg town cop's cruiser sat in our yard. He had been notified that there was a family emergency and that we should immediately call my parents' home in NH. The cop had no further information about the crisis, and our imaginations ran wild thinking about the possibilities.

I drove up Rt. 209 toward Bath as Mary checked her phone for a strong enough signal. Finally, at the Post Office parking lot we were able to get through to Mom. We were stunned at the news of Dad's death since he had no serious illness that we were aware of. For several years I had been taking him to the VA hospital in Manchester for general physical checkups and medication prescriptions. Most of Dad's known medical problems were those associated with old age. We quickly cleaned up the cabin and drove straight to our house, where we called Mom to find out more and to console her.

Dad was cremated, and a funeral was held at the New Rye Congregational Church in Epsom. In time, a granite grave marker was delivered to us from the Veterans Administration. Mary and I set the marker and buried his urn between his mother's and Larry's in the Nichols plot at the Loudon Ridge Cemetery.

While in the process of finishing this final chapter, it's time for late reflections:

In earlier chapters of this memoir, I related bonding friction between Dad and me, especially during my teen years. The friction continued to a somewhat lesser degree for several years as I moved through my late 20s and beyond. As with most relationships, we can link the causes of our troubles to both of us. No one is faultless. I was certainly no model son. We were both strong-minded and unyielding in our divergent opinions. Generational differences certainly shape the way most of us look at the world and our place in it, but so do one's life experiences. Powerful influences! I disagreed with Dad's conservative Republican beliefs. Over time, I learned to let some of Dad's assertions float by without arguing my differing ideas. Nothing could be gained by arguing, I finally realized. Better late than never, the adage goes.

Dad's authoritarian ways, his strict nature, quick temper and conservatism often led to verbal abuse. Mom bore the brunt of most, but not all, verbal vilification. Often while growing up and for years afterwards during visits, I resisted speaking out in Mom's defense from some of Dad's hurtful remarks. It seemed less confrontational for me to remain silent. I believe that the main causes for the negative sides of Dad's makeup stem from influences of his early years. I know that Dad loved Mom deeply, he just had a hard time showing it at times.

Born in 1918, Dad's childhood was plagued by severe poverty compounded by the Stock Market Crash of 1929 and the Great Depression that followed.

He grew up in family conflict and had few opportunities for fun. He had few reasons to laugh or even to smile. Dad was several years older than his brother and sister, and therefore he had to provide major caretaker duties. These responsibilities magnified after his mother and father divorced. His mother became mentally ill, requiring institutionalization.

Adding to earlier stresses came the bombing of Pearl Harbor and Dad's experiences in World War II. At differing intervals following the war his brother and sister both moved to Florida where their dad, Ned Nichols, also lived. This left my Dad to care for his mother until decades later when she was moved into a Florida nursing home. She died there in 1989 and is buried at the Loudon Ridge Cemetery in the Nichols plot.

And then came the devastating sickness and loss of Larry, a

time Dad almost never mentioned. Well, maybe he did rarely to Mom. But the weight of the tragedy sapped life from Dad, as it did to the rest of our family.

During the declining years of Dad's life, he often described it as "winding down." Especially since his death, I developed a deep appreciation and respect for many of his admirable qualities. Dad was physically strong, hard-working, diligent in whatever he did, reliable and honest. His patriotism ran deep. He had great respect for the natural environment and wildlife. He proudly took the best possible care of his property. Dad was quick to give a person in need anything he had. He provided a ride to many a hitchhiker, especially late at night as he drove home from work. Dad was one who could be counted on to lend a hand.

Dad and I were from very different generations with many opposing points of view, though we saw some things alike. He mellowed quite a bit in his late years. He even said that he had voted for Democratic presidential candidate Bill Clinton! We could lightly discuss his war and mine, though from the safe distance of the edges. Dad expressed passive acceptance, at least outwardly, of my 1990s revisits to Vietnam. But when I returned from my 1995 trip and spoke emotionally of Vietnamese friendships and forgiveness I had experienced, he became angry and belittling. I recall him shouting that we're the United States of America, and we don't need forgiveness. This outburst was very hurtful to me. I never again spoke with him about either of my profoundly healing journeys, nor did I show him any photos I had taken.

I wish we could have had more cordial, mutually respectful talks about world issues and life happenings, but unfortunately such talks got past us until it was too late. Sadly, this kind of relationship is fairly common between fathers and sons. I'm hopeful that this memoir might someday help fill some voids in my immediate family's understandings. I remember the last time

I saw Dad. I can visualize him sitting on a fairly flat boulder on the stone wall facing our house. I think of him when I walk past that rock.

Mom was not a stern disciplinarian parent. Through all my growing up years at home and during the decades since, Mom remained a very nurturing, accepting, generally nonjudgmental person with a positive, uplifting personality. She did tend to be quite worrisome, sometimes over things that seemed trivial to me. Mom did her best to avoid conflict, yet she was wise, perceptive, strong and independent in her own way. And she listened. Like my father, Mom was most generous in her giving, whether in a material way or otherwise lending a helping hand. I consider Mom as being close to saintly all during her long life.

In many significant ways my mom's childhood drastically contrasted from my dad's. Mom was born on July 28, 1923, into a big, loving farm family near the southeasterly end of Loudon Ridge Road. The family was monetarily poor, as were most farm families before, during and after the Great Depression.

She had a very wholesome upbringing with few frills, but the farm provided nearly everything that was needed. Mom's countless memories of growing up were mostly fond and happy. She recalled, as a six-year-old child, the first time a light switch was turned on providing the farmhouse with electric power. Before then, light was provided by kerosene lamps. Mom spoke of taking heated stones to bed on frigid nights to help her stay warm under the covers. We also heard about drafty visits to the outhouse! The house was roomy, and her parents welcomed family visitors for extended stays, especially during summer months.

Mom often spoke and wrote (on her own computer) about her cherished youth. She told of attending the "Brown" one-room schoolhouse on Loudon Ridge Road in grades one through eight and being the sole student in her class. Mary and

I loved hearing the many family stories that she shared. Mom was deeply saddened when the big homestead burned flat on a frigid April night in 1992. She was eternally grateful that none of the Cate family who lived in the revered farmhouse was killed in the late-night fire, though that outcome came perilously close.

Now, decades later in my life, I think back to my childhood experiences at the old Cate farm, and I can better understand why Mom treasured her memories of growing up there. Values that I didn't fully appreciate in my youth.

I remember the family Christmas celebrations in my grandparent's living room, crowded with so many gathered. And how incredibly hot that room was on those occasions with dry heat drifting up through a huge floor register from the monstrous cellar wood furnace. Also, the big old untuned piano topped with framed photos of family members.

On weekends during several sapping seasons Mom, Dad, Nan and I traveled to the farm and helped with the syrup making process. This was more fun than it may seem, with a pair of huge workhorses hauling the sap-gathering scoot with big galvanized gathering tanks through the woods, stopping at trees with hanging buckets so we could collect the sap.

With full tanks, the scoot was hauled to the most elevated side of the rustic sap house. Sap flowed from the tanks through a galvanized trough conveying it into a bigger capacity holding tank inside the sap house next to the evaporator. My elderly grandfather controlled the sap volume flow into the wood-fired evaporator. He tended the boiling process. Eventually, farm tractors replaced the horses.

At season's end we helped wash the hundreds of sap buckets for use the following year. As I write, I still sense how precious this childhood sapping experience was. (Separately in an essay, I've written more about the adventures I had as a youngster sapping at the farm.)

On rare occasions when Mom and Dad went away for a few

days, Nan usually stayed at the Cutter farm in Epsom, so she could play with her girl cousins. I stayed at the Cate farm. I recall the cot I slept in and exactly where it was located beside a downstairs window. And early breakfasts, which were always Nana's wonderful oatmeal with fresh raw milk and maple syrup that were produced on the farm. The big cast iron wood fired kitchen stove, the roomy pantry with a blend of pleasant smells, the barn full of cows and 10-gallon cans of milk standing upright in the cold water of the metal cooler.

I remember floundering in the hay and getting hot and itchy from the chaff. And I remember my elderly grandparents, my Uncle Earle and Aunt Betty and my Cate cousins who all lived at the farm in those days. Yes, I can understand the adoration and nostalgia Mom held from her years growing up on the farm.

Following Dad's death, Mom remained in their Chichester home for a couple years, but over time it became too much for her to keep up with, and she was lonely. In spring 2008 she sold the house and moved into a brand new independent elder living apartment building in Loudon Village called the Richard Brown House. Through the years, Mom was happy there with many resident friends and with Mary and me living just a few miles north of her. With age, Mom became increasingly frail and had to get around with use of the cane that I had made for Dad. Then a walker after her fall in April of 2018, which resulted in a broken hip followed by surgery and rehabilitation.

In the fall of 2009, Mary and I took a road trip across the country lasting more than 6 weeks. From home on September 18 (our 33rd wedding anniversary), we drove to Ottawa, Canada where we enjoyed a wonderful supper at an Asian restaurant. Over the next days we drove west through several states eventually stopping in Enumclaw, Washington to visit Mary's sister Annie and husband Dave. From Seattle, we ferried to Canada's Vancouver Island where we toured gorgeous Butchart Gardens. Back in the US we continued our journey through western states and the southwest, spending a couple fun days with Travis and Dara in Austin, Texas. Our final family visit on the way home was in South Carolina where we had a good time with cousin Judy and her husband Bear. At many locations on our trip, we camped at parks in our tiny North Face tent. We kept a journal along the way, and for Christmas 2011 Mary gave me a spectacular photo album covering some of the highlights of our memorable vacation.

Over the many years since Travis graduated from college in Houston, Texas, occupation opportunities led him and Dara to Kansas, New Jersey, and Austin, where they now live with their two beautiful young kids, Reese and Brady. All others in our immediate family live in close proximity to us in surrounding towns, so Mary and I are fortunate to see them often.

During both winters of 2012 and 2013, Mary and I spent a couple months in Horseshoe Bay at a plush Texas lake house, about a 45-minute drive from Travis and Dara's house. The place on Lake LBJ was owned by Dara's relatives, and she lined up the rental for us prior to our drive to Texas. This was an ideal arrangement at very reasonable rental costs. Downstairs sat a full-sized pool table, and we four had many raucous games during our times there.

In addition to our clothing and other stuff on our 2012 trip, our Toyota and Thule were packed to the brim with produce from our gardens plus Mary's sewing machine, fabric, etc. With overnight stops along the way we hauled the vegetables and sewing machine into our hotel rooms to prevent freezing. Mary sewed a child-sized quilt for baby-to-be Brady, and we ate lots of Ridge-grown food while we were visiting. Both years, we had wonderful times getting together with our Austin family every weekend. Mary and I took several jaunts while there, including hikes at various locations. At age 88, my mom flew out to be with us for a week in January during our 2012 stay.

On the drive back to NH, in late February 2012, Mary and I

spent a couple fun days in New Orleans. We stayed at the Hotel St. Marie located on Toulouse Street in the French Quarter, and we visited several famous places in the city. The abundance of good bars with live musicians attest to the revelry of the city. Evidence of the recent Mardi Gras festivities was everywhere.

While at the lake house in 2013, we decided to drive to San Antonio for a couple days. We visited the Alamo and a couple other Spanish missions at the National Historic Park, we took the River Walk and made an emotional stop at the Vietnam War Memorial.

In late February 2013, while on our drive home, we stopped in Savannah, Georgia for a couple days. This was another delightful visit following goodbyes with our Austin family. Like New Orleans, this port city is rich in history with plentiful parks, restaurants and bars.

Mary and I have been fortunate to vacation in various Northeastern states and at Canadian locations in addition to the travels previously described. We have coordinated the timing of some of our journeys to escape the big NASCAR races held each year down the road at the NH Motor Speedway. We strongly dislike the speedway and enjoy traveling, which has given us added impetus to leave home for a while. We've also benefitted from years of healthful retirement, allowing us to travel.

A nasty, often chaotic Republican primary took place during 2016 with Donald J. Trump determined the presidential candidate to run against Democrat Hillary Clinton. Much was said and written during the time leading up to the November election. Being Clinton supporters, on October 28, 2016, Jean Stimmell, John Jones, Steve Fowle and I stood on the plaza at Market Square in Portsmouth holding Old Glory, POW flags and a clearly worded banner stating, "Trump Disgraces Veterans." Public responses we got were mostly positive and few were negative.

*Protest against Trump at Market Square
in Portsmouth October 28, 2016*

Days later, the presidential election was won by Trump based on electoral college vote count, with Mike Pence as Vice President. This, though his opponent, Hillary Clinton, received 3 million more popular votes from the US citizenry. It's interesting to note that Mom and Mary's parents, John and Alice Ortakales, despised President Trump for his total lack of integrity and his boastful bullying nature. Mom mentioned that most elder residents at the Richard Brown House where she lived disliked Trump too.

During Trump's four-year term, the US was beset by tyrannical authoritarian rule. His continual lies, racism, sexism, and corrupt policies have forever marked Trump and his administration as being extremely dangerous and damaging to our country, our democracy, and to the greater world. Trump was impeached on two counts by the US House of Representatives in late 2019 but was acquitted by the Republican controlled Senate in early 2020. Henceforth, he finished his disgraceful term, but was later impeached and acquitted by Senate vote a second time.

Mary's dad, John Ortakales, began suffering from back pains during 2017, and by that fall he had swollen lymph nodes in his neck. In November he underwent surgery in Laconia, and a biopsy was performed showing that he had multiple myeloma. Following all possible treatments, John was admitted to the Belknap County Nursing Home in April 2018. Eventually his cancer worsened, and he was treated at the nursing home by hospice workers until his death on September 29, 2018, at age 89. John almost never complained about his illness and confronted his terminal cancer with courage and grace. He was a very commendable man, deeply proud of his Greek heritage. John's wife Alice, of French-Canadian lineage, remains at their Laconia home. Alice is currently 92 years old and is a very caring and skillful woman.

A serious viral disease was believed to have first infected citizens of Wuhan, a Chinese city, in late 2019. By early 2020 the coronavirus, labeled COVID-19, had spread to countries across the world, including the US. The virus was highly contagious and before long surged to pandemic proportions. Eventual control was partially attained in most countries through business lockdowns, social distancing, and by mandating certain preventative sanitary steps to be taken by the populace. Wearing a cloth mask over nose and mouth proved to be a fairly effective method of preventing the respiratory virus from spreading.

Within four months the US, under the inept, deranged guidance of President Trump, became the world's leading country in both the number of infections and deaths from the pandemic.

The virus eventually mutated, resulting in more highly contagious strains causing additional concerns. Life in general was turned upside down, with many holiday gatherings canceled, small businesses closed, and learning institutions disrupted. The pandemic's tentacles cast far and wide throughout society. Except for wealthy Wall Street investors and certain major corporations, the economy reached near depression levels.

Toward the end of his presidency, Trump instituted Operation Warp Speed to promote development of a COVID vaccine. Eventually, protective vaccinations were developed and approved for all folks aged five and above.

Abiding by guideline timeframes, Mary and I got Moderna versions of the vaccinations, including the booster shots. The COVID virus mutated, and each variant brought its unique characteristics. Huge, often violent protests across the US and in other countries against wearing masks and getting vaccinations caused the virulent viral strains to continue infecting people old, young, and in between. In the US, most COVID deaths are occurring among the right-wing anti-vaccination population. The last major pandemic occurred in the World War I era, between 1917 and 1919 and was known as the Spanish Flu. There is no end in sight for the current pandemic, and the US death count exceeds one million as I write in May, 2022.

During the spring of 2020, Mom let on that she was having considerable pain whenever she swallowed. This led to doctor visits, hospital lab tests and two biopsies. A tumor at the base of her tongue on the left side and a swollen lymph node below her left ear were diagnosed as oral squamous cell carcinoma, estimated to be at stage 3 of 4. Surgeons determined that an operation on Mom's tongue area was not an option because it would be far too expansive. She opted out of chemotherapy, leaving radiation treatments as the option performed under palliative care. She underwent four radiation treatments of the ten scheduled and decided not to undergo any more. The COVID-19 pandemic added to the difficulty of appointments and treatments, as well as life in general.

Mom was admitted for hospice care under the Concord Regional Visiting Nurse Association while living at the Richard Brown House in Loudon Village. Her physical condition due to the cancer became quite dire requiring doses of morphine and other meds.

On August 27th Mom moved in with us. We rearranged our sunroom to accommodate her hospital bed and related terminal illness needs. Mary quickly sewed and hung curtains for each of the sunroom's five windows, making sleep easier for Mom. At Mom's request, Mary played tunes on her Native American flute. I read Mom one of my favorite childhood stories, "Mr. Bear Squash-You-All-Flat." All of our local kids, their spouses, and our granddaughters stopped by our house during Mom's last days for a final visit. This was very meaningful to Mom. At separate times, my cousins Linda and Peg visited Mom, kindly giving Mary and me opportunities to rest and to leave the house for errands.

Nine days after moving in with us, Mom passed to the spirit world. Mary and I were at her bedside that afternoon. We feel somewhat at peace knowing that Mom was with us during this painful ordeal, dying at the opposite end of Loudon Ridge Road from the farm where she was born, was raised, and was married to Dad.

As Mom had desired, we held a graveside service at the Nichols lot at the Loudon Ridge Cemetery the morning of September 26, 2020. All wearing cloth masks for coronavirus protection, family members and friends attended the service officiated by Rev. Jim Young, pastor of the New Rye Congregational Church, where Mom and Dad had been members for several years. Mary and I buried Mom's urn containing her ashes Sunday, September 27th. I dug deep into the earth, exposing the edge of Dad's urn that we had buried years ago. The two urns rest side by side as they wished. My hand-written journal contains much more detail regarding Mom's ordeal leading to her death.

Later, Mary and I bought a sundial and mounted it on a slab of pink granite, which we had inscribed at Swenson Granite Works. In the early spring of 2021, we set the sundial tribute amongst the flowers in our "nursery" garden down over the hill near our pond. Each springtime I had driven Mom to this general location in our car so she could marvel at the bright yellow cowslips in bloom on the banks of the brook exiting the pond. During these times, Mom loved to see the wide array of colorful daffodils that Mary had planted on the sidehill leading to the pond.

The family sieges with cancer and all the associated suffering from life-ending bouts with various forms of the disease by Mom, my brother Larry, sister Nancy, two uncles as well as close friends and several Vietnam Veteran brothers triggered my PTSD. Traumatic dreams made sleep difficult and generated feelings of grief and helplessness that I had worked to dilute since America's Southeast Asia war years.

The 2020 presidential election featured the incumbent Trump/Pence campaign and the opposing Joe Biden/Kamala Harris campaign. The Biden team won the contentious election by over 7 million popular votes plus a considerable electoral vote victory. Leading up to inauguration day, Trump and his right-wing followers spread numerous conspiracy theories claiming electoral fraud and ballot tampering, asserting that Trump won the election.

Sixty or so court battles and bipartisan recounts did nothing to uphold the Republican charges of a rigged election. When, on January 6, 2021, Congress met to confirm the electoral ballot count recognizing Biden the soon-to-be 46th president, the US Capitol was charged and breached by violent white supremacists and far-right militia groups. Serious destruction to the magnificent building occurred, and legislators' lives were put at risk. Injuries and a few deaths also occurred in the brutal melee. Four DC policemen ended their lives by suicide following the trauma of the violent incident. This Trump-instigated mob attack became the first time that the Capitol had been besieged and damaged since the War of 1812.

During a January 13th session in the House of Representatives, Trump was impeached by a wide margin on the count of "Incitement of Insurrection," marking him with the ignoble distinction as the first president in US history to be impeached twice. Incredibly, Trump was acquitted of criminal charges February 13, 2021, by the Senate, which requires a 2/3 majority to convict. Seven Republicans joined all Democrats, but unfortunately the vote fell short.

Following the violent January 6 attack, the US Capitol resembled a fortress. It became surrounded by a 9-foot-high steel fence and razor concertina wire coils. It was protected around the clock by an increased police force and a National Guard detachment. FBI warnings of continued threats from numerous right-wing Trump-supporting militia groups were issued. Despite further investigations, Trump's big lie continues to divide our country, adding to the possible demise of US democracy. Democracy is increasingly in danger of extinction in our country if a re-run of Trump or with any of his rabid followers happens in the presidential election of 2024. Our country could be at a turning point toward long term autocratic rule.

Nowadays, life is hectic, fast-paced, expensive, and complex. Vastly different in so many ways, since the 1960s, 70s and early 80s. Compared to life in today's world, I've realized that those of us who grew up during the Sixties and Seventies were very fortunate. Other than assassinations, nasty racial turmoil and the senseless Vietnam War, my generation had it made. We could attend college without racking up insurmountable debt, apartment rental was available and affordable, cars were generally priced within ranges that were reasonable, labor unions were common, occupations offered generous pensions and benefits.

In more recent times, designation of an American as a hero by religious zealots, politicians and media outlets has created a somewhat diminished stature. Today, so-called heroes are everywhere, often labeled hero for quite insignificant, run-of-the-mill acts. Certainly, there are those deserving that honor in current times, but the term is now bestowed in such a watered-down manner, as if the US is full to the brim with heroes. The belief in "American exceptionalism" unduly influences the casual label of hero. True heroes used to be few and far between, and for good reason — it took an extraordinary deed, a brave or noble feat to earn that respectful tribute.

The ever-changing dynamics of communication through the internet using computers, tablets, cell phones, and smart watches allows emailing, texting, researching, and social media networking through Facebook, Twitter, Instagram, and Snapchat to name a few. These have positive and negative impacts worldwide. It's increasingly difficult to determine what information is true and what is false thanks to the internet. Computer hacking runs rampant everywhere, and monetary scams of all descriptions are a constant concern resulting in stress and disruption to many innocent victims.

Google has taken the place of traditional encyclopedias. Online newspapers and magazines have really hurt printed news options as they struggle to survive. Audiobooks have become a popular alternative to hardcovers and paperbacks. Merchandise purchased through Amazon has resulted in the demise of scads of small retail businesses and even some big long-established box stores. Access to music and movies constantly changes thanks to hyperspeed technology. Digital cameras have all but replaced 35mm film cameras. Photoshop software provides amazing image possibilities, some of which are artistic and helpful, while others are hurtful and scary. GPS navigational units have reduced the use of road maps. New cars and trucks have unlimited components driven by minute computer chips. Drones and robots are replacing people, as that form of automation takes over tens of thousands of civilian jobs, including highly specialized positions.

Military drones, with names like "Predator" and "Reaper," are routinely used for surveillance and as killer-weapons in the continuing wars in Afghanistan and Mid-Eastern countries. At remote command centers in the US, terrorists in faraway countries are instantly obliterated by unmanned drones unleashed through distant push-button attacks. This saves the lives of our fighter pilots. However, identity mistakes from afar have resulted in untold numbers of innocent civilian deaths. Those pushing the death buttons in safe isolation suffer grievous PTSD from lifelong guilt after killing family members, wedding parties, etc. The "Beast" travels differing routes.

Robots are often used to destroy land mines and bombs, saving the lives of demolition personnel and others. This is a great alternative in situations where robots are available and under conditions where they can be used. Like most good ideas these have limitations.

Especially since the occasional attacks by terrorists in the US and in other countries across the globe, fear has been taken to extremes. Surveillance devices are everywhere, making it almost impossible to piss behind a tree on a remote country road without showing up on some damned camera. Moreover, such a piss picture can easily be transmitted across the globe! Not much is private in this intrusive, fearful and suspicious high-tech security world. Boarding a plane has become somewhat intrusive due to required security scans and entry into federal buildings is restricted until cleared of possible danger.

There is no stopping such spiraling technological changes, whether we like them or not. This computer driven world is a runaway train with nothing to stop it, less Earth's destruction. There's no going back. Here's hoping that the positives outweigh the negatives.

The ramifications of all this are mind-blowing. There are definitely pros and cons to living in the 21st century with all the rapidly changing technology versus long ago decades. But weighing the many positive advantages, I think I'd prefer living in the culture of the distant yesteryears. However, writing this memoir by hand or even typing it on a manual typewriter, as was done in the past, would be tedious. Such methods are obsolete. Here I sit in 2022 typing these many pages on our iMac computer with spellcheck, copy and paste, and other convenient features. Yet I have remained a rare holdout for not using a cell phone. Maybe I too have become obsolete!

To me, the most menacing threat to life on planet Earth is climate change, sometimes referred to as global warming. Human degradation of the natural environment has been my most urgent concern since I wrote my *Heed the Warning* poem in the early 1970s as Earth Day approached. Nearly all scientists in the world realize and have communicated the credible research proving that climate change is now spiraling out of control. The pace of human-caused climate change increases each year, and its effects are devastating. Scientific evidence proves this to be true. However, one does not need to be a scientist to recognize obvious changes that are taking place. Clearly evident if living in the countryside, on any coast, in a city or in the Arctic. Natural disasters of all types are more numerous across the world, and the results are usually severe, often unprecedented in scope.

Unfortunately, there are mindless deniers of science and

climate change who blindly confuse "weather" with "climate." Also, there are those who are self-centered, greedy and shortsighted, who refuse to consider the plight of future generations. Former President Trump, his right-wing administration and supporters fell in that abhorrent category. Our country's natural features were degraded. Protection of our national monuments was assaulted. Endangered plants and wildlife were disregarded. Donald J. Trump was definitely a dangerous threat to the US and to the planet. Climate change, with the natural disasters it creates, gets more intense each year.

In the fall of 2021, Mary and I signed a contract with Fuat Ari, owner of Sun Dial Solar, Inc., to have 24 ground mounted solar panels installed in our field below the barn. Winter conditions prevented the project until spring, but in time the panels should deliver the electrical power we need. Several of our friends have operating solar systems and have experienced positive results in getting free of major power grid networks.

I understand the fervor that for decades has driven the slogan, "Never Again." It became a common two-word phrase as World War I ("The war to end all wars") ended. And later by survivors of the Holocaust in their tireless *never again* efforts. These survivors have been significantly diminishing with passing years.

Fortunately, there have been no comparisons to Hitler's atrocities. However, genocidal massacres have since taken place in Pol Pot's killing fields of Cambodia, in Rwanda, Bosnia-Herzegovina, Iraq, Syria and elsewhere. America's villainous war against Vietnam spawned destruction to so many US troops—killed in battle, maimed, poisoned by Agent Orange, missing, suicide, incarcerated, homeless and those of us still breathing. And to the millions of Vietnamese people, to their culture, their historic monuments, their natural environment and to their beautiful countryside. Laos and Cambodia bore similar consequences from the American war in Vietnam. *Never Again* has morphed into an almost universal phrase denoting various tragedies, including senseless mass murders at schools, theaters, churches, etc. by wackos with guns designed for war. *Never again* reruns occur again and again. So does the curse.

Many of us Vietnam veterans have used the *never again* theme in our gut-wrenching talks to today's youth, and through films and writings. If only an honest openness could have been articulated by more World War II vets, perhaps my generation would have been less eager to follow in our fathers' footsteps. But, understandably, that seldom happened because the war they fought in was necessary and honorable. With more first-hand classroom exposure to war's ugliness, possibly veterans' kids would be less willing to answer our country's beckoning call. In the context of present-day conflicts though, this is a naive thought. Especially since there is no conscription in effect.

Regardless of the era, regardless of the justification, and regardless of the outcome, every war is horrific. As General Dwight D. Eisenhower said in early 1946, "I hate war as only a soldier who has lived it can, only as one who has seen its brutality, its futility, its stupidity."

Did it take a Vietnam experience to expose history and disrobe war's mythical glory? Now, nearly five decades after the last US combat troops left Vietnam, many former supporters of that war have come to grips with the fact that it was disgracefully wrong. Through all the turmoil since becoming active in the peace movement, I've gained wonderful new friendships, including a few veterans of Korea and World War II. And yet, the US has become ensnared in war after war since then. The *never again* lesson has not been learned.

In 2022, as I type the final paragraphs in my memoir, war crimes are being committed by heartless troops under Russian President Vladimir Putin. His powerful military is laying siege to the adjoining country of Ukraine. As the country is blown apart, untold numbers of Ukrainian women, children, and the elderly are being maimed and killed, as are Ukraine's military personnel. Millions have become refugees in Poland, Hungary and other European countries.

Never Again banner in Washington, DC April 1987

Ukrainian men aged 18 to 60 are required to remain and fight the Russians. Ukrainian President Zelensky is courageously staying in the capital city of Kyiv leading his country as the slaughter continues each day. Strongly nationalistic citizens are fighting the Russians valiantly. President Biden and all other North Atlantic Treaty Organization (NATO) nations are providing humanitarian and military assistance to Ukraine, and heavy sanctions have been enacted to disrupt Russia. The fear of starting World War III looms close, especially with the threat of nuclear weapons. Thousands of Russian citizens have been beaten and imprisoned for protesting against Putin's horrible war. The scourge of war is again denying *never again* dreams from becoming reality.

Romio Shrestha, Buddhist master of enlightenment art, expressed words similar to this that are worth our consideration: As long as our actions are dominated by anger, ignorance and pride, we are lost in a world of illusions, spinning in an endless cycle from which we will not escape.

The United States is an astonishingly beautiful country, and I have seen much of it. I believe the majority of its citizens are decent, kindhearted people. However, as is the case with most countries, many shameful and violent chapters blemish our history. For an honest, no-frills chronicle of historic events throughout our country's past, I recommend reading *A People's History of the United States: 1492 - Present* by the late Howard Zinn. Serving as a bombardier during World War II, Zinn later became a renowned historian and college professor. Some of his writings are outside of the establishment's historical accounts and are essential reading. I have the book as well as his follow-up book titled *The Twentieth Century: A People's History*, and I have referred to them often over the years.

This brings me to the summer 1989 NH Alumnus magazine quote from UNH Professor Harvard Sitkoff: *"Our maturity as a nation also requires an end to the delusion of American omnipotence which, like Agent Orange, lies dormant and then later appears to claim its victims. There are limits to our power. We cannot always accomplish anything we wish, anywhere in the world."*

I intend to extend a hand toward a more peaceful world in any way I can until I am dust. Not as a true pacifist, for I'd readily fight to protect my family, the land we live on, our way of life or the country we live in from direct assault. I'm most proud of the USMC as an elite branch of the military, though I disagree with nearly all post-WW II reasoning for its deployment in the affairs of other countries. But in an actual life-or-death situation, I would again opt for the Marines. Like my dad did.

In civilian life, all these years since my enlistment, I've met many men who had once been in the Marines. When talking about our varied military experiences, it surprises me to hear a few former Marines expound on what great adventures they had while in the service. These were not the experiences of combat but were instead those from peacetime enlistments at some cushy secure assignment in the US or in some friendly country. Or like serving aboard a ship on a Mediterranean cruise with numerous stops at European ports. Hearing about such fond memories always makes me want to ask why they didn't stay in the Corps if it was so great. Why didn't they become USMC "lifers"? Most all got the hell out just as soon as their enlistment was up, glad to be free of the regimentation and continual bullshit.

I feel at peace knowing that none of our four children have joined the military and gone to war. As they were growing up readying for college, I did all I could to keep them from entering military service. I hope none of our six beautiful grandchildren join, nor any of their children's children! That cycle in our family has been broken. The torch won't be passed anytime soon. Hopefully never.

These few lines from Maya Angelou's poem "A Brave and Startling Truth" beautifully speak to the kind of peace I seek and try to promote:

> *When we let the rifles fall from our shoulders*
> *And children dress their dolls in flags of truce*
> *When land mines of death have been removed*
> *And the aged can walk into evenings of peace*
> *When religious ritual is not perfumed*
> *By the incense of burning flesh*

During each of our kids' childhoods, I've taken them to visit the Portsmouth Naval Shipyard to obtain dependent ID cards and for a glimpse of the infamous abandoned military prison, which has fallen into serious disrepair. They have no ghostly connections—no Marine Barracks pettiness, no guard duty, no hospitalization, no orders to ship out. The place carries historic family footprints, but fortunately for our kids it conjures up no direct military experiences. Sometimes what goes around doesn't come around! If fate prescribed that earlier generations had to bear war's pain, then we must *never again* turn back to old solutions, only forward. Hopefully, this is not just wishful thinking!

At just under age 77, I've come to the final paragraphs of my memoir. I realize that in many ways I could have done better as a husband and as a dad. Too late to turn back the clock. There are events that I probably should have included and surely many lie ahead that I could write about if my narrative continued. I feel that the time to end it is now.

I offer the following statement as an ending thought from Paul Tritschler, psychology professor and author:

Why Stories Matter

"Storytelling, recognized in every society as a way of making sense of cultural roots or social reality, is an elaborate form of metaphor, and memoir is its masterpiece: life stories enable us to share insights and enhance mutual understanding in a social, political, psychological and spiritual sense. Memoir is revolutionary precisely because, when shared, it's a way towards the truth."

Grateful Acknowledgements

To Mary, my soulmate, for standing by me and offering encouragement in getting to the end of my long memoir-writing adventure. For jarring my memory and reminding me of things I hadn't gotten quite right and for editing with the eyes of a hawk. Also, for her expertise with computer issues, and for getting me out of many hi-tech fuck-ups along the way.

To daughter Jessie for reading and commenting on the excerpts I sent along the way, and for her continuing encouragement.

To Tom at Piscataqua Press for his patience, sound advice and proofreading during the publication process.

To Vietnam brothers and sisters and many supportive friends.

To Tran Tra and Pham Duc Phong for their kindness and for helping me find my way through the mire of emotions during my 1995 and 1998 revisits to their country. And for subsequent communications of cultural exchange.

To my old sea bag for holding some of the things I carried helping me to get through.

Appendix I

Partial list of significant events of the early 1960s to mid-1970s

Women's liberation: Feminist movement influenced by Betty Friedan's book, *The Feminine Mystique* published February 19, 1963. National Organization for Women (NOW) established in 1966.

Dr. Martin Luther King, Jr.: Delivered famous "I Have A Dream" speech on August 28, 1963 in front of the Lincoln Memorial during the *March on Washington*. Largest demonstration ever in the nation's capital with estimated 200,000 – 300,000 in attendance.

President John F. Kennedy: Assassinated November 22, 1963 in Dallas, Texas.

The Beatles in America: *Meet The Beatles!* album was released in the US January 20, 1964. 73 million people watched the Beatles perform on *The Ed Sullivan Show* February 9, 1964. This extraordinarily creative British band swept in a tsunami of rock bands bringing about major changes in the music scene, leading to the psychedelic era of the mid-60s - mid-70s.

The Civil Rights Act of 1964: Initiated by President Kennedy in 1963, this landmark legislation was signed into law by President Lyndon B. Johnson on July 2, 1964. It prohibited discrimination on the basis of race, color, religion, sex or national origin.

The Wilderness Act of 1964 signed into law by President Lyndon B. Johnson on September 3, 1964. It created the National Wilderness Preservation System, which protected millions of acres of national forest wilderness land. Considered as being one of America's greatest conservation achievements.

Malcolm X: Assassinated February 21, 1965 in New York City. Controversial Muslim minister, spokesman for the Nation of Islam and outspoken African American rights activist.

Voting Rights Act of 1965 signed into law by President Johnson on August 6, 1965. This civil rights legislation prohibited racial discrimination in voting.

Super Bowl #1: Green Bay Packers beat the Kansas City Chiefs on January 15, 1967, by a score of 35-10.

Students for a Democratic Society (SDS): Leftist student activist movement having antiwar and counterculture influence particularly during the last half of the 1960s.

Muhammad Ali (formerly Cassius Clay): US Olympic boxing gold medalist and World Heavyweight Champion boxer. Refused to be drafted into the Vietnam War in 1967. Stripped of his boxing title and boxing license was suspended. Quotes: "Why should they ask me to put on a uniform and go 10,000 miles from home and drop bombs and bullets on brown people in Vietnam while so-called Negro people in Louisville are treated like dogs and denied simple human rights?" "I ain't got no quarrel with those Viet Cong." Regained his World Heavyweight Champion title in 1974.

Vietnam Veterans Against the War (VVAW): Founded in June 1967 in New York City. Members demonstrated against war, exposed war's atrocities, worked for veterans' rights and benefits, and taught the lessons of the Vietnam War. Still active with many chapters.

"Summer of Love": During 1967, most notably in San Francisco, California — also extended to many big cities across the US, Canada and Europe.

Monterey Pop Festival: June 1967 in Monterey, California.

Nominated by LBJ, Thurgood Marshall became the first African American to serve on the US Supreme Court in October 1967. Served honorably as Associate Justice until 1991.

Yippie Movement (Youth International Party), a countercultural revolutionary organization, raged during the late sixties into the early seventies. The most prominent Yippies were Abbie Hoffman and Jerry Rubin. Well known close associates were poet Allen Ginsberg and attorney William Kunstler.

American Indian Movement (AIM): Activist Indian advocate organization founded in 1968 with the purpose of securing Native American rights and preserving indigenous culture. Most notable AIM actions took place in the early to mid-1970s.

My Lai massacre by US troops in Vietnam, March 16, 1968.

Rev. Martin Luther King, Jr.: Assassinated April 4, 1968 in Memphis, Tennessee.

Senator Robert F. Kennedy: Assassinated June 5, 1968 in Los Angeles, California.

1968 Democratic National Convention: Unprecedented disruption by massive demonstrations, August 1968 in Chicago. Violent, destructive confrontations between activists and police.

LSD banned federally in the US on October 24, 1968. Iconic psychologist Timothy Leary actively continued his advocacy of the hallucinogenic drug.

New York City police raid the Stonewall Inn, a gay club in Greenwich Village on June 28, 1969. Known as the Stonewall riots, the event was followed by several days of protest and violent clashes. It served as the catalyst leading to the gay liberation movement and years later, the advance of LGBT rights in the US.

First Moon landing, US Apollo 11, on July 20, 1969. Astronaut Neil Armstrong became the first human to walk on the Moon, July 21, 1969. Edwin "Buzz" Aldrin joined Armstrong for the moon walk.

The Woodstock Festival: August 1969 in Bethel, New York.

Altamont Free Concert: December 1969 in northern California.

Weather Underground (the Weathermen): Radical revolutionary offshoot of SDS active in late 1960s into the early 1970s. Strong opponents of Vietnam War. See *Fugitive Days* by Bill Ayers.

Black Panther Party: Powerful force for racial equality and social justice during the mid-1960s into the early 1970s. Strong opponents of Vietnam War. Members Fred Hampton and Mark Clark were shot to death in Chicago during a police raid in

December 1969. *Black Power* movement hammered by FBI and cops.

Earth Day: Founded in US April 22, 1970, as an environmental teach-in promoting awareness, appreciation and stewardship of the natural environment. Sparked the beginning of the modern environmental movement.

No-fault divorce: Laws passed in early 1970s making divorce in the US easy to obtain and much more numerous. Courts grant divorces based on "irreconcilable differences."

Lottery draft: US Selective Service System inductions began in 1970 by lottery drawings.

Kent State University, Ohio: During an antiwar demonstration May 4, 1970, four student protesters (two women) were shot to death by Ohio National Guardsmen. Others wounded.

Festival Express: June 1970 musical train trip across Canada (E. to W.).

The Environmental Protection Agency (EPA) established December 2, 1970, by President Richard M. Nixon. Its goal was to protect the natural environment through pollution reduction and energy conservation.

Pentagon Papers: New York Times began publishing excerpts June 13, 1971. Daniel Ellsberg's release of these papers exposed decades of lies and deception by high-level US government officials leading to and throughout America's vile war in Vietnam.

Watergate burglaries: Nixon Administration break-in scandal, June 1972.

Nixon's infamous "Christmas bombings" of Hanoi, December 18–29, 1972. Over 20,000 tons of ordnance dropped on Hanoi, mostly by B-52 Stratofortress bombers, killing over 1600 Vietnamese. Included in the bombings were an elementary school and the Bach Mai hospital. Nixon declared, "Peace is at hand."

Draft ended in US: Conscription discontinued in 1973. Converted to an all-volunteer military.

Roe v. Wade case: US Supreme Court legalized abortions January 22, 1973.

All parties of the Paris peace talks signed a pact leading to the withdrawal of US military forces from Vietnam and leading to the release of all American POWs from North Vietnam, January 27, 1973.

Summer Jam at Watkins Glen: July 1973 in Watkins Glen, New York.

The "Endangered Species Act" authorized by the 93rd US Congress was signed into law by President Nixon on December 28, 1973.

Nearly all US military personnel out of Vietnam by December 31, 1973.

President Richard Nixon: Resigned in disgrace August 9, 1974, to avoid impeachment and likely criminal charges. Pardoned by President Gerald Ford on September 8, 1974.

Suggested references to many of the historic events listed can be found in the following books and magazines in my library:

The Sixties: Years of Hope, Days of Rage by Todd Gitlin

Fugitive Days by Bill Ayers

Witness to the Revolution: Radicals, Resisters, Vets, Hippies, and the Year America Lost Its Mind and Found its Soul by Clara Bingham

You Say You Want A Revolution?: Records and Rebels 1966 - 1970 edited by Victoria Broackes and Geoffrey Marsh

The 60s: The Story of a Decade by The New Yorker

High Societies: Psychedelic Rock Posters of Haight Ashbury

Appendix II

Glossary of commonly used terms and acronym identification

(some acronyms and terms used have long and complicated definitions, which can be further understood through research)

"782 gear" — basic USMC issuance in boot camp, clothes, personal hygiene items, a bucket, etc.

1-A — Available immediately draft classification

2-S — Student deferment draft classification

4-F — Unfit for military service draft classification

AFB — Air Force Base

American Legion — an organization supporting US veterans

ARVN — Army of the Republic of Vietnam (South Vietnamese Army)

ASCS — Agricultural Stabilization and Conservation Service, former name of a USDA agency

AWOL — Absent Without Leave while in the military, also called UA, unauthorized absence

BLT — Battalion Landing Team

C-4 — Plastic-like explosive, can be shaped into a highly explosive charge

C-ration — Canned meal issued to troops during wartime, now called MRE, meal ready to eat

CIA — Central Intelligence Agency

COVID — Viral pandemic and variants spread throughout all countries of the world, killing millions

DAV — Disabled American Veterans, a national organization supporting rights, medical and mental well-being and compensation for veterans suffering from physical and/or mental wounds

DD-214 — Important record of military service

DEROS — Date Eligible for Return from Overseas, a duration of 13 months for Marines in Vietnam

Det. cord — Detonation cord, highly explosive and rope-like. Used as an individual explosive or to detonate other explosives

DI — Drill Instructor

DMZ — Demilitarized Zone, — a demarcation line dividing a country, such as North and South Vietnam. The DMZ divided North and South Vietnam roughly along the 17th parallel

DNA — simplified as a chemical name of a molecule that carries genetic identifications in living things

DSM — Diagnostic and Statistical Manual of Mental Disorders

DVD — Digital Video Disc used for information storage and video entertainment

FBI — Federal Bureau of Investigation

Flak jacket — A form of body armor, but not bullet proof. A vest made of heavy nylon material lined with fiberglass panels to protect from shrapnel

FNG — Fuckin' new guy — a newly arrived military person in Vietnam — one having no experience in war

Fragged — Murder or attempted murder usually of an unpopular officer or sergeant

Free fire zone — Areas determined to consist of enemy forces or enemy sympathizers were considered to be open killing zones from US weaponry. All living in these areas were considered to be enemies, regardless of sympathies or noncombatant status. This was the equivalent of open season!

Field of fire — An area from a fixed position which can be covered by a weapon, such as a machine gun, or by group of weapons

Friendly fire — Wounds and death occurrences to American servicemen and women caused from mistaken identity by others in the US military. Such accidents could be from the air, artillery or from small-arms fire from American forces.

Head shop — A store associated with the 60's generation, selling marijuana-related supplies, psychedelic posters, patches, and magazines, and hippie-type items of clothing, etc.

Hooch — Thatched living quarters common in Vietnamese villages, sometimes with an attached shelter for animals

I Corps — Northernmost strategic area in Vietnam from the DMZ south consisting of five provinces. Leading southward are II Corps, III Corps and IV Corps, taking in all of the country

ITR — Infantry Training Regiment in the USMC

KIA — Killed in Action

KP duty — Kitchen Police, lower ranked military kitchen staff work for a specified period of time. Also called mess duty

LCU — Landing Craft Utility, a Navy landing craft departing from a larger ship

Lifer — A derogatory term for one who makes a career of the military. Usually seen as someone who puts his/her military career ahead of the security of lower-level troops.

LSD — Landing Ship Dock

LST — Landing Ship Tank

LZ — Landing Zone, an area positioned and cleared enough for helicopters to land and take off from. Enables troop insertion, resupply operations and medevac

Medevac — Medical evacuation of casualties by helicopter. Sometimes called "dustoff"

MOS — Military Occupational Specialty, signified by a set of numbers

MP — Military Police

Napalm — Napalm is jellied gasoline. Big canisters of napalm were dropped from US aircraft, which lazily tumbled to earth. Upon impact, the canisters exploded, engulfing huge areas in flame and sucking up oxygen in the vicinity causing suffocation. Napalm was also used in flamethrowers. The properties of napalm make it cling to whatever it comes into contact with.

Attempts to wipe it off only spread it around, expanding the burn area. The intense heat can cause suffocation and can produce severe burns even without actual contact. The noise, smoke and smell are horrifying

NATO — North Atlantic Treaty Organization established as a defensive organization of nations following WW II, a collective security group of nations

NCO — Non-commissioned Officer — enlisted personnel ranks of Corporal and Sergeant

NVA — North Vietnamese Army headquartered in Hanoi

PC — A heavily-built 3/4 ton military truck

PDRL — Permanent Disability Retired List from military service

PFC — Private First Class, E-2 rank

POW — Prisoner of War

PRC-6 — A military walkie-talkie, often called a prick-6

PRC-25 — A military portable field radio, often called a prick-25

PTSD — Post-Traumatic Stress Disorder, includes moral injury. Referred to as the Beast in this memoir

PX — Post Exchange on a military base where a variety of items can be purchased

R&R — Rest and Relaxation (or Rest & Recuperation or Rest & Recreation), a period of release from the war into another country's civilian environment, usually lasting from 5 to 7 days

SCS — Soil Conservation Service, an agency of the USDA

SDS — Students for a Democratic Society, a nationwide 1960s - early 70s student activist organization focusing on antiwar and social issues

SEAL — US Navy component, stands for Sea, Air and Land, elite special military operations forces

Search and Destroy — US military operations to destroy villages suspected as supporting the enemy, but not to hold ground. Destroying hooches, food supplies and crops, killing domestic animals, poisoning water sources and rounding up suspected VC sympathizers

STB — Special Training Branch, USMC boot camp area for recruits temporarily removed from training platoons who are considered unmotivated or fat and weak

TBI — Traumatic Brain Injury

TDRL — Temporary Disability Retired List from military service

Tet — Date signifying the new year and advent of spring. Vietnam's most important holiday

The Wall — The Vietnam Veterans Memorial in Washington, DC where the over 58, OOO names of Americans killed in Vietnam are inscribed in the black granite wall

The World — Serviceman/woman's term for the USA during one's tour in Vietnam

UCMJ — Uniformed Code of Military Justice — US foundation of military law

UDT — Underwater Demolition Team, a specialized combat Navy Seal team

UNH — University of New Hampshire

USDA — United States Department of Agriculture

USO — United Service Organizations which offer performances by celebrities to entertain military personnel

VA — Veterans Administration, now known as the Department of Veteran Affairs

VC — Viet Cong or alternatively, Vietcong

VD — Venereal Disease — sexually transmitted diseases

Vet Center — VA community-based centers which provide readjustment counseling services to veterans and their families covering wide-ranging support

VFP — Veterans for Peace, a national organization founded in 1985

VFW — Veterans of Foreign Wars — a national veterans organization for vets who served on foreign lands, waters or in the air

VVA — Vietnam Veterans of America, a national organization in support of Vietnam veterans and their families

VVAW — Vietnam Veterans Against the War, a national organization formed in 1967 in support of Vietnam veterans and their families. Obviously opposed to America's war in Vietnam!

WIA — Wounded in Action

Appendix III

Some of my special Vietnam vet brothers and sisters from New England:

*Jean Stimmell, Brown Water Navy — lifelong friend since high school, writer, artist, therapist, serious PTSD

*Dave Robinson (Davey), USMC — shot three times in I Corps, long-time friend, serious PTSD

*John Jones (Jonesy), Army Green Beret medic — returned to Vietnam twice after the war, serious PTSD

*Randy Zoll, Army infantry — NH resident formerly from NY

*Steve Fowle, Army — Saigon graves registration lab, Portsmouth, editor of "The NH Gazette", serious PTSD

*Gary (Bear) Jenisch, Army intelligence — flight crew member based at Tan Son Nhut - flew surveillance missions over South Vietnam in 1967 - 68 — died from Agent Orange diabetes and cancer September 25, 2019

Ken Leidner, Air Force and Army 173rd Airborne Brigade, died December 19, 2017, serious PTSD

Buzz Gagne, Army — helicopter gunner, Agent Orange cancer survivor, serious PTSD

*Paul Hague, Navy — on ship in August 1964 where Tonkin Gulf incident lies took place

*Gary Rafferty, Army — artillery, published poet and memoir author, serious PTSD

*Pauline Hebert, Army — triage nurse in Vietnam — published poet, serious PTSD

*Neil English, Navy — published poet, craftsman, built our house on Loudon Ridge

*Karl Bergeron, Army medic — refused to carry a weapon during the war, serious PTSD

*Rick Ducey, Army — serious war wounds, died August 30, 2007 from Agent Orange cancer, serious PTSD

*Dwight Graves, Navy Seabee — artist, musician, activist, humanitarian, died from Agent Orange September 3, 2013, serious PTSD

Bobby Corliss, Army — jailed in Tennessee, died September 5, 2012 at home in Barnstead of Agent Orange cancer, serious PTSD

Mike (Bull) Towle, Army MP — died at home in Pittsfield in spring of 2016

*Ed Tasker, Army — from Barnstead, wounded in Vietnam (amputee)

*Don Rollman, USMC — wounded in Vietnam, hospitalized with me at Portsmouth Navy Yard

*Robert Daigneau, USMC — suicide November 9, 1991 (see my poem), serious PTSD

Kerry Stimson, USMC — AWOL, suicide, serious PTSD

Gary Locke, USMC Recon — suicide

*Richard (Dickie) Brooks, USMC — died in Quang Tri Province, I Corps, April 25, 1968, age 20

*Walter Murzin, USMC — KIA in Quang Nam Province, I Corps, October 2, 1966, age 20

Russell Dunn, Army — infantry, multiple war wounds, died November 28, 2009 from Agent Orange cancer, serious PTSD

*Martin Carney, Army — infantry, Central Highlands, serious PTSD

Nat King, USMC infantry — from NH Lakes Region, serious PTSD

Ed Bowser, Army — VFP member, serious PTSD

Col. John F. Barr, USMC — Korea & Vietnam veteran, VFP member, died September 22, 2014

*Michael Wilson, USMC — from Brattleboro, VT, my late sister's former husband died in 2015

Paul Camacho, USMC — from Concord, worked with the

William Joiner Center, Boston

John F. Markle, Jr. (Twoey), Army combat engineer — lost a foot to a land mine. Died February 11, 2019, serious PTSD

*John Brock, Army infantry — Vietnam veteran, Manchester Vet Center therapist

Ed Myers, Army — Vietnam veteran & Manchester Vet Center therapist

Russell Wilson, Navy Corpsman — Vet Center group, shot at Khe Sanh, died March 27, 2010, serious PTSD

Andy Roy, Army — Vet Center therapy group, multiple tours in Vietnam, serious PTSD

Dave Alley, USMC — Vet Center group

Ed Batjer, Air Force — Vet Center group

Glen Fox, USMC — Vet Center group, serious PTSD

Joe Higgenbottom, Army — Vet Center group, serious PTSD

George Fleming, USMC —Vet Center group, serious PTSD

John Morrissey, Army — Vet Center group

Ed Connolly, USMC — Vet Center group, serious PTSD

Richard Jean, Army — Vet Center group

Julius, Army Green Beret — Vet Center group, wounded in Vietnam, serious PTSD

Bob Miner, Army — Vet Center group, wounded in Vietnam, lost son to suicide, serious PTSD

Scott Robart (from Andover, NH and Alaska), Army — Democratic Party & antiwar activist

Dale Cox, Navy Corpsman — combat with Marines, originally from the Iowa, serious PTSD

Bruce Lake, USMC — helicopter pilot, ASCS employee, memoir author

John Riff, Army — ASCS CED in Coos County.

*Dave Connolly, Army — from South Boston, MA, — three purple hearts, VFP and VVAW member, published poet, featured in *Voices in Wartime* video, author of *Lost in America* book of poetry, serious PTSD

Winston Warfield, Army — from MA member of the Smedley Butler Brigade, VFP, serious PTSD

Jim Packer, USMC — from MA member of the Smedley Butler Brigade, VFP, serious PTSD

*Michael Casey, Army — from MA, published poet, serious PTSD

Preston Hood, Navy Seal Team Two — from Maine, published poet, lost son to suicide, serious PTSD

<u>Special notes:</u>

* signifies vets mentioned by name in memoir narrative

All vets listed were from NH when I knew them except Dave Connolly, Winston Warfield, Jim Packer and Preston Hood.

*Charlie Richmond, USMC — Vet Center group member in his 80's, WW II vet wounded in battle of Okinawa who, though not a Vietnam vet, joined our Vet Center group and contributed experiences, wisdom and understanding, serious PTSD.